THE URBAN WEST SERIES

EARNING POWER

ups and downs and heard more than they ever wanted to about this project. I owe my greatest debt, however, to my family. They gave me their unstinting support (emotional, intellectual, and often financial) whenever I needed it. Alice, David, Lorraine, and John Wallis—this book is as much yours as it is mine.

ACKNOWLEDGMENTS

As projects tend to do, this book has grown and evolved over the years. It began as my doctoral dissertation at the University of Utah. I am deeply indebted to the late Dr. Dean May, who encouraged me to pursue my interest in women in the urban West and who saw this dissertation through its formative stages. I also want to thank Dr. Eric Hinderaker, who stepped in as chair following Dr. May's untimely passing, and Dr. Elizabeth Clement, Dr. David Igler (now of the University of California–Irvine), Dr. Rebecca Horn, and Dr. Lars Rodseth for their help and advice. I would also like to thank the staff, faculty, and graduate students of the History Department at the University of Utah and the 2002–2003 Tanner Humanities Center fellows for their unfailing support and helpful feedback.

Extra special thanks goes out to the faculty and staff of the History Department at California State Polytechnic University in Pomona, where I have been happy to work for the past several years. I could not ask for more supportive colleagues.

I also owe a debt of gratitude to the staff of the five institutions where I conducted much of my research: the Urban Archives Center at California State University in Northridge; the University of California at Los Angeles's University Research Library, Department of Special Collections; the University of Southern California's Special Collections Department in Los Angeles; the Southern California Library for Social Studies Research in Los Angeles; and the Huntington Library in San Marino, California.

Research for this project was funded in part by an Andrew W. Mellon Foundation Fellowship at the Huntington Library, an HSSC/Haynes Research Stipend from the Historical Society of Southern California, a Graduate Fellowship from the Obert C. and Grace A. Tanner Humanities Center at the University of Utah, a University Teaching Assistantship from the University of Utah, and awards from the Department of History at the University of Utah.

No woman is an island, and I send special thanks to my friends Anna Blaine, Cristina Honles, and Susan Hwang, who have seen me though all the

PREFACE

This book grew out of my scholarly interest in the lives of women in the urban West. With one side of my family rooted in Nebraska, the other side in Texas, and as a second-generation Angeleno, I have long been fascinated with how women survived, physically, emotionally, and particularly economically, in the American West. Many of our family stories revolve around the struggles my grandmothers, great-grandmothers, and great-great-grandmothers faced in providing for themselves and their families. Shortly after advancing to candidacy at the University of Utah, I thus suggested women's work in the urban West as a possible dissertation topic to my graduate committee. They gave me their blessing.

But which city to study? Relatively little had been written about the urban West, and even less on women in western cities. Just about any location would have proved a rich field for study. It was during a holiday break, while on a visit to my family in Southern California, that I hit upon the idea of studying Los Angeles. Like most Angelenos, even though I had been born and raised in the area, I knew little about its history prior to World War II, save the stories my father and grandfather had told me. More important, Los Angeles and the surrounding area also provided a case study with racial diversity, tumultuous labor relations, and complex politics. These dynamics added to my study of gender to make for an exceptionally rich and complex story about the many ways such variables can impact daily life.

It is my hope that other scholars and students will pick up where I have left off, and reconsider the role of gender in shaping America's cities, particularly those west of the Mississippi River.

We now know a great deal about women's roles in the historical development of East Coast cities like New York. But only now is a picture of their western counterparts—in Denver, in San Antonio, in Seattle, and, yes, in Los Angeles—beginning to emerge. Further research may create a picture of the many roles played by women in the western United States and their vast contributions to regional history.

ILLUSTRATIONS

Illustrations
(following page 148)

Cover of *Sunset* magazine, January 1905

Portrait of Mrs. Robert Burdette

Maria de Lopez, 1913

Bessie Bruington Burke, 1924

Meeting of female employees, Bullocks Department Store,
Los Angeles, ca. 1920

The Los Angeles YWCA Clark Memorial Home

Women working in a garment factory in Los Angeles, ca. 1928

Mexican American woman workers at the
Side Way Baby Carriage Company, 1922

English class for Korean women at YWCA International
Institute, 1922

CONTENTS

For Alice and David
and for
Dean L. May

THE URBAN WEST SERIES

Series Editors: Eugene P. Moehring and David M. Wrobel

University of Nevada Press, Reno, Nevada 89557 USA
Copyright © 2010 by University of Nevada Press
All rights reserved
Manufactured in the United States of America
Design by Kathleen Szawiola

Library of Congress Cataloging-in-Publication Data

Wallis, Eileen V.
Earning power : women and work in Los Angeles, 1880–1930 /
Eileen V. Wallis — 1st ed.
p. cm. — (Urban west series)
Includes bibliographical references and index.
ISBN 978-0-87417-813-5 (hardcover : alk. paper)
1. Women—Employment—California—Los Angeles—History.
2. Women employees—California—Los Angeles—History.
3. Women—California—Los Angeles—Social conditions—History.
I. Title
HD6096.C3W35 2010
331.409794′94—dc22
2009039721

The paper used in this book is a recycled stock made from 30
percent post-consumer waste materials, certified by FSC, and meets
the requirements of American National Standard for Information
Sciences—Permanence of Paper for Printed Library Materials,
ANSI/NISO Z39.48-1992 (R2002). Binding materials were
selected for strength and durability.

FIRST PRINTING

19   18   17   16   15   14   13   12   11   10
5   4   3   2   1

EILEEN V. WALLIS

EARNING POWER

Women and Work in Los Angeles 1880-1930

UNIVERSITY OF NEVADA PRESS   RENO AND LAS VEGAS

EARNING POWER

Introduction

In 1933 Los Angeles police arrested striking garment worker Anita Castro for distributing union literature. She found herself in a city jail cell surrounded by other women:

One women is sitting, young woman, and she's crying and I says, "Why are you crying? But why are you in jail?" And she says, "because I was soliciting." But I didn't know what soliciting meant. So [she says] "and what were you doing?" And I says, "Well, I was distributing." [Laughs.] She's soliciting, I'm distributing. So I ask her what she was soliciting so she told me. So I says, "Oh, gosh, why do you have to do that for? You shouldn't do that," I said . . . "I tell you what," I said, "I belong to the union," I says, "we're garment workers, and we have a strike, but when the strike is over then there will be plenty of jobs." I says, "You come over and see us at the union and you can get a job sewing, you don't have to go looking for men."[1]

Castro still vividly recalled this encounter when she was interviewed decades later. Perhaps she remembered the young prostitute because it was her first exposure to the seamier side of women's work in the city. Or perhaps Castro remembered her because she had so desperately wanted to help the other woman find a better line of work. In either case, this encounter clearly illustrates the struggle that Southern California's women faced when trying to make their financial way in the world.

This study was designed to recover stories like Castro's and to explore women's contributions to the region's history as political and social actors, as employers and employees, and as wives, mothers, and daughters. In order to do this, we have to go back a century, to when Greater Los Angeles was experiencing its most rapid growth. The population of the city more than quadrupled in the 1880s, growing from 11,183 in 1880 to 50,000 a decade later, faster than any other city in the United States. By 1920 the population of the Los Angeles metropolitan area was five times as large as it had been in 1900. By 1930 metropolitan Los Angeles had "about twice as many people as San Francisco, three times as many as Seattle, and four times as many as Portland and Denver."[2] It ranked fifth among the nation's cities and fourth among its metropolitan areas. This ferocious rate of growth has dominated the city ever since. Plagued with explosive growth, urban sprawl, and visual clutter, Los Angeles contradicts our cherished cultural myth of the West as an open, rural frontier. Instead, the city that has always dominated Southern California has become the prototype for the cities that now dominate the West: Denver, Houston, Phoenix, Seattle, Portland, and Salt Lake City. Whether California can truly be considered a "western" state in any way other than geographically remains a subject of some debate in western historiography. But nonetheless, California's cities played and continue to play crucial roles in the development of the region. Cities in the Far West did not evolve from rural beginnings but rather grew side by side with ranches, farms, and mines. As the fastest-growing and now by far the largest of such cities, Los Angeles is a potent symbol of both the potential and the pitfalls of urban growth.

This study seeks to expand our understanding of how women negotiated both issues of gender and issues of ethnicity to gain an economic foothold in one western city. The years between 1880 and 1930 affected not only the spatial development of Los Angeles but also the opportunities and challenges facing its residents. Looking at women's roles as workers as well as wives, mothers, voters, reformers, and so forth is critical if we are to fully understand Greater Los Angeles's rise to national prominence. Women contributed at every level to the economic, political, and cultural life of the city, but their actions and motives were often quite distinct from those of men.

Tackling women's work in Los Angeles also helps redress the imbalance between the East and West coasts, and between North and South, in the existing scholarship. I argue that Greater Los Angeles was distinct from other American cities for three reasons. First, Los Angeles encompassed more ethnic diversity within its boundaries than more established cities like Boston, New York, or even Los Angeles's rival city to the north, San Francisco. Mexicans and Mexican Americans, Chinese, Japanese, African Americans, and

European immigrants shared the city with native-born Americans from the midwestern and eastern United States. This tremendous diversity complicated and sometimes confounded attempts to rigidly structure the economy by race or ethnicity and by gender. Ultimately, however, both the city's economy and its social structure privileged white men over white women, white women over minority men, and (in some but not all cases) minority men over minority women.

Second, by 1890 Los Angeles's population had a nearly equal ratio of women to men. In contrast, by 1890 San Francisco, Denver, Portland, Seattle, and Spokane all had more men than women. More of California's women worked outside the home for wages than in other parts of the western United States. This was in part a reflection of larger statewide trends. As early as 1870 more than half of the 172,145 women living in the western states and territories lived in only one state: California. This concentration of women had a direct impact on employment. By the end of the nineteenth century California also had one of the highest rates of single women aged twenty-five to twenty-nine (the prime years for employment) in the country.[3] In fact, in 1880, 1890, and 1900 in the Pacific and mountain states of the American West the highest percentages of females working outside the home for wages were found in California. Nevada and Colorado had the next highest percentages, while Idaho and New Mexico had the lowest.[4] The increasingly urban nature of Greater Los Angeles made the city particularly attractive to female migrants. Given the limited economic opportunities available to women in rural areas, young single women across the United States migrated at a higher rate and at an earlier age than men to towns and cities in search of work. By 1900 women living in cities were more likely to work for wages than were women in the United States as a whole. These trends accelerated in the last decade of the nineteenth century, and may explain why so many women were moving to Los Angeles. With women making up a greater proportion of the population than in many other cities, Los Angeles becomes an ideal Far Western city to explore life for women in the urban West.[5]

Third, rapid urban growth in Greater Los Angeles generated a great deal of economic, social, and political instability.[6] Women, in particular, found it particularly difficult to find steady, well-paid employment in the city. Unlike either their western male counterparts or women in the East, working women in both the urban and the rural West found work primarily in service industries. Rapid growth frequently created new opportunities but destroyed others. As John Putnam explains, "Growth in a short time span [exposes] in greater relief the conflicts and struggles Americans faced in the industrial age."[7]

Reintroducing women workers to the narrative demands that we reconsider some of our assumptions about the nature of Greater Los Angeles's economy. This includes its image as a bastion of the "open shop" where unions were powerless in the face of capital. I argue that when it came to female workers, the "victory" of the open shop was never as definitive as some have claimed. Women's search for an economic role in the constant flux of Greater Los Angeles meant that some women found remarkable success. But women also frequently ran afoul of ethnic and gender biases that limited their economic opportunities.

In order to better explore these dynamics I have chosen to use a broad definition of "worker" and "working class" in this study. My definition includes those women working outside the home for wages and, in the case of "working class," the wives and daughters of wage-earning men below the level of professionals. Working and nonworking women's volunteer efforts, such as club work and suffrage campaigning, will also be considered.[8]

By the late nineteenth century Greater Los Angeles had a central downtown business area. It housed a wide range of enterprises providing job opportunities for women: several major department stores, thousands of offices, and businesses ranging from banks and schools to cafés and saloons. Los Angeles was also home to the region's garment businesses and many of its steam laundries. Downtown Los Angeles housed the first local branch of the Young Women's Christian Association (YWCA), and most of the major women's clubs would build their clubhouses there. Not surprisingly, downtown Los Angeles was thus at the center of many women's working and social lives. But a working woman did not have to live in downtown Los Angeles. Boyle Heights, a fashionable Anglo residential district on the east side of the Los Angeles River, the "westside" neighborhoods of Bunker Hill and Echo Park, and the area around Temple Street north of downtown were filled with stately homes and more modest bungalows; residents had an easy commute to downtown. Los Angeles had also begun to creep westward toward the ocean, where newer wealthier communities and beach towns appeared. Like spokes on a wheel, Los Angeles was surrounded by dozens of smaller cities such as San Gabriel, Pasadena, and Santa Monica. Many residents there also worked in and around downtown Los Angeles, commuting back and forth on a variety of available trolley lines. The women in this study thus enjoyed a relative amount of mobility across the rather sprawling network of cities, towns, and neighborhoods that made up Greater Los Angeles at the turn of the century.

Whether she had arrived on her own in the city, had a sick relative to support, or needed to supplement the family income to meet mortgage payments, a woman working outside the home for wages was by the 1880s no longer an unusual occurrence. The years following the end of the Civil War saw a steady increase in the number of women working and living away from home. Three factors influenced the growth of women's employment in this period. First, as industrialization spread, families increasingly purchased goods (soap, textiles, clothing, canned goods, and so on) that used to be produced in the home by wives and daughters. Second, as economic opportunities at home and on the farm shrunk, labor demand in cities expanded. Urban families sought servants, and employers often sought female rather than male labor. Because employers assumed women did not support families, women's wages remained considerably lower than for men in the same jobs. Many mills, factories, and offices thus turned to female employees as a cheap source of labor. Third, a relatively large population of young women increased the likelihood a woman would be available for employment. Prior to 1900 the majority of American women remained single until the age of twenty-five. This stimulated a new trend of independence for women between the end of adolescence and the advent of marriage and motherhood.[9]

U.S. Census data shows the same upward trend in the numbers of women working in California found in the rest of the country. Although workforce participation for California women as a whole increased between 1880 and 1900 (from 13 to 18.7 percent), several variables determined who was most likely to be found working outside the home for wages. First, wives were less likely than single and widowed women to be working. Age also influenced the decision to work: women between the ages of twenty and twenty-four were more likely to work outside the home than any other age group.[10] Unfortunately, most women found work in low-paid, traditionally female occupations. The average weekly pay for an American urban female worker in the late 1880s was $5.68; when adjusted for illness and layoff it fell to just $5.24. An 1889 report by the U.S. Department of Labor estimated an average cost of living for a self-supporting woman to be $5.51 a week. If these figures can be trusted, an American woman thus made roughly $0.27 less a week than would be required to support her if she lived alone.[11]

This gap in pay, along with overwork, lack of advancement, sexual exploitation on the job, and racial as well as gender discrimination, stimulated a larger social debate about women's work in this period. Often referred to as the "problem of the working girl" or of the "woman adrift," it was quite simply this: if women were going to be independent economic actors, how much would American society have to change to accommodate them? The variety of different ways Angelenos answered that question will also be explored in this study.

Scholars now recognize the late nineteenth and early twentieth centuries as a pivotal time for women in the workforce. While women have always worked in one form or another, historically American women's work was largely unpaid and done in the home. Domestic service and work in the mills of New England were exceptions. Superb studies such as Alice Kessler-Harris's seminal *Out to Work: A History of Wage-Earning Women in the United States* and Christine Stansell's *City of Women: Sex and Class in New York, 1789–1860,* as well as more recent work by Maureen Flanagan, Joanne Meyerowitz, Nancy Hewitt, and Eileen Boris, have done a great deal to recover the history of America's working women. Broader studies of American women's political and cultural history, such as those by Estelle Freedman, Paula Baker, Kathy Peiss, Elizabeth Alice Clement, and Rebecca Edwards, provide insight into how both women who worked and those who did not understood their roles in society and in politics.

But scholars of working women have tended to focus on the eastern, rather than the western, half of the country. This has created an unbalanced picture of the nature of women's employment patterns in this period. Living in the American West produced patterns of women's work that look different from those found in other parts of the United States. The work of Glenda Riley, Linda Peavy, and Susan Armitage, among others, has done a great deal to publicize the variety of roles rural women played in the history of the region. These ran the gamut from pioneer wives and mothers to rural entrepreneurs to prostitutes. However, the lack of attention paid to women in western cities becomes especially problematic when one considers that by 1880 almost as many westerners (if not more) lived in cities proportionate to population as their northeastern counterparts. Moreover, gender balances in western cities were far more likely to be equal or nearly equal than in rural areas. Mary Lou Locke's work, for example, compares the western cities of Los Angeles, San Francisco, and Portland in 1880 and finds that women in the urban West experienced far more diversity in backgrounds, jobs, and living arrangements than their eastern counterparts, due largely to late and incomplete industrialization. Edith Sparks's work on female proprietors in nineteenth-century San Francisco reveals women (many of them immigrants) who carved out opportunities in small business. John C. Putnam's excellent study on class and gender politics in Seattle explores the interplay of women and organized labor in an urban environment. Studies by Joan M. Jensen, Gloria Ricci Lothrop, Gayle Gullett, Judith Rosenberg Raferty, and Sherry Jeanne Katz have done a great deal to reintroduce California's women to the historiography. The works of William Deverell, Tom Sitton, Mark Wild, Douglas Flamming, Josh Sides, George Sanchez, and Ricardo Romo have likewise pushed for a closer examination of the role that race and ethnicity have played in Southern California's development.[12]

The historiography also weighs much more heavily toward the nineteenth than the twentieth century. This has created, in the words of Joan M. Jensen and Darlis A. Miller, "a nineteenth-century picture album of women in the West." A small but growing body of scholarship is slowly altering this picture. The work of Vicki Ruiz, Sarah Deutsch, Janis Appier, Natalia Molina, and Lee Simpson takes California and western women's history through to the mid-twentieth century. If the ultimate goal of such scholarship is not just to add more pictures to the album but to modify our view of western history as a whole, then the urban West is an excellent place to begin.[13]

A study of working women in Los Angeles forces us to move beyond issues of pay and opportunity to a reconsideration of the workers themselves. Work, gender, ethnicity, and class are often examined independently of one another, resulting in studies that often see workers as simply black or white, male or female. Instead, we must consider the more complex issue of how these variables combined to shape opportunity. Barbara J. Fields points out that any attempt to privilege race over class (or vice versa) in shaping daily life will invariably ring false. These concepts do not occupy the same analytical space and thus, Fields argues, "cannot constitute explanatory alternatives to each other."[14] Rosaura Sánchez takes this idea one step further by adding gender to the mix. She writes that "there can be no essential gender discourse, only gender discourses in articulation with other discourses, like those of nation, race/caste, religion, family, class, and sexuality, all of which articulate with one another and generate a variety of social identities." Class, gender, and race also became entangled with, and in some cases drove, politics and political behavior. The editors of *The Challenge of Feminist Biography* are even more blunt: "No matter how 'free' of gender-specific conditions a woman may think she is, these conditions nonetheless affect her. In addition, of course, other aspects of her identity—class, race, religion, ethnicity, sexuality, region—also play critical roles."[15]

Certainly, the race or ethnicity of an individual played a key role in this process. The binary of the black versus the white worker that first developed in the southern and eastern United States was eventually applied to other ethnic groups. Asians, American Indians, Mexicans, and often eastern and southeastern European immigrants became characterized as "nonwhite." Historians, most notably among them David R. Roediger, have argued that racism directed at African Americans prevented American workers from mounting any cross-racial opposition to capital. White male workers joined unions organized along lines of both craft and race, shunting African American male workers to largely unskilled, segregated jobs.[16] The identity of "worker" increasingly went hand in hand with a "white" racial identity. I argue that racial exclusion and subjugation offered white female workers in Los Angeles some very real material advantages, from inclusion in some unions to the attention of social reformers. The city's pervasive ethnic divisions also served the needs of capital because it helped keep the female workforce fragmented and often unable to organize effectively.[17]

But racial-ethnic discrimination does not operate independently of class and gender. A multiethnic, multiracial city with an equal or nearly equal gender balance reveals how these interconnected variables impacted the female labor force as well as women's larger economic and social opportunities. Looking at Los Angeles in this era reveals a city that was unusually diverse but also unusually fractured. At times, gender consciousness could and did trump other considerations, but just as often it could not.

Trying to hear the voices of Los Angeles's working women through existing sources is extremely difficult. As in other American cities at this time, the lower a woman was in economic and social status, the less likely she was to leave any records behind her. Most of the largest employers of women, such as steam laundries and independent canneries, no longer exist. I have made extensive use of articles and reports in local newspapers and periodicals that covered women's issues and activities. Local, state, and federal statistics on employment, wages, hours, and population proved invaluable in providing context for this project. Collections left behind by female reformers both shed light on this time period and gave me new leads. Finally, federal census data helped me flesh out some of these women's stories and trace their movements over time.

Chapter 1 focuses on how the economic boom of the 1880s shaped the future of women's work in the city. Economic developments in this period helped shape future patterns of occupational segregation. While Los Angeles's economic and social structures provided many opportunities for determined entrepreneurial women, they also sharply curtailed who would have access to white-collar jobs and, once in them, how far a woman would advance.

Chapter 2 looks at both the least and the most desirable jobs open to women without professional training: domestic service and retail work. Comparing and contrasting the two allows us to explore connections across different segments of the labor market. Greater Los Angeles had a large population of servants, the women whose work made professional and club women's lives easier. Special consideration is given to why so few women were willing to work as domestics, and how that relates to the battle for autonomy and better conditions that domestics waged. The desirability of retail work and the larger social debate about it are also covered here.

Chapter 3 considers the city's women's club movement and its relationship with working women. Both the history of the clubs themselves as well as some of the more notable successes and failures when it came to reaching working women are discussed. This chapter sheds light on how class, ethnicity, and gender combined to shape reform efforts.

Chapter 4 compares and contrasts two different strategies for female unions in Los Angeles: the mixed male-female union and the female-only union. The relationship between unions and women, between male and female union members, and between working women and the city's open-shop proponents illustrates the limitations of collective bargaining to create lasting change.

Chapter 5 examines the tenuous cooperation between working and non-working white and nonwhite women in the 1911 suffrage campaign, and its aftermath. Women's suffrage in California led to the first widespread attempts to investigate and reform industrial work, but this again often put working women and reformers at odds with one another.

Immigrant and nonwhite women at work and in the community are the focus of chapter 6. The connections between residential and occupational segregation, which impacted nonwhite and immigrant workers far more than white workers, are considered here. This chapter places an emphasis on nonwhite and immigrant women's relationship with the power structure and the limitations placed on them both due to gender and ethnicity.

Finally, chapter 7 looks at the new industries that emerged around the time of World War I. By this period Greater Los Angeles's economy was almost fully developed, and each new industry that arrived had to adapt itself to and grapple with existing hiring patterns. The nascent film industry provides a case study of how this worked. Motion pictures simultaneously offered new employment opportunities to women but also exposed old fault lines about gender, ethnicity, and the "proper" role for women in American society.

While it would be impossible to cover the myriad of different jobs, roles, and struggles of Los Angeles's women in the years preceding World War II, this study hopes to create a more complete picture of how urban women's work influenced the economic and historical development of both California and the modern American West.

1

Women in White-Collar Work

"THE SPIRIT TO DARE AND DO"

Beginning with its March 1911 issue, *Sunset* magazine regularly devoted space to profiling women across the American West and their work. As might be expected for a magazine born as a promotional effort, the women profiled seem to have been selected for their potential to represent how women in the West were different from their eastern counterparts.[1] As Los Angeles–based journalist Bertha H. Smith noted in the very first article:

What women are doing in the West might be told in one word—everything. . . . The woman in business, the professional woman, the woman in philanthropic and civic work is common everywhere. But the West, with its abundant and varied natural resources, its youth and its promises, appeals to the imagination of women as of men and offers them the same diverse and tempting opportunities. . . . In the air of the West is a subtle and potent essence which creates in the soul of man the spirit to dare and do. Men and women are pretty much alike, though each resents the accusation, and that women are influenced no less than men by the elixir of the West this series of sketches bears witness.[2]

Female ranchers, farmers, canners, teachers, and entrepreneurs, many of whom lived and worked in Southern California, all earned space in these columns over the next ten years.

Such profiles existed in part thanks to developments almost twenty years earlier. The boom years of the 1880s had opened up new opportunities for women, often in unexpected ways. These new opportunities allowed women to make real contributions to their family economies during a time of unstable regional growth. Professional women, in particular, benefited from a combination of timing, demographics, and structural opportunities. *Sunset* painted a rosy picture of women succeeding purely on their own merit. But such a view masked the complex economic, social, and political shifts at work across the region.

The last two decades of the nineteenth century were a time of profound change in Southern California. Anglo-Americans had solidified their control over the region, and Los Angeles was growing from a small town to an American city. For the descendants of the *Californios,* these were particularly bitter decades in which many saw a steep decline in both their economic and their political clout. Although ethnically and racially diverse, Los Angeles was highly stratified, and its economy was far from being a level playing field. Women, in particular, found it hard to make a respectable living. Few categories of jobs were open to women, and competition for them could be fierce. But economic necessity continued to propel women from all walks of life into the workforce. By 1880 15 percent of the women in Los Angeles worked for wages, slightly lower than the national average but higher than the average for the West as a region or for California as a whole.[3] In 1883 a new wave of rapid growth began, one that further exacerbated the problems of ethnic discrimination, geographic segregation, and a lack of job opportunities for women.

By the early twentieth century a woman's best chance to ensure both her economic and her social future was to enter professional or white-collar work: teaching, medicine, law, business, and other jobs that required advanced education, specialized training, and access to capital. Los Angeles attracted more than its fair share of professional women who took advantage of the city's rapid growth to carve out positions for themselves in the local economy. However, for most women in professions, such work did not translate into equal earning power or the ability to advance in the chosen career. On the contrary, Los Angeles's white-collar workers remained sharply segregated by gender. A dearth of manufacturing and large numbers of white-collar immigrants made jobs scarce, particularly for women of color and those without the training for skilled professions such as teaching.

One of the greatest challenges facing the scholar of women's employment is how to identify and group occupations. While each job has its own particular set of skills, in order to make meaningful comparisons similar jobs need to be grouped into some sort of larger organizational scheme. Where one chooses to place a particular occupation can have profound implications for the larger study, as this can partly predetermine the pattern of social stratification and social mobility one will find. For this project I have chosen to use the occupational classification scheme developed by Mary Lou

Locke for her study of working women in San Francisco, Portland, and Los Angeles in 1880. Locke developed eleven categories based on a consideration of a job's skill level and required training, its status, and its working conditions.[4] Under this scheme professional and other white-collar jobs include teaching, medicine, editing, the law, and university teaching. Women who worked as wholesale merchants, as manufacturers, and in business are also included here. This chapter explores the interplay between the historical development of Greater Los Angeles and the role of women in its economy, with a particular focus on how the boom of the 1880s shaped women's white-collar work.

The Boom of the 1880s and Its Impact on Women's Work

Women's entrepreneurship in Southern California was not a new phenomenon. During California's Spanish and Mexican periods, women had been able to obtain or inherit ranchos. This not only provided an income but also, in keeping with *Californio* tradition, elevated the owner's status considerably. Such women occupied the highest rungs of Los Angeles society. Many bought, sold, traded, and invested their holdings. Some also borrowed and loaned money. A *ranchera,* like her male counterpart, supervised the raising of cattle; managed dairies, vineyards, and orchards; and sold ranch produce. She usually presided over a large household of family, relatives, servants, and guests. Many elite *Californios* had further consolidated wealth by encouraging the marriage of their sisters and daughters to American and European men. Even more middling townswomen in the pueblo of Los Angeles had been able petition the city council to receive grants of land. During this period the council allocated plots of land to residents, preferably heads of households, who needed it to graze animals and grow food. With these smallholdings a woman could usually raise enough food to feed her family.

The decades immediately after the Mexican-American War saw the beginning of Los Angeles's transition from a Mexican pueblo to an American city. But it was really the economic boom of the 1880s that completed that change. The significance of the boom to this story is twofold. The boom economically and culturally incorporated Los Angeles into the rest of the United States. It also attracted the first great wave of American men and women intent on settling, and not just speculating, in Los Angeles. Because the area's economy in that decade centered on tourism, land sales, and health, it did little in the short term to create economic opportunities for the city's women. But because most of these immigrants to Los Angeles intended to stay in the area permanently, most arrived as families or sent for them soon after arriving.

This in large part explains Los Angeles's almost balanced ratio of women to men. Los Angeles also had fewer middle-aged persons of either sex and large numbers of elderly.[5]

Many characteristics of the boom contributed to these women's need to seek paid employment, and the influx of American women would have a significant impact on the city's occupational structure in the decades to come. For *Californios* and *Californianas,* however, who suddenly found themselves in the minority, the boom often deepened economic and social inequalities.[6]

The initial trigger for the boom of the eighties came with the completion of the Southern Pacific Railroad line to Los Angeles in 1875. The Central Pacific founded the Southern Pacific in 1865 specifically to tap the new markets of Southern California. The new line ran down the center of the state from San Francisco to Los Angeles. By 1881 this California line joined the Texas and Pacific at Sierra Blanca near El Paso, and by 1883 the line extended all the way to New Orleans. With the line extended to New Orleans winter migration by eastern and midwestern Americans to California became a regular occurrence. Boosters hired by the Southern Pacific Railroad proved adept at recruiting new travelers. Publications and advertisements circulated by the railroads lauded the climate and rich agricultural land of Los Angeles. These men wrote, lectured, and organized exhibits about California all over the world.

In 1885 Angelenos celebrated the completion of the city's second railroad connection, this one belonging to the Santa Fe Railroad. The two competing railroads promptly entered into a rate war that further fueled migration. Normally, a one-way trip from the Mississippi River to California would cost around $125, but the two lines now dropped their prices in an attempt to capture each other's business. Prices hit rock bottom in 1886, when $1 would take a traveler from Kansas all the way to Los Angeles. In addition to cheap fares, the railroads offered other attractive features to the would-be traveler. So-called emigrant cars offered poorer travelers seats that could fold down into beds and included cooking accommodations. In some cases he or she could purchase a "land-seeker's ticket," in which the fare paid would be applied to the purchase of railway-owned western land. The excursion, or specially directed trip, became the most popular option. The Santa Fe line started excursions on a large scale in 1886. These trips became so popular that by 1887 three to five excursion trains entered California each day.[7]

Many of the new arrivals enjoyed relative wealth. Newspapers of the day remarked on the affluence of these visitors. One observer commented, "The quality of the newcomers is not less noteworthy than their numbers. They are almost invariably persons of American birth, good education, and some means. . . . [T]his is the best American stock; the bone and sinew of the nation; the flower of the American people."[8]

This influx of population and money in turn attracted land speculators. These men flooded the city, triggering a buying frenzy unlike anything the state had ever seen. During June, July, and August 1887 an estimated $38 million in land transactions occurred in Los Angeles. Investors bought up land and then subdivided it and offered tracts for sale to the public. Buyers rarely paid cash. Instead, they purchased land on contract, paying anywhere from one-third to one-fourth down and the rest in installments. Land changed hands so frequently, however, that many transactions were never recorded.[9]

New businesses sprang up across the city, coupled with the rapid growth of old ones. Land prices downtown climbed steadily upward. Speculators noticed the city growing in a southwesterly direction, toward the Pacific. The westside of Los Angeles, they predicted, would become the wealthier section of the city. East Los Angeles and Boyle Heights, however, also attracted buyers once the new Buena Vista Street Bridge over the Los Angeles River connected the area to downtown. Newcomers, rather than natives, made up the bulk of purchasers, and many wrote to relatives back East urging them to move to Los Angeles and join the fun.[10] But not every newcomer found bliss in Los Angeles. Perhaps the city did not always live up to the promises of boosters, because some one thousand people left the city each month during the boom years of 1885–1887.[11]

In spite of promoters' promises that the boom could continue indefinitely, by the winter of 1888 it had collapsed. Easterners had tired of the hysteria over the city, and fewer and fewer arrived. Tourism dropped off dramatically that winter. Fortunately for the speculators, banks had handled the boom conservatively, and few failed. The collapse left the landscape dotted with undeveloped townsites and unsold lots, but many of the city's suburbs can trace their birth to this period. Northern cities like San Francisco and Sacramento for the first time looked at Southern California as a real competitor rather than a dusty cow town.[12]

Although the end of the boom signaled the end to the greatest period of speculation, it also permanently reshaped Southern California. Most notably, Los Angeles County's population, which had increased some 30 percent between 1860 and 1870 and then doubled the following decade, now more than tripled during the 1880s—all this in spite of the subtraction of some thirty thousand citizens with the creation of Orange County in 1889.[13]

But the boom had failed to attract many manufacturing concerns to the city. The reasons were purely economic. Southern California's still relatively sparse population did not provide enough local demand for most manufacturing businesses to survive. The distance from eastern markets made costs for shipping Los Angeles–made goods across the nation prohibitive. Investment capital could be difficult to obtain. Those already living in the area, as well as easterners looking for investments, chose to put their money elsewhere, most notably into real estate. The professional orientation of immigrants also meant that the city had a very limited labor supply: its new residents were doctors or businessmen, not unskilled laborers or craftsmen. Because of such problems, in 1890 Los Angeles, with its fifty thousand people and 750 firms, manufactured only $9.9 million in goods. This placed the city behind not only larger western cities like San Francisco and Denver but even smaller ones like Portland and Seattle.[14]

While retail and a few light-manufacturing enterprises dotted 1880s Los Angeles, most employed few if any women. Relatively few women worked in dressmaking, millinery, tailoring, and general needlework because workers in San Francisco filled much of the demand for these consumer items.[15] But unlike previous regional "booms," by the end of the 1880s Southern California's economy was now sufficiently well developed to offer a relatively broad range of opportunities to women.[16] White Anglo and European women who worked did so largely in teaching and domestic service, with a few also finding work as clerks or in the skilled trades, such as printing. African American and Mexican American women who sought paid employment outside the home were limited by the openly racist hiring policies of the late nineteenth century. Most could find work only in service occupations like domestic service and tending the sick. However, other factors, such as easy transportation to California, widowhood, and the high cost of housing in Southern California, ensured that women of all ethnicities would still be looking for work and to build new lives in Los Angeles.

Women as Migrants, Women as Workers

The boom of the 1880s provided the underpinnings for much of the region's subsequent economic development. It also had a profound impact on how and why women migrated there. In order to understand women and work, we must pause briefly to consider who these women were and why they came to Southern California.

One of the reasons Southern California attracted so many women, including single women, in these years was the availability of railroads. Unlike previous generations of women, who endured arduous journeys by wagon, ship, and even foot to reach California, by the early 1880s many women had only to buy a ticket and spend a few relatively pleasant days on a train to reach Los Angeles. Railroads had in fact quickly learned how to make travel appealing to women by emphasizing its safety, its respectability, and its convenience. In her superb analysis of gender and American railroads, Amy G. Richter argues that railroads were in fact tapping into the "New Woman" ideal of the 1880s and 1890s: "Capable yet feminine, strong yet demure, she embodied the possibility of a public life that maintained gender differences without burdening men with the protection of women." By the 1890s the New Woman was cropping up regularly in railroad advertising, engaging in "vigorous, albeit respectable, activities . . . playing sports, posing on beaches, or walking the seashore with binoculars." These sorts of combinations, Richter argues, were key to the success of railroad advertising. The New Woman might travel to California for the winter, or even move to California and luxuriate in a tropical garden, but she could never completely separate from more traditional "Victorian" womanhood.[17]

The Southern Pacific Railroad in particular frequently made attractive young women the centerpiece of some of its advertising. One ad from 1904 featured a photograph of a rosy-cheeked, fashionably dressed young woman with the slogan, "I'm going to spend the winter in California—why don't you come, too?" A 1905 cover of *Sunset* magazine featured a lovely woman standing in a lush California garden, her arms laden with large breastlike fruit. If one believed the promotions and advertising, Southern California was no Wild West frontier. It was a Mediterranean Eden that women could easily reach and where they would be welcome.[18] As Lee Simpson notes, women themselves often played key roles in creating and promoting this image of the region, first as boosters and later as budding politicians.[19] If a young woman was looking for a fresh start or an adventure, traveling to Southern California could not have been easier or seemed more appealing.

But Southern California had another, more tragic, attraction: its reputation as a place to heal the sick. Some Anglo-American women who relocated to Los Angeles in this decade came either as invalids or with an ill family member. Here again advertising played a role. One doctor suggested the climate would cure persons of "delicate constitution," dyspeptic troubles, chronic kidney and bladder trouble, nervous prostration, chronic rheumatism, and asthma. Tuberculosis (or consumption, as it was known at the time) could purportedly be cured by a trip to Los Angeles, where the pure air would heal the invalid just through breathing. Several thousand tuberculosis sufferers relocated to Los Angeles, creating a minor health crisis. Many advanced cases arrived alone in a city without adequate hospital or medical facilities to care for them. In 1886 the Sisters of Charity opened St. Vincent's Sanitarium in the hills above the city, designed to accommodate the sick at reasonable rates. The Los Angeles Sanitarium on South Hill Street soon opened for business as well.[20]

Overwhelmingly white, American, and professional, the "health-seeking" immigrant also had a unique impact on the city's occupational structure. Semiprofessional and professional jobs filled quickly, while openings in the skilled trades or even manual labor often went unfilled. "The towns and country are overstocked with lawyers, doctors, merchants, and clerks," one visitor observed.[21] The wives and daughters of men who either could not find jobs or were too ill to work added to the ranks of the city's working women.

Not surprisingly, Greater Los Angeles also became a mecca of sorts for widows. Some were women who had lost their spouses shortly after relocating. Others moved after widowhood, looking for a warm climate and, often, a lower cost of living. In either case being a widow in Southern California often precipitated a crisis. A woman, separated from her extended family back East, now had to struggle to find the means to support herself and her children.

This was exactly the challenge that faced Clara Wheeler. She had received a college education and had worked as a teacher. But Wheeler had left the workforce when her son, Roy, was born in the early 1880s. Her husband, H. Milman Wheeler, was a professor of Greek at a midwestern university before he developed tuberculosis. In 1885 the family moved to Los Angeles, where Milman Wheeler taught for at time at the University of Southern California (USC). Within a year, however, he succumbed to the disease. Left alone with a young son, Mrs. Wheeler was fortunate to have connections among some of the elite women in the city. She was given the position of matron at the new Flower Festival Home and the job of overseeing the new Women's Exchange (see chapter 3). "Board and twenty-five dollars a month just seemed like a gift from heaven," she later wrote. "Of course I accepted the position with gratitude in my heart and one black dress in my wardrobe." To further ensure her and her son's future she traded a set of her late husband's encyclopedias for a lot near USC. She later sold it at a profit. This was the beginning of what would become vast real estate holdings, to which Wheeler would add during her two subsequent marriages, to Col. Presley C. Baker in 1890 and to the Reverend Robert J. Burdette in 1899.[22]

Other widows were even luckier. Jesse Benton Frémont had recently lost her husband, "Pathfinder" John C. Frémont, and was nearly broke when she and her daughter, Elizabeth, arrived in Southern California. The women of Los Angeles were so thrilled to have such a notable personage in their midst that they raised money to have a house built. It was then presented as a gift to Frémont and her daughter. The two women lived quite comfortably as large fish in the rather small society pond that was late-nineteenth-century Los Angeles. Mrs. Lucretia Rudolph Garfield, widow of President James A. Garfield, also settled just outside Los Angeles, in Pasadena, in the early 1900s. Local society heralded this as another great coup.[23]

Competition for available housing and the rising cost of housing may also have pushed many women into the job market during the boom. The trickle of newcomers in 1885 had become a veritable flood in 1887, and the city's population was estimated to have jumped in this two-year span from eleven thousand to eighty thousand. An estimated one hundred new houses a month went up around the city in the boom years. The cost of housing grew faster than the overall cost of living. Landowners generally preferred to build to sell, not to rent, out of fear they would not recoup their investment. This meant a family either needed to have cash in hand when they arrived or had to come up with some way to meet steep mortgage payments. For some families, this meant sending wives and daughters to work outside the home.[24]

Women in White-Collar Jobs: Teaching, Medicine, and Law

If a woman had to or wanted to work, obtaining a white-collar job or owning her own business was probably her best option. "White-collar" jobs that would have been available in the 1880s included professional jobs (teachers, physicians, editors, lawyers, university professors, wholesale merchants and manufacturers) and semiprofessional jobs (public nurses, artists, music teachers, and so on).[25] Greater Los Angeles did provide many opportunities for this sort of work, as did other western cities. With only 5 percent of the nation's population and only 4 percent of its adult women, in 1890 the western states had 14 percent of all female lawyers and 10 percent of all female doctors and journalists. Almost twice as many women living in western states engaged in professional work than elsewhere in the country.[26]

Ethnicity was one major factor in determining who could and could not enter white-collar and professional work. But it appears to have played less of a role in Los Angeles than elsewhere. Los Angeles's European immigrant women, in particular, often found positions in white-collar work such as teaching, a phenomenon virtually unknown in other cities of the period. Young single immigrant women working in Los Angeles in 1880 were more than twice as likely to hold white-collar jobs as immigrant women working in Portland or San Francisco. Proportionally fewer jobs existed for young women in semiprofessional or clerical and sales white-collar work in Los Angeles than in San Francisco. But immigrant women also had good luck in finding jobs in these professions. In fact, white immigrant women actually had more success in finding these positions than American-born Anglo- or Mexican American women. In 1880 a quarter of native-born women held white-collar jobs in Los Angeles, compared to 32 percent of foreign-born women. This may have been because most of the merchants in the city had immigrated there themselves. They thus preferred hiring women from their own communities, when they hired women at all. German women had the highest rate of employment in white-collar jobs, at 52 percent. Irish women had the lowest, with 27 percent, but this is still higher than the rate for native-born American women. Another study suggests that because of the expense involved in migrating to Los Angeles, European immigrants may have been more affluent and less "foreign" than the majority of immigrants in East Coast cities. They thus may have entered into the professional ranks more easily than their poorer countrymen and women elsewhere. In fact, European-born workers of both sexes found work in white-collar occupations in Los Angeles at much higher rates than those who lived in the East or even other western cities.[27]

The single largest category of white-collar work for women in Los Angeles was teaching. Its new residents stressed the importance of expanding Anglo-American culture in the area, and therefore schools took on particular importance in the community. Although there had been several privately operated schools during the Mexican period, the first city-owned and operated public school opened in 1855. Students were divided by gender, and therefore one teacher was male, the other female. The teachers were William A. Wallace and Louisa Hayes.[28] The city's first public high school opened in 1873, and the first kindergarten in California opened in the city three years later. As the boom of the 1880s took hold, the number of schools in the city and county multiplied. Los Angeles County, which in 1860 had only seven schools and an enrollment of just 460 students, by 1885 had 11,368 students divided between two hundred school buildings.[29]

The development of schools took place against a larger national gender shift in the teaching profession. Teaching increasingly became a "woman's" job. School boards embraced female teachers because they could be paid less than males. Reformers promoted teaching as a respectable job for single women who needed to work. Los Angeles–area schools followed this trend.

By 1875 women filled fourteen of the twenty-eight teaching positions in the city, and twenty years later women taught almost all of the elementary classes in Los Angeles. By 1898 the male schoolmaster was an endangered species: a survey that year of Los Angeles County schools found 679 female teachers but only 121 male ones.[30]

Beyond its respectability, teaching in Greater Los Angeles offered some clear advantages for female teachers. For young people living in Los Angeles, Orange, Riverside, or San Bernardino counties, their proximity to the Los Angeles branch of the California State Normal School, opened in 1881, made it relatively convenient to train for a teaching career.[31]

In 1874 an act of the California state legislature had declared that female teachers should be paid the same as male teachers, provided they held the same qualifications. The reasoning behind this act remains a bit opaque. Legislators may have viewed it as a way to attract and retain as many qualified teachers as possible to meet the growing demand, or it may have been the outcome of the growing women's rights movement in the state. In spite of this act, the average salaries of women teaching in the state remained substantially lower than those of men. But Los Angeles still offered advantages: classes were relatively small, and salaries for women more closely equaled those of male teachers than in other cities.[32]

There was little upward mobility for ambitious teachers. Few women taught at the high school level, and fewer still carved out careers teaching at the college level or as school administrators. The most notable exception was Dr. Susan Dorsey, who started her teaching career at Los Angeles High School in 1896 and worked her way up to vice principal. In 1913 she became Los Angeles's first female assistant superintendent of public schools, and in 1920 the Board of Education hired her as superintendent of the Los Angeles school system. Dorsey was the second woman in the country to head a large urban school district. Because married women were not allowed to teach in Los Angeles's schools, most contemporary accounts of Dorsey's life claimed she was a widow. In reality her husband had taken the couple's only child and abandoned her.[33] In 1916 Dr. Ethel Percy Andrus of Los Angeles's Lincoln High became the first woman in California hired as a principal for a secondary school.[34]

Female teachers made more money than women in many other jobs, and worked shorter hours as well. However, the seasonal nature of teaching often meant that a woman needed some financial flexibility. For three months of the year she needed to fall back either on family support, on her savings (if she had any), or on another temporary job.[35] Teacher Mary Lang complained to a local newspaper that she and her fellow teachers had to turn to either taking in sewing or selling real estate during the summer to make ends meet. Lang also reported that many women would have liked to work as waitresses in the summer months but that doing so might have cost them their teaching jobs. Unlike teaching, waitressing was of questionable respectability in the late nineteenth century (see chapter 4).[36]

Teachers were also vulnerable to the caprice of school superintendents and local school boards. In the nineteenth and into the twentieth centuries these bodies had complete control over the hiring and firing of teachers. As David Tyack notes, teachers often became the unfortunate victims of power struggles between school boards and superintendents. A teacher who lost her job had virtually no recourse.[37] Although many teachers belonged to the National Educational Association (NEA) or the Los Angeles Teachers' Association or both, they lacked any central body that might pressure the community to raise wages.[38]

Los Angeles's teachers resisted unionization. In 1893, for example, the Los Angeles Council of Labor approached local schoolteachers, urging them to organize. The council promised that the unions would support teachers in a dispute with the Board of Education, which now insisted that all teachers be qualified to give music lessons. The teachers, however, refused to become entangled with the city's organized-labor movement. They no doubt feared that siding with organized labor in a period of tense capital-labor relations in the city could erode sympathy and support for them in the community.[39] They preferred to rely instead on the Board of Education. "We feel it will only be necessary for us to study into conditions [sic] and formulate measures for the common good of teachers," Helen Matthewson, president of the Los Angeles Teachers' City Club noted, "and . . . these measures will be acted upon favorably by the board at our suggestion, and without necessity for demand on our part." Threatened with a shift to a merit-pay system in 1912, the Teachers' City Club sent only a letter of protest to the board. Fortunately for them, the board evidently dropped that plan.[40]

Like teaching, librarianship was also a white-collar profession with the right mixture of steady pay and respectability. While Los Angeles's two previous librarians had both been men, in 1880 the city's library board decided it would only hire a "lady librarian." This decision may have been guided by the fact that women heavily patronized the library and had objected to the "intemperate" behavior of the previous male librarian. It was also part of a larger national trend of employing young women as librarians for economic reasons. Los Angeles's first city librarian, John Littlefield, had made $100 a month when hired in 1872, but in 1878 the board dropped his salary to $75 a month. Some board members argued in favor of dropping the salary for the job, which included janitorial as well as library duties, even lower. The library board may have assumed they would not attract a respectable male librarian for the salary they were willing to pay.[41]

Journalist Elizabeth Banks, visiting Southern California in 1904, nonetheless expressed pleasure at seeing "so important a public institution in the hands of my own sex." She found that city libraries employed more than forty women who worked seven hours a day and earned anywhere from $30 to $150 a month, depending on position and seniority. The city operated its own training school, which was free but open only to applicants between the ages of eighteen and thirty. "Under eighteen they are too young to begin," Banks observed, "and beyond thirty they are too old."[42]

Like female teachers, female librarians often faced challenges from male superiors. The career of one of the most notable of these new "lady librarians," Mary Emily Foy, illustrates how much power the all-male library board could exert over a female librarian's job. Foy had been born into an elite local family in 1862. She took over the Los Angeles Public Library, consisting of three rooms on the second floor of the Downey Block, at Main, Spring, and Temple, in September 1880 at a salary of $75 a month. Foy set up a catalog system, kept the library accounts, acted as hostess in the Ladies Reading Room, and settled bets made in the downstairs saloon. The library board renewed Foy's appointment for three years, undoubtedly due in part to pressure on his fellow board members from her neighbor and family friend, Mayor John Toberman. But in 1884 the new mayor, C. E. Thom, reorganized the library council. This time the council decided to give Foy's job to another woman more in need of it: Jessie Gavitt, whose father had recently died and who needed to support her mother and siblings. Perhaps sensing this move had more to do with politics than Miss Gavitt's financial need, Foy published a valedictory in the newspaper, which criticized the board for a lack of involvement with and interest in the library. Undaunted, Foy made a successful move from one white-collar job (librarian) to another (teacher). She trained as a teacher at the Los Angeles State Normal School, taught in the lower grades, and later served as an elementary school principal. She joined the English Department of her alma mater, Los Angeles High School, in 1893. Foy's case, while perhaps exceptional, illustrates that a white, educated, and well-off woman could move with relative ease from one white-collar position to another in Los Angeles, at least so long as she knew the right people.[43]

But while American and European women could find work in white-collar and professional jobs, the city's minority women, particularly its African American women, often received a cold shoulder from potential employers. However, African American women in Los Angeles who needed a positive example had before them the example of Biddy Mason, a prominent member of the community who had been born a slave. Mason's owner had moved her and her three daughters from Missouri to Utah to San Bernardino, California. Once in California Mason and several other slaves had sued for and won their freedom in 1856. Mason then decided to remain in Los Angeles. She went to work as a nurse and acquired a reputation as a skilled midwife. She delivered hundreds of babies for both the elite and the city's poor. Mason invested money in land downtown, sections of which she sold during the boom of the 1880s. She also became a significant force in the African American community where she helped found the First African Methodist Episcopal Church in 1872 and provided financial help to the African American community.[44]

By the 1880s African American women in the West were better positioned for entry into white-collar work than perhaps anywhere else in the nation. First, they benefited from greater educational opportunities in the West, where many families kept their daughters in school longer than they did in other parts of the country. Second, with so many coming from middle-class families, fewer African American women had to work outside the home for wages. When choosing a profession, women who worked for personal reasons, rather than pure economic need, could afford to be selective. Douglas Flamming's study found that from 1900 to 1920 women made up about half of the black workforce in Atlanta, New Orleans, and San Antonio. "In Los Angeles, women represented less than one-third of the black workforce in 1900, and slightly more than one-third in 1920."[45]

African American women initially found some opportunity for work as teachers in the segregated school system of California. By the 1880s, however, lawsuits had integrated most schools, leading to a decline in the numbers of black female schoolteachers. In its first twenty years the Los Angeles State Normal School graduated only two African American women: Alice Rowan in 1888 and Grace Harrison in 1903. Neither young woman taught in Los Angeles's public schools. Rowan worked in the predominately Mexican American Trujillo School District in Riverside and as a music teacher. Harrison was recruited to teach at the Tuskegee Institute.[46] It was not until 1911 that another Normal School graduate, Bessie Bruington Burke, became the first African American, male or female, to teach in Los Angeles's city schools.

Burke later became the first African American principal in the city.[47] By 1920 there were twenty-five African American teachers in Los Angeles's public schools, all teaching on the east side in predominately white schools. But for the majority of the city's African American women, such jobs remained the exception, not the rule.[48]

Mexican Americans also faced challenges. Some Mexican American women found jobs in teaching, particularly in Spanish-language instruction. This is particularly interesting because in this era both Mexican American and Mexican immigrant children across Southern California were increasingly being pushed into segregated schools. The same does not appear to have been true of Mexican American teachers.[49]

The relatively small numbers of Mexican American women who successfully entered teaching may be due to several factors. A woman usually needed both financial and familial support to get the training required for a white-collar job like teaching. In the face of persistent economic as well as racial discrimination it may have been more difficult for Mexican and Mexican American families to make this sacrifice. Mexican and Mexican American women also had to grapple with Southern California's tendency to locate them solely in California's romantic past rather than as part of its economic and political future. Many potential employers may not have taken Mexican and Mexican American job applicants seriously.[50]

One family that overcame these challenges was the de Lopez family of San Gabriel, approximately thirty miles east of downtown Los Angeles. Guadalupe Maria de Lopez and Ernestina de Lopez were the two youngest children in a large family. Their father had been a blacksmith. The family's oldest daughter, Belen, had lived at home and worked as a seamstress. No doubt she had been contributing to the family's income, and the de Lopez sons probably did the same. Two other sisters had married and left home. But by the late 1890s, with all of their older children grown and out of the house, it may have been financially easier for their parents, Nepomiceno and Guadalupe, to keep their youngest daughters in school.[51] Both Maria and Ernestina completed high school and then graduated from the Los Angeles Normal School. Maria went on to the University of California. When their father died in 1904 the two women returned home to San Gabriel to live with their mother. To support her financially both worked as Spanish teachers.[52] Of the two sisters, Maria de Lopez eventually carved out the more distinguished career. In 1902 she became the youngest instructor at the University of California, she was a Spanish-language translator for the suffrage movement during the 1911 statewide campaign, and eventually she taught at the University of California at Los Angeles (UCLA), making her possibly the first Latina ever to do so. After her marriage, she became Maria de Lopez Lowther, or sometimes Maria de Lopez de Lowther.[53]

By the 1910s the family's adobe house was just a few doors away from the theater that housed one of Southern California's most popular tourist attractions, *The Mission Play*. This was a heavily romanticized, semifictional account of the region's Spanish and Mexican past.[54] The author of that play, John Steven McGroarty, knew the house, the Casa Vieja, "an old adobe of the best type," well. Maria and Ernestina operated a Spanish-language school there as a side business. McGroarty was one of their students. His teachers were, McGroarty told *Los Angeles Times* readers in 1914, "olive-cheeked, dusky-eyed, and raven-haired: in every way lovely. . . . Spanish made easy? Si, senor: and very pleasant, too."[55] To supplement their income, both de Lopez sisters also worked as translators for a variety of authors, including McGroarty himself.[56]

In nearby Pomona, Manuela Ornelas also struggled to reconcile her need to make a living with the cultural expectations placed upon her as a Mexican American. Ornelas was the daughter of a grocer, and like the de Lopez sisters, she attended the Los Angeles Normal School. She, too, carved out a career teaching Spanish in the public schools, and was heavily involved with a variety of clubs and organizations.[57]

Ethnic discrimination may also have been a contributing factor in the relative dearth of Mexican American teachers in this period. Although there are no surviving records that break down Southern California's teaching population by ethnicity, it is entirely possible that potential employers preferred to hire Anglo teachers for everything other than Spanish-language instruction.[58]

Outside of the public schools, many employers would not hire Mexican American or Mexican immigrant women for white-collar jobs. Mexican American men encountered similar problems. By 1880 only slightly more than two-fifths of the city's male Mexican American population worked in white-collar or skilled jobs. More than two-thirds of Los Angeles's European American workers and four-fifths of its non-Hispanic native-born population worked in such jobs. Hispanic women entered the workforce in increasing numbers throughout the 1880s, but most young, single Mexican-American women could find work only as servants or in the needle trades. Ironically, even when a storekeeper advertised for a clerk who could speak

Spanish, he expected the applicant to be "American," which generally meant non-Hispanic.[59]

While training for a career as a teacher required some specialized training, women who wanted to enter the "classic" male-dominated professions of medicine and law faced even greater hurdles. The practice of barring women from these professions limited women's opportunities across the United States throughout the nineteenth and early twentieth centuries. But California's new state constitution (drafted in 1879) had incorporated provisions outlawing discrimination against women in education and in "any lawful" business or profession, making the state seem friendly to professional women. Having this law on the books, however, did little to prevent de facto gender discrimination in business or higher education. Such practices lasted well into the twentieth century.[60] With a growing (and sickly) population, Los Angeles attracted several female doctors, many nurses, and even a few lawyers.

Reform-minded women created a public-health nursing association in 1894 as part of the new Los Angeles College Settlement (see chapter 6). Settlement workers also persuaded the city to pay their in-house nurse a salary of fifty dollars a month. Under the guidance of Pittsburgh-born Maude Foster Weston, the Instructive District Nursing Association for the City of Los Angeles, as it became known, served the area of downtown near the settlement and along both sides of the Los Angeles River. In its first nine years it provided care to an estimated seven thousand people. The association later merged into the Los Angeles Health Department.[61]

Like most woman doctors of the era, Dr. Rose Talbott Bullard trained in the eastern United States. She moved to Los Angeles in 1886. Two years later she married another physician, with whom she had one daughter. Dr. Talbott Bullard not only ran a private medical practice with her husband but also taught gynecology at USC and served on the board of the Los Angeles branch of the Young Women's Christian Association. Dr. M. Evangeline Jordon started her career as a teacher, but eventually earned a degree in dentistry from the University of California. She opened a private practice in Los Angeles in 1899 and became the first dentist in the United States to specialize in the care of children's teeth. Like Dr. Talbott Bullard, Dr. Jordon also devoted some of her time to teaching at USC. Los Angeles got its first female lawyer in 1897 when Elizabeth L. Kenney set up her practice. Kenney specialized in probate matters and in administering estates, and also became prominent in the local women's suffrage movement. She also served as the attorney for the Women's Pacific Coast Oil Company, a short-lived, all-woman enterprise that speculated in Kern County's oil district.[62]

Women in Business and Real Estate

Women with access to capital, a good idea, or a service to offer might choose opening their own businesses over other white-collar work. Like teaching, medicine, or law, owning a business could be a path to better pay and higher social status.

Of all the female entrepreneurs in postboom Los Angeles, none was more celebrated than Emma A. Summers, the "Oil Queen of Southern California." A native of Tennessee, Summers had moved to Los Angeles in the 1870s and worked as a music teacher. When oil was discovered in the Los Angeles basin, Summers began investing her savings into oil wells she tended herself like "a sick babe's cradle." The wells did not immediately produce, and she was soon more than ten thousand dollars in debt with a family of seven to support. But her wells eventually paid off. She soon became a key independent oil producer and broker in the region, working primarily with Iowa Standard Oil. By 1900 Summers controlled half of the oil production in the original Los Angeles Field. By 1911 she had made enough money to build a grand house on fashionable Wilshire Boulevard and to maintain a suite of three offices in downtown Los Angeles.[63]

Like Summers, June Rand was another woman with a good idea. When a placement agency proved unable to find her any sort of employment, Rand decided to try to sell the dresses and aprons she had long made for herself. Traveling from shop to shop, Rand drummed up enough orders to launch her business. She named it Sassy Jane, after one of her most popular dress designs. By 1918 Sassy Jane products were so popular that Rand oversaw a downtown factory with eighty employees. She claimed that male dry-goods salesmen and bankers had deliberately tried to bankrupt her by offering her too much credit. But "by buying goods on sixty days' time and selling on thirty she has managed to keep going without capital," one article crowed. By 1921 Rand employed two hundred people, and her factory occupied almost an entire city block downtown.[64]

With racist hiring practices often limiting their access to other professions, African American women seized the opportunity to open businesses of their own across Southern California. The nature of African American migration to Los Angeles made this possible. As Douglas Flamming notes, "Most of the migrants were city people, by birth and upbringing, and most arrived with some savings."[65] A Mrs. Davis not only owned her own hairdressing parlor on the corner of Pico and Main but also employed and trained young African American women in the beauty trade. Maxine Leeds Craig notes that the sale of hair-care products and services (particularly those produced by Madam C. J. Walker and Annie Turnbo Malone) gave African American women across the country their entrée into small-business ownership. Francis Dawson built and operated her own grocery store and ran a poultry business on the side. In the early twentieth century Nannie Reynolds Hall was probably Los Angeles's best-known caterer.[66] Charlotta Spears (later Charlotta Spears Bass) arrived as a health seeker. She found a job with Los Angeles's local African American race paper, the California *Eagle,* and ultimately became its owner and managing editor. When she married reporter Joseph "Big Joe" Bass in 1914, he became "editor" in charge of editorial content and Spears became "managing editor" in charge of the business operation of the newspaper.[67]

Like their male counterparts, women across Southern California also actively speculated in real estate. When a 1905 study of property owners in Los Angeles estimated that women owned one-third of all property across the city, the *Los Angeles Times* offered an explanation for the phenomenon. Women, "energetic and full of business push, have been strong in the belief that fortunes come quicker to those who hustle while they wait. . . . [They] have kept their nest-egg rolling until, like the boy's snowball, it has increased to enormous proportions." However, Lee Simpson argues that for most women, real estate speculation was not simply a product of "hustle." She believes that for many women, taking advantage of their legal right to own property actually came slowly, and only after what Simpson calls an "apprenticeship" period, in which they often shared ownership with male family members. In time, such "apprenticeships" made women confident enough to strike out on their own.[68] Among the major players in local real estate that the *Times* singled out were several *Californianas,* such as Mrs. Maria Antonio de Woodworth, who still controlled part of her family's original holdings. But they also found relative newcomers, such as Clara Wheeler Bradley Burdette, making considerable fortunes buying and selling property as the market fluctuated. African American women also speculated in real estate. For those shut out of white-collar jobs, owning, selling, or renting real estate provided a "risky but rewarding" living.[69]

Given the interest women had in buying and selling property, female real estate agents soon followed. In 1902 Adelia Edwards Hickman became the first women to establish her own real estate office, Union Square Realty, in Los Angeles. Mary Vititoe followed in Hickman's footsteps and became Hollywood's youngest real estate agent by targeting female buyers. "[Male agents] took it for granted that only the men had money," she explained. "Maybe so—but the men buy what their wives, their mothers, want. So I determined to sell to the women, to advertise to the women, to develop the personal touch and the personality angle which stern businessmen tell you you must smother into a routine machine-like dignity if you are to succeed." By the time *Sunset* magazine profiled Vititoe she was making thirteen hundred dollars a month in commissions alone. Other women used real estate as a springboard to other careers. In the early 1920s Consuelo Castillo de Bonzo, a native of Aquas Caliente, Mexico, who had moved to Los Angeles as a child, was a successful real estate agent. In 1923 she invested her savings in a Mexican restaurant, located first on South Spring Street, and later on Olvera Street. The restaurant, La Golondrina, is still in business today.[70]

By the 1920s women who wanted to open their own businesses in Southern California benefited from an array of specialized services, including a women's banking department in Los Angeles's branch of the Bank of Italy. The Bank of Italy assumed that women needing bank loans, start-up capital, or investment advice would be reluctant to approach male tellers. Its new women's banking department had seventeen female staffers headed by Miss Grace Stoermer. Stoermer had been the first-ever female secretary for California's state senate; she eventually became an assistant vice president for Bank of America. Stoermer was active not only in a variety of local businesswomen's clubs but also in the National Association of Bank Women. She took her role in Southern California's financial life very seriously. "I can honestly say that nowhere [do] I find women so keen in business, so alert, progressive, and full of personality as the businesswomen of Los Angeles," she reported. "California women . . . should never underestimate their business ability. It is a liability so to discount one of your greatest assets."[71]

African American businesswomen also forged their own networks of support, including the Sojourner Truth Industrial Home and the Day Nursery of Los Angeles (see chapter 3). The latter provided safe day care for the children of working African American women. The Women's Business Club encouraged African American women to pursue economic independence, and the local branch of the National Association for the Advancement of Colored People (NAACP) fought against job discrimination.[72]

But the limits of opportunity, even in a booming economy, can be seen most clearly in the case of the region's Chinese and Chinese American women. An area just east of the Plaza had became the nucleus for Los Angeles's first Chinatown. Many Chinese had originally come to California in search of gold or as labor on the railroads, but by the 1870s some had settled in Los Angeles. The Chinese were an exception to the city's gender balance: in those early years only about 16 percent of the Chinese population was female. Chinese men, their opportunities curtailed by racism and discriminatory laws, worked in laundries, sold vegetables, and cooked for elite families.[73] Whites grudgingly tolerated the Chinese because they satisfied the city's demand for cheap labor, particularly as servants. Reflecting on life in the city in the 1850s, businessman Harris Newmark remembered, "It was not easy in the early days to get satisfactory domestic service. Indians, negros and sometimes Mexicans were employed, until the arrival of more Chinese and the coming of white girls." Chinese women's lives were often even bleaker. It was generally not culturally acceptable to send a wife or daughter out of the home to work, no matter how pressing the family's need may have been. Most Chinese women probably contributed to the family income in other ways, such as taking in boarders and helping out in family businesses. Unfortunately, census workers of the day did not recognize or record such contributions. This makes it difficult to move beyond speculation about Chinese and Chinese American women's working lives before the turn of the twentieth century.[74]

Conclusion

By the end of the 1880s Los Angeles's occupational structure for women looked different from that of many other cities. With relatively few manufacturing jobs available, many women pursued white-collar work in the professions or business. Working as teachers or librarians or running their own businesses provided some women with respectable ways to earn a living. Larger numbers of immigrant women entered white-collar jobs than in other cities of the period, but there remained more women looking for such work than there were openings. African American, Chinese American, and Mexican American women often faced racism when they attempted to enter such jobs.

At the other end of the spectrum from white-collar work were service jobs, such as domestic work and retail. In the decades after the boom the numbers of women working as domestics in Los Angeles actually bucked national trends by going up, not down, as women continued to crowd into the city. Although higher in social prestige than domestic service, the next step in the city's developing female economy, retail work, presented many of the same problems: low pay, long hours, and the possibility of exploitation on the job. After 1890 reform-minded elite women in the city increasingly turned their attention to improving conditions for working women. They did so through private charities and organizations such as the Friday Morning Club and the Young Women's Christian Association. These women largely ignored domestic servants, but they often singled out women who worked in retail for aid. The next chapter considers the challenges that domestic and retail workers faced on (and off) the job.

2

Servants and Retail Workers in Los Angeles

"TO KNOW HER PLACE AND KEEP IT"

Few employment options existed for the vast majority of women who either arrived without professional training or whose ethnicity barred them from white-collar work. The real estate boom of the 1880s had increased Los Angeles's population from eleven thousand to eighty thousand people in the space of a few years, but the newcomers still struggled to integrate themselves into the local economy.[1] By the late nineteenth century the city of Los Angeles was just beginning to advance itself as a serious rival to San Francisco's economic dominance of the Pacific Coast. The Chamber of Commerce and the Merchants and Manufacturers Association (M&M, as it was known locally) simultaneously offered economic incentives to industries willing to move to the area and prevented widespread unionization of the city's workers (see chapter 4). But industrialization, and the jobs it would have created for women, still lagged far behind other cities.

Compared to eastern cities and towns, where as early as the 1830s women could find work in mills and small-scale manufacturing, the urban West provided few such jobs for women. Numbers of women employed as servants nationally dropped steadily after 1870. But this trend did not apply in the Pacific states: in fact, more than two-thirds of working women in San Francisco, Portland, and Los Angeles in this period held low-paid jobs in service occupations.[2]

As we saw in chapter 1, the entry of women into some occupations and not others was shaped by numerous factors: the larger regional and national economy, level of skill and education, ethnic and racial background, social class, and so on. But the sex and racial segregation of a labor market, with distinct jobs assigned either to women or to racial or ethnic groups, never emerges fully formed. Instead, as Ruth Milkman explains, it must be "created and maintained."[3] In the last two decades of the nineteenth century we can see Greater Los Angeles's segmented labor force being created. Even so, it was still more flexible than in other American cities.

In order to make a living, many women of all ethnic backgrounds turned to domestic service. Perhaps because of its ready availability, however, domestic service was considered the least-desirable form of employment by women across all ethnic and racial groups. Instead, the job many women aspired to was retail work, as a clerk or shopgirl. Looking at these two jobs together provides an opportunity to explore how intimately connected different segments of the labor market really were. Domestic service and retail work were, simply, two sides of the same coin. One was the job nearly everyone could get but few wanted; the other was the job many wanted but few could get.

Domestic Service in Greater Los Angeles

The Anglo-American migrants to Los Angeles brought with them a mind-set new to the region, what one historian has called a "village mentality."[4] The new residents did not want a cosmopolitan city like San Francisco. Rather, they wanted a series of connecting villages or communities. The vast majority owned their homes or eagerly pursued home ownership. This meant that, unlike eastern and midwestern cities, where industrial conditions largely determined land use, Los Angeles shaped itself around communities of home owners, many of whom expected to employ servants.

Domestic service had been the most common form of employment for women for most of the nineteenth century. Most middling as well as elite families employed servants of some kind. The use of servants had deep roots in America's agrarian past. Traditionally, farm families had depended on some form of female "help" to keep the concern economically viable. Sisters, cousins, nieces, and neighbor girls assisted a family during busy times of the year or when the family needed extra hands. Although such arrangements often included the exchange of money as well as room and board, few on either side of the exchange recognized such arrangements as wage work. While in her temporary job a woman working as "help" suffered no social stigma. She lived as another member of the family. Even though she may have prepared the meals, for example, she also sat and ate with the family.[5]

For women in cities who needed to support themselves, working as "help" seemed a natural solution. However, women throughout the United States found that the social climate in cities did not lend itself to replicating traditional patterns. The very dynamism of cities that made them so attractive to women also meant they could be anonymous places with rapid population turnover. Moreover, the increasing emphasis on the home as a sanctuary from the hustle and bustle of urban and commercial life created a new set of needs that required a new kind of "help": the domestic servant. With the home no longer a site of economic production for most Americans, it increasingly became a way to display status to the outside world. In order to do so, newer houses hid any and all evidence of work, including the servant herself. Basement kitchens, back stairs, and freestanding "summer kitchens" increasingly separated the world of the servant from the world of the employer, while simultaneously increasing the distance a servant had to travel to perform his or her duties. Throughout the country the highest wages and greatest demand were for specialized servants. A cook, chambermaid, or butler made more money than a maid-of-all-work. Nationally, the largest single ethnicity of female domestic servants was Irish. More young single women emigrated from Ireland than from other European country, and Irish women faced no language barrier to employment. So ubiquitous was the Irish servant that the stereotype of the faithless, feckless "Biddy" dominated discussion of the "servant problem" in eastern cities. In some parts of the country Scandinavian women also entered service in large numbers, as did free blacks in northern cities.[6]

For those Los Angeles women facing ethnic discrimination, a lack of specialized skills, or simply a dearth of jobs, domestic service became the easiest form of employment to obtain. Ethnicity helped determined who would be working as servants in Los Angeles's households, but not to the same degree seen elsewhere in this era. For example, in most other cities African American women were most likely to work as domestic servants. But this does not seem to have been true in Los Angeles. One explanation for this is that Los Angeles's African American community remained much smaller and relatively better off financially than its counterparts in other cities: as late as 1900 only two thousand African Americans lived in Los Angeles. African American women in Southern California thus may not have needed to find work outside the home as frequently. They may also have been doing other less visible kinds of service work, such as taking in laundry. This would have been consistent with findings for other states in the region. In 1890 some 92.9 percent of all black women in the Rocky Mountain and Pacific Coast states worked in domestic service or as laundresses, even though they made up only 1 percent of the females in these states.[7]

Census records note unusually high numbers of native-born women working as servants in Greater Los Angeles. However, it must be remembered that until the waves of new immigration from Mexico after 1910 the bulk of the city's Mexican American population had been born in the United States. Period accounts certainly mention native-born Anglo-American women working in domestic service, but given the social and educational limitations placed on Mexican American women these women appear to have been at least as likely to work as servants in the city as their Anglo counterparts. Unfortunately, since census takers did not distinguish between Mexican Americans and Anglo-Americans in the city, this is largely supposition.[8]

Among the city's European immigrants, Scandinavian and German women seem to have been the most likely to work as domestic servants. Nor did Los Angeles's servant population consist of only women: although as of yet few Japanese had moved to Los Angeles, some young Japanese men worked as servants in local homes. Known as "Japanese schoolboys," young Japanese men often earned tuition and board by working as servants. Anglo employers also applied this term to any Japanese apprentice servant, whether a student or not. Seen by employers as a benevolent opportunity to teach Japanese immigrants English and useful skills, such positions offered only token wages. Journalist Elizabeth Banks admired the neat white coats or jackets worn by "the superior and educated Japanese boys," while noting that the "commoner class of Japanese servants look anything but neat." According to Evelyn Nakano Glenn's study of Japanese schoolboys in San Francisco, where they were far more common as servants than in Los Angeles, these young men made as little as $1.50 a week in 1900.[9]

A brief survey of some notable households in Greater Los Angeles reveals the multiethnic nature of the servant population. Clara Wheeler Bradley Burdette depended on servants after illness forced her to leave her job at the Flower Festival Home. At first it was a Chinese man she remembered only as "Jim" who helped her care for her son, Roy. The man was "devotion itself— 'Jim' . . . fed Roy and watched after him with the help of the nurses and such little attention as I could give him. He was so loyal to me that when I was very ill without my knowledge he slept in a comforter on the floor outside my door—he 'not trust nurses' he said—so it was time there was a woman permanently in the house." Given the shortage of qualified servants in the city Burdette had to rely on friends to help her find a well-trained, English-born housekeeper named Jennie (or Jeanie) Butterworth. Burdette lured Butterworth away from her job in Tacoma, Washington, with an offer of a "tempting" increase in monthly pay. Butterworth worked for Burdette for the next fourteen years.[10]

Noted club woman Caroline Severance had a Canadian-born housekeeper, but her gardener and paid companion were both American-born Anglos. In the early 1890s booster Charles Willard employed "a colored girl of about 15" and, later, a young married couple with a month-old baby. Of the latter the wife was "well and strong," but the husband, like Willard himself, suffered from tuberculosis. Nonetheless, Willard wrote, "they will live in two of the rooms which are rather shut off from the rest of the house. She will do the bulk of the house work and he will do chores about the place for their board. So you see," he concluded, "the arrangement is a moderately advantageous one." By 1908, although his private nurse, Mrs. Delive, was an Anglo, the two other household servants were Japanese men.[11]

Los Angeles's servant workforce might have been multiethnic, but employers singled out one type of servant for criticism: the American. Seen as demanding, irresponsible, and poorly trained, employers laid the blame for the city's "servant problem" squarely at the feet of the American girl. They understood that she viewed domestic work as beneath her and therefore only a job of last resort. One employer told a reporter that she would accept anyone but an American in her house: "Irish, German, Swede, Dane, Japanese or Chinese, but I won't have an American who doesn't know how to boil a potato nor understand the difference between a scrubbing brush and a knife sharpener."[12]

The struggle between servants and their employers over the pace, pay, and status of domestic work illustrated the problems confronting Los Angeles's women as they began working outside the home in increasing numbers. Servants, Anglo-American female servants in particular, resented the attitudes of employers, the low pay, and the poor conditions endemic to domestic service. When unions failed to organize them, some servants formed self-help organizations. But the job remained the first choice of few women. As new segments of the economy opened up to women, by and large those women who could left domestic service for other kinds of work.

Angelenos' assumptions about the proper relationship between master and servant fitted into prevailing cultural assumptions about such work. For elite American women, employing a domestic servant came to mean much more than freedom from the drudgery of household work. As Sarah Deutsch explains, these women believed that domestic service "benefited the employee with moral uplift and benefited society, binding class into a single family, albeit unequal." In eastern cities, where the poor lived crowded together in tenements and girls often shared the home with unrelated male lodgers, elite women saw service as a safer alternative for vulnerable young women. In service, they argued, girls would be under the watchful, caring eye of a respectable woman—their employer. Nineteenth-century Americans viewed factory, store, or office work as existing in opposition to domestic service. While reformers tried to regulate the first three through legislation, vocational training, and supervision, they assumed domestic servants to be inherently protected by working in homes. Domestic work in the United States thus remained "normative, idealized, and unregulated." Deutsch notes the irony that women in domestic service were frequently exploited sexually by the men in the household, but elite women never acknowledged this possibility.[13]

But just as Los Angeles's economy did not fit prevailing national patterns, neither did the city's domestic servants. In eastern cities fluctuations in the business cycle caused periodic expansions and contractions in both the availability and the wages of servants. In Los Angeles, although the strength of the area's economy certainly varied from year to year, both the demand for and the wages of servants remained high. A lack of women available for employment as servants remained a frequent complaint of Los Angeles housewives, and indeed housewives all over the western United States.[14]

Perhaps because of such difficulties, visitors remarked on how few families in Los Angeles had servants at all. They also noted that those who employed servants had difficulty keeping them. London-based journalist Elizabeth Banks found to her astonishment many local housewives making due without servants:

The women of Los Angeles are a continual source of wonder and pride to me— wonder that they can accomplish so much and be so fresh and happy in the accomplishment, and pride that they are my own countrywomen, many of them coming from the state I call my own, Wisconsin. . . . Instead of servants they have telephones and modern conveniences. The Los Angeles houses seem to have been built for the purpose of solving this servant problem. What I call the "push in system" between kitchen and dining room, is one of the delightful contrivances for doing away with walking to and from the dining room and the kitchen. The dish cupboard with its shelves and doors opening into both rooms makes the setting of the tables and the clearing of it away an easy matter.[15]

Banks also attributed the easier life of both Los Angeles's housewives and its servants to such practical inventions as the dumbwaiter, hot running water, and a door connecting the dining room and the kitchen.[16]

The primary causes of friction between employer and employee were autonomy and job performance. Banks noted in another article that "I have

been talking with Los Angeles women about their servants, which they call
'help,' and which they say are that only in name."[17] (It is fascinating to note
that area women still used the word *help* to describe their servants. I would
suggest this is a holdover from many employers' midwestern origins.) Unlike
their eastern counterparts, women who employed servants in Los Angeles
could not make the argument that they were sparing their female employees
from the sexual threat of tenement life. Los Angeles did not yet have anything comparable to tenement life, where not only a large family but also
often unrelated individuals crowded into a single apartment. In fact, many
women who entered service in Los Angeles had arrived in the city not with
their families but on their own. Some more reform-minded organizations
argued that these "women adrift," as they were known, should be in domestic
service rather than in other forms of employment. But they based their argument on the high cost of housing in the city, and not on any inherent moral
threat. The YWCA, for example, sometimes placed female retail clerks who
had trouble paying their rent in domestic service positions.

Employers complained that servants dressed inappropriately for their
tasks. The young women allegedly favored extravagant dresses and hats over
what employers regarded as sensible work clothes. For her part, Banks tried
to point out that the issue was often one of basic hygiene: fashionable wool
dresses could not be as easily cleaned as the calico dresses and long aprons
encouraged by employers. Another complaint was that women who applied
for jobs as domestics in Los Angeles often could not or would not provide
references. Banks noticed that many applicants had the audacity to sit in the
presence of their employers or quit without notice, both of which would have
been unacceptable in most other cities.[18] Even women who got along well
with their servants faced dozens of tiny annoyances. Clara Wheeler Burdette
remembered of her housekeeper, Jennie Butterworth:

There is a type of people—with limited education and social contacts—who think
it defends their social standing to be addressed as "Mr." or "Mrs." or "Miss"—Jennie
belonged to that type and not to be called "Mrs." was a sore trial to her pride, I discovered. Also the habit of being dressed up on Sundays and going out the front door
denoted her pride in her church life—a sort of feeling that when one is in their best
clothes and is going to church there can be no distinction for all are brothers and
sisters—especially in the Methodist church. So we compromised—I called her Jennie
and once a week she marched proudly out the front door, and no harm was done to
me. . . . [H]er singing is a bit annoying . . . but the matter of being expected to wear
long white aprons in the afternoon—as was the custom then for those in service—

was something for prayer and overcoming of one's pride that time alone had to bring to pass.[19]

While their employers complained about their behavior, servants in Los Angeles also found much to complain about. Anglo-American women, most of whom had not come to the city expecting to work as servants, were the most vocal in airing their complaints both to employers and in the local press. The booster literature of the day promised abundant and well-paying jobs to anyone willing to move to Los Angeles. One can only imagine these women's bitter disappointment when such jobs did not materialize. American women's primary objection to domestic service was not the work per se, but that it violated their sense of independence and autonomy.

But servants of all ethnic backgrounds faced similar problems. Regulated by time, not by task, their working lives could be extremely demanding. Employers expected a servant to be at work constantly until explicitly told otherwise. Not only did a woman in service work longer hours than a woman in another occupation, but she also spent the rest of her time "on call" in case the family needed her. She also had to do several hours of work before receiving her customary one afternoon and evening off each week. Banks weighed in against such treatment in her newspaper articles, arguing that women would be far more likely to choose and stay in service if they could be assured of the kind of personal freedom enjoyed by women employed in stores and offices. Domestic servants complained of the strain of constantly having to work under the supervision of their employers. This twenty-four-hour supervision became the heart of the struggle between domestics and their employers. Working women also generally preferred to seek employment near friends or relatives if possible, something easier to find in factories, in retail, or elsewhere. Servants complained of isolation and loneliness on the job, particularly the lone maid-of-all-work, or "house girl," the most common type of domestic in those Los Angeles households that employed servants. Turnover remained high. By 1890 the average tenure of a domestic servant in the United States was less than one and a half years.[20]

Employers and employees frequently argued about what "fair" pay for such work might be. In fact, no one at the time appears to have agreed on what a servant in Los Angeles could or should earn. Banks's 1903 investigation found that a "really good house girl" in Los Angeles could earn somewhere between thirty and thirty-five dollars a month, and that specialized servants, such as cooks, made even more. These would be high wages for a servant in the period, and a sign of just how much the demand for good servants in the city outstripped the supply. Banks pithily observed that it was no surprise to her that so few Angelenos had servants: surely, only the rich could afford them. But after Banks published her findings, one domestic wrote to the *Los Angeles Express* newspaper to chastise her for listening too much to employers:

Our English friend seems to be under the mistaken impression that $40 is the usual wage for a common house worker to receive, while not more than $20 is a fair average for girls who take entire charge of the household duties, washing included, in nine places out of every twelve. And, pray, why should not the servant girl look down upon her hard position when those who employ her treat her as an utterly inferior being? They "teach her to know her place and keep it." They patronize, scold her and look things out of cold critical eyes that are even worse than the uttered words, and find fault with the slightest mistake. She is made to feel that she is so far beneath the level of her mistress that it is almost vain to look upon her as a human being with a soul and a heart that yearns for pleasant things as intensely as the fair daughters of the house she serves. Nothing matters. She is hired to labor, paid for same, and that ends it.[21]

The writer, whose name Banks withheld from publication, also reported that employers preferred "those ignorant foreigners" only because they were too ignorant and unskilled to protest mistreatment. Even those servants who conceded that their pay might seem high explicitly made the point that, given the amount of work, the supervision, and the isolation she was expected to tolerate on the job, no female domestic earned what she truly should.[22]

The inclusion of room and board in servant "wages" complicated matters further. Both reformers and the State of California included the value of room and board when comparing the wages of servants with the wages of other occupations. This inevitably skewed the numbers in favor of service. The actual cash wages of servants were extremely low. Moreover, domestics generally valued the room and board provided by an employer below that provided by a good boardinghouse. In a boardinghouse, after all, she would not have to eat in the kitchen or clean the whole house.[23]

The social stigma attached to domestic service added to servants' concerns about the value of the work. One woman, working as a stenographer and typewriter at ten dollars a week, told Banks exactly that. "Do houseworkers get an opportunity to associate with other women engaged in other work?" Banks quoted her as saying. "Can they join literary clubs? Do young men invite them to go to the theatre with them—I mean the same kind of young men who take saleswomen and typewriter girls out? Do ambitious young men marry them? If I were a houseworker would a floorwalker in a store marry me?" Although some domestics took advantage of the free room and board to save money for the future, if Banks's informant is to be believed, many women in Los Angeles feared work as a domestic servant would actually deprive them of a better life. The local labor newspaper, *Los Angeles Citizen*, weighed in on the side of domestic servants in a 1909 editorial, arguing that two-thirds of the "servant problem" in the city stemmed from the employers, not the employees. Most of the problem, the paper opined, would be solved by more humane treatment by and less recrimination from city housewives. The paper suggested that the name be changed from the "servant problem" to the "mistress problem."[24]

Whether a servant was an Anglo-American woman or a Japanese man, she or he had little recourse in disputes with employers. Local unions, already weakened by a savage battle with *Los Angeles Times* editor Harrison Gray Otis, had no interest in organizing the city's servants.[25] Instead, some female servants created self-help organizations in the hopes that networking with other servants would help ameliorate some harsher aspects of life as a domestic servant.

Self-Help for Servants:
The Hermosa Club and the Progressive Household Club

Los Angeles's unions, like those elsewhere, ignored the plight of working women and particularly that of the local servant population. Historically, unions focused on organizing skilled or industrial workers, and regarded women as at best temporary workers and at worst competitors for male jobs. Because of servants' high rate of job turnover and isolation from other workers, unions generally regarded them as impossible to organize. David Katzman points out the irony of this argument. Had servants organized, their job-turnover rate might have dropped.[26]

Some domestic servants in Los Angeles refused to wait for unions to take up their cause. Instead, they formed self-help organizations to fill the gap left by isolation, hard work, and low pay. The first of these organizations, the Hermosa Club, organized in 1893. When Joanna Sanger arrived in Los Angeles from Buffalo, New York, looking for work, she consulted a Dr. Spencer at the Salvation Army. Spencer, who ran an employment office for women, suggested the "working girls" form a club. Sanger evidently found this idea appealing. Finding work as a "janitress" for the local branch of the Young Women's Christian Association, Sanger recruited several other young women into a club. Nurses, laundresses, and hotel help all belonged to the club, but it made a special effort to reach out to female servants.

Wealthy families wintering in Los Angeles judged California help to be less malleable than eastern help, so they usually brought their servants with them. Employers made no provision for their servants' amusement, however, and as a consequence large numbers of women often passed their free time in public parks, particularly the park on Sixth Street. Sanger and other club members visited the park on Sundays, inviting these women to take advantage of the YWCA's facilities. While employers often brought a servant with them to Los Angeles, they just as often left her behind when they returned home. Some employers seem to have objected to paying the women's fare home. Others may have assumed they were doing the women a favor by leaving them in a warm, sunny climate rather than taking them back to the gloom of an eastern or midwestern winter. The Los Angeles YWCA became a center for these newly unemployed servants.[27]

The as-yet-unnamed club took as its goal the creation of a vacation home for working women. The brother-in-law of one of the members offered to loan the women some land in Sierra Madre, twenty miles northeast of downtown Los Angeles. Sierra Madre did not yet have streetcar service, and the nearest railroad station was Santa Anita's, but it nonetheless seemed an ideal location to the club. The women seized their chance: "Miss Sanger, Ida Dean and Mrs. Bailey went to Hamburger's [sic] Store, then on N. Spring Street. . . . There they bought bolts of unbleached muslin, which they sewed together in strips, the boyfriends agreeing to put up the framework. . . . Hammocks, couches, and folding beds were donated to the Club and were used willy nilly by the girls on their trips to the tent."[28]

Club members determined use of the tent in Sierra Madre by need and by the ability to pay the club's sliding-scale fees. YWCA records detail the case of one children's nurse, Millie Brant, who made her home in the tent after illness prevented her from traveling abroad with her employers. While living in Sierra Madre, Brant evidently supported herself making preserves and jelly from fruit given to her by local orchards.[29]

When the club had saved up enough money through dues (fifty cents for initiation and twenty-five cents a month), it began searching for a suitable piece of land on which to build a permanent home. In 1904 one employer involved in planning the new community of Hermosa Beach offered Ida Dean, his housekeeper, and Mrs. Bailey, his cook, any piece of land they wanted for free. The two women selected a lot on Second Street near Manhattan Avenue between the town of Redondo Beach and the as-yet-uncompleted Hermosa

Beach. In spite of ankle-deep sand the club contracted for the house to be built for a thousand dollars. Donations from employers furnished the new home, and the club now took "Hermosa" as part of its name.[30]

Period accounts suggest why women so valued this beach cottage. Many Hermosa Club members came from Norway and Sweden and had found the dramatic change in climate unhealthy. Some developed tuberculosis. If a period of rest and the fresh sea air did not improve a member's condition, other members cared for her, either at the cottage or in a hospital, until the end of her life. In at least two cases the club raised enough money to send members back to their homes "across the Atlantic." When the new YWCA building opened downtown in 1908, the Hermosa Club met there regularly twice a month and offered social teas in the building on Sunday afternoons. The supposition that many Scandinavian women were employed as domestic servants in Los Angeles is supported by the fact that in 1913, when the Progressive Housemaid Club was organized, its bylaws were read to the assembled women not only in English but also in Danish, Swedish, Finnish, and German.[31]

In 1913 domestic servants created the Progressive Housemaid Club, another self-help club. As Hannah Anderson, the Swedish-born vice president of the club, pointed out:

We housemaids are in a class by ourselves and must help one another.... [S]omeone has said that the YWCA or the Mary Clark Home would be the best place for the stranger to go, but frankly such homes are too expensive for the girl who does housework. Then, too, we girls would not feel at home there. These homes are filled with the girls who clerk in stores and while we would not for a minute regard this line of work as better than ours, the girl who works downtown for five or six dollars a week and supports herself won't look at the girl who works in families, but who gets more money and has a better place to live.[32]

To this end the Progressive Housemaid Club's clubhouse at 1309 South Alvarado Street in Los Angeles provided several low-cost rooms for its unemployed members, as well as a library, sewing room, and laundry. The club's in-house employment agency so impressed members of the Women's Christian Temperance Union (WCTU) that they shut down their own bureau and began referring women to the Housemaid Club. Within a year the club had more than five hundred members and a clubhouse on West Ninth Street, furnished with money the members themselves raised. Educational lectures and member meetings were often conducted in both English and Swedish, and sometimes in Finnish and German as well. The club even joined forces with the Los Angeles City Teachers' Club to offer classes in English to members. The seeming failure of the Progressive Housemaid Club to reach out to Mexican American, African American, or Asian servants, however, is indicative of how gender and ethnicity divided these workers. YWCA records are silent on the subject, but given the surnames of the women involved with the Hermosa Club and the fact that the YWCA itself was segregated at this time, it would have been extremely unlikely that these servants pursued any ethnic inclusiveness beyond white European women.[33] This gulf only deepened as the city moved into the first decades of the twentieth century.

But while servants had to rely largely on their own self-help organizations, the same was not true of retail workers. Like domestic workers, the retail workforce was heavily female, largely underpaid, and often overworked. But unlike domestics, women working in retail quickly drew the attention of club women and reformers. The increasing visibility of women in retail work forced Angelenos to confront a whole host of issues—salaries, unions, and sexual exploitation on the job—new to the debate about women at work. Not only were retail jobs open only to certain women, but gender discrimination prevented most women from advancing professionally within retail organizations. Gender divisions between male and female retail workers as well as employer resistance kept the profession largely unorganized in Los Angeles. Private charitable organizations showed more concern over the morality and education of female retail workers than in improving their hours or wages. In fact, club women worked so hard to try to ameliorate the suffering of retail workers that they largely undercut any other attempts to organize these women.

Shopgirls and Working Women: Retail Work in Los Angeles

The entry of women into retail work in large numbers after the Civil War made women more visible in both Los Angeles and in the American economy as a whole. This era saw the ascendancy of the department store in American life. These stores offered an unprecedented combination of size and variety of goods to the buying public. Although men had initially filled sales positions, by the 1870s many store owners recognized that fashionable Parisian stores successfully used women as salesclerks. Moreover, female salespeople offered several distinct advantages to the store owner: they were young and usually had at least a partial high school education, they added "class" to retail establishments, and, most important of all, they worked for less money than men.

As the ready-to-wear clothing industry grew, so did department stores

and the number of women employed in them. The number of women working as saleswomen in the United States jumped from 7,462 in 1880 to 142,265
in 1900, an increase of 1,800 percent in twenty years. By 1901 Los Angeles
boasted four major department stores, all located between the 200 and 400
blocks of Broadway. These were the Broadway Department Store, the Ville
de Paris, the Boston Dry Goods Store, and Coulter's Dry Goods. There were
also numerous smaller specialty and five-and-dime stores. When it came to
education, store owners appear to have been correct: retail workers in Los
Angeles were more likely than even those in San Francisco to have attended
high school. Forty percent had at least an eighth-grade education. But education had little impact on a woman's earning ability in Greater Los Angeles's
retail trade. Only if she had completed business school or university did her
pay reflect her education.[34]

Marital status and family need shaped women's retail work. Given the
long hours demanded of workers in shops and department stores (twelve-
hour days and often sixty- to eighty-hour weeks), it is not surprising that
almost three-quarters of Los Angeles's female retail clerks were single. Married women were a distant second, at slightly more than 12 percent of workers. Widows, however, earned the most money: 48 percent of widowed retail
workers earned twelve dollars or more a week. These women may have been
older, on the job longer, and thus earning more, but the records are silent on
this subject.[35]

Women seeking to balance the demands of the job with the low pay often
had to adjust their living arrangements. Based on the interviews she conducted, reporter Banks estimated that about half of Los Angeles's female
retail clerks lived with parents or other family, while the other half had to
make do as best they could. Local store employers, she wrote, preferred to
hire women who lived with their families, so the employers "might have an
easy conscience in offering low wages." The *Los Angeles Times* put a different
spin on the same trend, explaining that it wasn't low wages that made retail
employers choose the "home girl," but rather that these men "have found it
good policy to employ girls living either at home or with relatives, as they
are then certain of good influences, and as a rule, stay longer with the firms
they start with." Official statistics put the number of retail workers living at
home even higher, at more than 75 percent. Those who lived at home consistently earned less than those who lived on their own. This raises the question
of whether most female retail clerks continued to live at home by choice or
simply because they did not yet earn enough to move out.[36]

Race and ethnicity shaped these job opportunities. Los Angeles was hardly unique in the powerful influence these two factors exerted on retail employment. In her superb history of women in American retail work, Susan Porter Benson points out that in the southern and eastern United States African American women almost never worked on the sales floor. Instead, they were confined to jobs as elevator operators or behind-the-scenes personnel. In Los Angeles, Mexican American women working as salesclerks could be found only in the smaller shops centered around the Plaza district, or in Anglo businesses that catered exclusively to the Mexican population. Racism kept them out of jobs in the larger department stores. Although no data about Los Angeles's Asian American women in retail work have survived, it seems likely that similar patterns would have applied, and they would have been able to find such work only in Asian-owned businesses.[37]

Place of birth also seems to have been an important factor in hiring patterns for Los Angeles. Native-born Americans, rather than white European immigrants, made up the bulk of the city's retail labor force. This was the opposite of hiring trends in white-collar work (see chapter 1). It was also the opposite of patterns found in retail labor force in Los Angeles's competitor to the north, San Francisco. More of those retail workers who lived independently in Los Angeles were native rather than foreign born, the reverse of conditions in San Francisco. This pattern is likely attributable to the numbers of Anglo-American women that had moved into the Los Angeles to look for work.[38]

Even by the standards of the day retail work did not pay very well. Salaries varied tremendously by gender and location within the store, but salesmen always made more than saleswomen. On average, a woman in a department store in the early twentieth century made only two-thirds what her male counterpart earned. The highest-paid women on the sales floor worked in millinery, cloak, or suit departments, where they usually worked on commission. Investigators at the time noted that this system tended to cause discord between workers. Forty percent of female retail workers in Los Angeles over the age of eighteen made less than ten dollars a week; more than half of those under age eighteen made less than six dollars a week. While she lived in the city Elizabeth Banks observed two distinct classes of shopgirls. The first, employed in the two or three largest stores, made an average of eight dollars a week. The women employed in smaller stores, however, earned five dollars a week or less. Apprentices who had just started a job in a store, she noted, made nothing at all. Due to the high cost of housing in Los Angeles, Banks explained to her readers, it would be impossible to afford a room at a respectable boardinghouse if you made less than five dollars a week. Rooming houses, where the lodger had to do her own cleaning, were slightly more affordable. But when Banks asked one interviewee about her finances, the woman reportedly scoffed, "Save! You don't expect me to save, do you? Is it not enough that I get myself room and food and clothes and car fare on twenty five dollars a month? If I save a dollar a month I am doing well."[39]

Many observers puzzled over the numbers of women who chose retail work over other forms of employment. Among women workers, saleswomen earned somewhat more than their counterparts in factories, but only in the southern United States were sales positions at the top of the pay scale for women. To local reformers' eyes, in particular, the disadvantages of such work seemed to outweigh the advantages. In addition to low pay, department stores demanded obscenely long hours from employees, often sixty to eighty hours a week, with even longer hours over holidays and at inventory time. Saleswomen stood on their feet for twelve or more hours a day and sometimes fainted on the job. The need to look fashionable on the job demanded a woman make considerable investment in both clothes and time. Beauty and fashion were valued almost as highly as experience and endurance. The *Los Angeles Times* even devoted an entire article to lauding the beauty of the local female sales force. Adding to the problems inherent in such work was its seasonality. Retail employment opportunities always peaked in December for the holiday sales and then quickly slacked off again in January. Nationally, saleswomen in 1909 could earn $6 to $7 a week, while stock girls might earn $3.50. Cash girls (who ran between the saleswomen and the cashiers with the customer's change) and the cashiers made only $1.50 to $2 a week.[40]

But local working women liked the variety of experiences offered by sales work. More important, shop work, particularly in department stores, enjoyed higher social status than domestic service. However low the pay or long the hours, the presence of customers gave the department stores and their employees an illusion of gentility. "Maggie" in the factory became "Miss" on the sales floor, one turn-of-the-century editor explained. The higher status conferred by retail work also influenced the life choices of young working women hoping to make a successful marriage. Articles of the day stressed the greater opportunities for retail workers to meet suitable mates, either their male coworkers or among the throngs of city shoppers. Those Los Angeles saleswomen who married presumably left sales work behind them, at least for a time. Not surprisingly, Banks herself observed that "this business of selling over the counter seems to be a popular and much-sought-after one in Los Angeles, and for every vacant position there are at least a dozen applicants." Los Angeles's saleswomen struck Banks as particularly well mannered, and she suggested most must have learned how to behave at home, not in the shops.[41]

The most direct solution to the low pay of department store personnel, organization into a union or unions, proved exceedingly difficult. Largely ignored by traditional craft unions, retail clerks of both genders who wanted to form unions faced tremendous difficulties. Department store owners across the country took the philosophy of the open shop very seriously. Employees were routinely fired and even blacklisted if their union affiliation became known. Some stores employed elaborate networks of spies to keep tabs on their employees.[42]

In spite of the city's general antiunion sentiment, Los Angeles's clerks did initially win several union victories. In February 1883 retail clerks in the city organized the Early Closing Association and persuaded thirty businesses across the city to close their stores at 6:30 PM. After achieving its objective, however, this organization soon became inactive. In 1893 the clerks joined the Retail Clerks' National Protective Association as Local 83. In 1895–1896 Local 83 mounted a campaign for shorter hours. Members collected five thousand signatures from city residents on a petition and demanded a 6:00 PM closing every day except Saturday. By October 1895 city stores had adopted these new hours. The clerks then demanded a Sunday closing. They sent a petition to the Los Angeles City Council that called for the Sunday closing of all businesses except drugstores, livery stables, hotels, and restaurants. The council, however, voted against the proposal. They argued that the law was religious in nature and thus in conflict with state law, as well as unfair to business owners. In 1902 Local 83 pushed to have the union card displayed in the window of all mercantile establishments in the city, but most stores continued to refuse to recognize the union.[43]

By 1907 city stores had abandoned the early closing. But clerks in the city had, since 1906, received a half-day off on summer Saturdays and an earlier closing on all other Saturday nights. One unidentified department store, however, announced it would return to the old Saturday closing time of 10 PM. This prompted an outcry from clerks across the city. In June 1907 retail clerks organized into the Clerks' Association to lobby for an early Saturday closing. Clerks who represented fifteen of the largest stores in the city held a mass meeting to attract attention to their plight. In published reports, however, these men and women quickly disavowed any suggestions that they had formed a union or that they planned any boycotts. Instead, they promised only to "develop sentiment" against long Saturday-night hours. Viewing this battle as a way to protect the health and well-being of workers, local church leaders, the YMCA, the YWCA, the Ebell Club and the Friday Morning Club, and the Consumers' League supported the clerks until they won their fight.[44]

However, relations inside the union between its male and female members appear to have been uneasy at best. In 1910 Local 83 reorganized into the Retail Clerks of Los Angeles, and vowed to win equal pay for equal work, a decrease in hours, and comfortable chairs behind the counters. Two years later the local sent Eva Sturtevant, its first female representative, to serve on Los Angeles's Central Labor Council. But some male clerks reportedly feared that if women made too much headway in the industry, employers would give the jobs now filled by men to lower-paid female clerks. To prevent this, male union members pushed for both genders to receive equal pay. The local even held male-only "smokers" as part of its open meetings.[45]

In addition to strife within the unions, some proprietors developed ingenious ways to frustrate employee organization. The most notable was to form employee associations. Large eastern department stores pioneered such programs: Filenes in Boston and Bloomingdales in New York City set up employee loan programs and gave out free turkeys at Thanksgiving. Los Angeles store owners followed this model. By 1902 Arthur Letts, owner of the Broadway Department Store, already provided his employees with a half-day holiday in July and August and overtime pay for those working more than nine hours a day. In 1904 he organized his clerks into a Mutual Benefit Association that provided sick and death benefits. With such benefits available in-house, retail clerks' unions understandably struggled to convince potential members to abandon employee associations for much riskier union activity.[46]

Given the failure of union activity to provide female retail clerks with a living wage, reformers both in Los Angeles and across the nation stepped into the breach. As such work had increased in popularity with young women, reformers became concerned with what they perceived to be the influence of department store work on women's morality. The young shopgirl, they argued, surrounded with luxuries she could not afford on her meager salary, might be tempted to sacrifice her virtue to obtain them. The potential spouses were also potential predators: department stores brought women into contact with male bosses, coworkers, and customers, any one of whom might tempt a naive girl to stray from the straight and narrow. The *Los Angeles Citizen* newspaper made the connection between retail work and vice explicit for its readers in a 1911 cartoon. The illustrations depicted a hardworking but underpaid salesgirl accepting dinner invitations from strange men just so she could eat, a road that led her to dance halls, prostitution, and, eventually, "a suicide's grave, unknown to mother or friends."[47] Clearly, then, at least some Angelenos worried about the morality of and influences on young women engaged in retail work.

Department store owners recognized the need to respond to such concerns, as well as to ensure a steady supply of trained salesgirls. To satisfy both needs, owners embarked on a series of cooperative programs with the local branch of the YWCA. In some cities store management resisted such attempts by the YWCA to reach their female employees, but Los Angeles employers seem to have welcomed the reformers as a way to mollify public concern over the plight of saleswomen without inconveniencing management.[48]

Stores in Los Angeles became educational institutions. Susan Porter Benson has identified two strands to this movement: one, welfare work; the other, training programs. Both allowed managers to devote time to reforming their employees without having to address the inequities of their hiring practices. Welfare work, in particular, could offer material benefits to employers. Store lunchrooms, for example, provided affordable, nourishing food for salesclerks, but also ensured women would return to work promptly. Department stores also took advantage of the positive publicity generated by such measures. In Los Angeles the Broadway Department Store took out a full-page ad in a local paper that boasted of the high salaries it paid its employees, its "large, clean, bright, airy cafeteria," and the courses on salesmanship it offered employees.[49]

In area department stores the YWCA organized social clubs, Bible study, and educational classes for working women that promoted health, domestic skills, and "proper" female morals. In 1905 it organized an extension department to oversee the activities of all of its outreach organizations. This new department took particular interest in the girls and women employed in the many department stores downtown. Thanks to the extension department, "not a fresh young girl starting out for her first venture in the business world, not a weary, disheartened women with strength almost gone but will find her welfare is a matter of moment to at least one person in the world," one newspaper applauded. The YWCA established an advisory committee in each store composed of three members of the firm and two members of the YWCA. These two women, Miss Chappell and Miss Sayre, made "calls" on the female store employees. In one reported case the two YWCA workers saved a young women who had been "on the brink of a life of shame." In another they helped a female dentist from out of state get her California license so she would no longer have to work as a shopgirl. The YWCA also organized clubs in each of the major department stores. The Victoria and Victoria II clubs at the Broadway Department Store and the Queen Esther Club at Hamburgers had educational work and cooking classes in the evenings, as well as basketball games. The *Times* noted approvingly, "The business woman of today is keen for education and nowhere is she more eager to acquire a valuable fund of information and accomplishments than here in Los Angeles. All she wants is a chance." Many women remained members of these clubs even after they had moved on to other jobs or to business schools.[50]

Conclusion

As women from a variety of ethnic backgrounds continued to migrate to Los Angeles, those who needed or wanted to work outside the home faced an economy that continued to discriminate against them on the basis of both race and gender. Some women, particularly native-born Anglo-Americans and European immigrants, found new opportunities in the city's expanding retail market, but many women continued to find work only in domestic service. Both jobs were problematic. Domestics were relatively well paid but deeply resented the low status of the job; retail workers were poorly paid but saw the job as a path to respectability.

The Los Angeles women's club movement and the YWCA tried to fill the void and provide some social and support services to working women. But the elite Protestant Anglo-American women who dominated the club movement brought to their work their own assumptions about gender and race. These women failed to reach out equally to their working counterparts. Club women largely ignored domestic work, leaving female servants to fend for themselves. The creation of servant self-help clubs suggests that domestics knew they could not wait around for someone from the outside to provide leadership. Servants also seem to have preferred those forms of assistance that did not infringe on their sense of autonomy and independence. Club women did, however, take an active interest in the lives of female retail workers because those women were seen as morally vulnerable in a way servants were not. Bread-and-butter issues such as salary or job advancement never appeared on the agenda of groups aiding retail workers. Whether this omission occurred due to pressure from employers or because club women considered morality and self-improvement more pressing issues, or both, will have to remain a subject of debate. But, either way, as we will see in chapter 3, such help did not come without a price.

3

Working Women and the Limits of Welfare Capitalism

"UNLOVED AND HALF PAID"

Writing for the *Los Angeles Express* newspaper in 1903, reporter Elizabeth Banks interviewed a cross section of the city's working women: servants, office clerks, retail workers, and so on. These women told Banks that a woman should expect to pay thirty dollars a month for room and board in a "desirable and convenient" place, and that clerical workers, for example, received on average twenty-five dollars a month. Puzzled, Banks mused in one of her articles that she had "put in all yesterday morning trying to do an arithmetical sum in simple division. I tried to make thirty go into twenty-five and have something left, and much to my disgust I could not manage it." Banks's informants directed her to the Los Angeles Young Women's Christian Association's building, where she was pleased and surprised to find a restaurant offering low-cost meals as part of the organization's "noon rest" program. The restaurant offered bread and butter for three cents. A "bit of fish" could be had for five cents. For those girls with no pennies at all, a free glass of water would wash down "a cracker from her pocket. . . . Here, God help her! She could go hungry and not be caught in the act!"[1]

The American-born Banks had gotten her start writing for American newspapers before relocating to Great Britain. Her work appeared regularly in London's *Weekly Sun,* and she continued to submit articles to American papers like the *Los Angeles Express.* During her sojourn in Los Angeles, Banks reflected on her own experiences as a working woman in London, when she had been too poor to fill up on anything other than crackers and cheap buns at lunchtime: "But that was in London, the great city of the world's poor. . . . I did not expect to find California working girls up to the tricks of the London girls in the matter of making both ends meet. It seems however, there is this touch of womanly nature that makes the London and Los Angeles girl akin. The girl who has no home and earns small wages gets a furnished room and proceeds to go hungry in order to dress and pay car fare. This is the first thing I have found out in my observation of the working girl problem in Los Angeles."[2]

The "working girl problem" Banks observed was only one of several changes that profoundly altered Los Angeles at the turn of the twentieth century. Women's clubs like the Women's Christian Temperance Union, the Friday Morning Club, and the Young Women's Christian Association did their best to promote their ideological vision of "reform" both for the city and for working women. But, like their male counterparts in the business world, club women did not see any value in organizing working women into unions. Instead, they created and promoted a system of charities, clubs, and evening classes to try to protect the health, morality, and well-being of female workers. "Club women wanted to ease their [working women's] lot and at the same time ensure that unattached women in the city were neither exploited nor exploiters of changing conditions and standards of behavior for women," Sandra Haarsager explains.[3]

This chapter looks at the creation of women's clubs in Southern California and at club women's relationship with working women. The Los Angeles branch of the YWCA is used as a case study of the often conflicting needs of these two groups of women. Clubs' charity networks excluded most minority women and those in the unskilled trades. In many instances middle- and upper-class women ultimately supported capital by using their unpaid "charity" labor to compensate for working-class women's underpaid labor.

First Steps: The Los Angeles Woman's Club

The growth of Los Angeles in the 1880s and 1890s not only produced changes in the spatial, economic, and ethnic composition of the city but also coincided with the growth of a new mass movement in the United States. Called "organized womanhood" to emphasize the power found in solidarity with one another, affluent native-born Anglo-American Protestant women across the United States sought to improve their political and economic position in society. While these clubs initially instituted a variety of measures and events they hoped would help female workers, they failed to create a successful cross-class alliance of Los Angeles's women. Their story illustrates how gender, class, and ethnicity could both unite and divide Angeleno women.[4]

The greatest boost to organized womanhood in Los Angeles came with the arrival in the mid-1870s of Caroline Severance.[5] A Bostonian, Severance had been active in both abolition and organized womanhood before the Civil War. When her husband's ill health forced a move to a warmer, drier climate, Severance brought her experience and organizational skills to Southern California. In 1878 the fifty-eight-year-old Severance organized the Los Angeles Woman's Club. Modeled after a similar club she had started in Boston, the Woman's Club was intended as a place where women could study together and present scholarly papers of general interest. But when Severance returned to Boston for several years, the club collapsed. When she returned in 1885 Severance started a second Los Angeles Woman's Club. The club now attracted enough members to ensure its survival.[6]

The members of the Los Angeles Woman's Club, like organized women elsewhere, wanted better conditions for and recognition of the work women already performed. They also wanted to expand women's opportunities for work, including "the work of the home, work for wages, social service, and political activism." The increasing industrialization of and continuing migration to Los Angeles fueled this development (see chapter 4). As industrialization separated home from work, industry became the center of capitalist masculinity, and the home became a sanctuary from it. As more and more women moved into work outside the home, female members of this "cult of domesticity" criticized what they viewed as the negative effects both on women's character and on future generations. Reform-minded women sought to use their moral influence to counteract these effects. The use of domestic servants made such activism possible. Servants freed some women from the demands of household work, and gave them a chance to pursue interests outside the home for the first time. Most women viewed club work as an extension of their private domestic sphere, the home, not as a challenge to the social authority of men. Others, however, sought to redefine the relationship between women and politics.[7]

In the 1880s and '90s Los Angeles developed a network of organized women in large part because the goals and memberships of women's groups in the city overlapped. Large numbers of Anglo women could find common ground in these groups. A core group of reformers, women's rights activists, and Socialists active in the region helped facilitate interorganizational cooperation. However, as most club members were Anglo-American and either middle or upper class, their efforts on behalf of working women tended to favor those (teachers, clerks, and others) most like them.[8]

Given the fast-changing social climate of American cities, and Los Angeles in particular, politics seemed to some organized women's groups the only way to maintain their influence over and guardianship of health and morals. First and foremost of these groups was the Women's Christian Temperance Union, which made explicit the connections between alcohol use and social problems. Los Angeles women organized the second branch of the WCTU in the state in 1884. The same year suffragist Elizabeth Anne Kingsbury organized the Los Angeles Woman's Suffrage Association (LAWSA). Socialist women, in particular, joined the LAWSA in large numbers. They served as officers or executive board members and encouraged popular support for other political groups, such as the Nationalists and the Populists, with whom they often collaborated.[9]

Local club women recognized that by 1890 nearly one in seven American women worked outside the home. One of their greatest preoccupations was how to protect working-class women on the job and from public dangers. One popular tactic, the construction of special homes for working women, allowed female reformers to "protect" young unmarried women from sexual exploitation but also to police residents' sex lives. The Los Angeles Woman's Club's Work Committee founded the first such home in Los Angeles following its investigations into the state of working women in the city. Among the elite women who served on this committee were the wife of a banker, the wife of a judge, and the wife of the business manager of the Times-Mirror Company. These women confirmed what journalist Banks had already discovered: that women arrived in the city and expected to find work immediately, but many actually remained unemployed for some time. For those who found jobs, wages were often inadequate. To this end the committee decided to build a subsidized women's boardinghouse. By 1888 some forty such homes across the country, many of them funded and operated by the Young Women's Christian Association, served working-class women.[10]

The Work Committee formed the Women's Cooperative Union to build the house. In 1885 the union organized a flower festival to raise the needed funds. The event was so successful that the group changed its name to the Flower Festival Society, and the festival became an annual event. The home, a three-story house with thirty-six "sleeping apartments," opened in 1887. The sliding-scale fees, based on a woman's income, kept rent affordable, and the house filled quickly. The first floor also contained a Women's Exchange, where women could sell anything they produced, and a Bureau of Information to help women find jobs. The club hired newly widowed Clara Wheeler to serve as the exchange's business manager. The Flower Festival Society boasted that, within a year, its bureau had helped three hundred women find employment, and that another two hundred supported themselves through what they sold at the exchange. Like their counterparts in other cities, clearly the ladies of the Flower Festival Society sympathized with Los Angeles's working women. "What right have we," society president Mary Barnes Widney asked, "with money always at our command, to look with contempt upon the frail, helpless, unprotected, unloved and half-paid girl who, in a moment of desperation, for want of money, yields to the tempter's voice?" However, the presence of a matron, as well as a curfew set by the society, suggests the ladies might not have been as confident in the morals of their charges as they claimed. With the collapse of the economic boom in 1888, however, the society had to cancel the festival, and club women's interest in the home waned. At the end of the nineteenth century the Flower Festival Society gave the home to the Salvation Army.[11]

Women's Clubs and Working Women

The Flower Festival Society had drawn off much of the interest in the Los Angeles Woman's Club, and this club, like its predecessor, died. But in April 1891, Caroline Severance helped found the Friday Morning Club, the most important and longest-lived women's club in the city's history. The success of the Friday Morning Club can be largely attributed to the burgeoning population of the city: the club attracted two hundred members in its first year alone. It also attracted a diverse group of women: the wives and daughters of senators and bankers rubbed elbows with suffragists and other politically radical women.

The Friday Morning Club first weighed in on behalf of the city's Anglo white-collar working women in a dispute between teachers and the Los Angeles School Board. In July 1891 the Teachers' Committee of the school board summarily fired twenty-one female teachers without warning or explanation. The club women assumed the women were fired so political appointees could have their positions and, outraged, confronted the board. Within three months the club had managed to have half the teachers rehired. It then launched a successful campaign to have a woman appointed to the school board.[12]

The Southern California branches of the Ebell Club, which also first appeared in Los Angeles in the 1890s, ran a close second in significance. The club took its name from German immigrant Dr. Adrian Ebell, who had founded the first one in Oakland in 1876. The Ebell Club made the educational development of its members an explicit goal, "with the idea that women, the world over, should be better fitted in knowledge and culture, to fill the over-broadening spheres of life, to which they were being called by the advanced civilization of the age." There were soon multiple branches of the Ebell across the city, each with its own departments or sections devoted to a variety of educational topics.[13]

Religion was another important nucleus for club formation. The city's Young Women's Christian Association, the most powerful Protestant organization of women in the city, became the parent of numerous smaller YWCA-affiliated clubs. These were devoted to special topics such as Bible study or Spanish-language instruction, or for women and girls employed in department stores.[14] Catholic women could join the Catholic Women's Club, which not only provided a variety of educational and social activities but also was one of the primary sources of support for the city's two Catholic settlement houses. Originally known simply as the Woman's Club, it appears to have changed its name to the Catholic Women's Club sometime in the 1910s.[15]

Last but not least, depending on an individual woman's interest, she might also join any number of clubs devoted to a particular topic or interest. If she fancied art history, she might join the Ruskin Art Club; if she longed for exotic vistas, she could attend meetings of the Los Angeles Travel Club; or she might be attracted to clubs devoted to a variety of political causes, from education to women's suffrage.[16] The Los Angeles Woman's Suffrage Association, for example, spurred on by its Socialist members, focused on the needs of working women. In 1893 it successfully worked to ensure that clerks in local stores gained the right to sit down and rest between sales.[17] Most club women, even those who worked outside the home, belonged to several clubs simultaneously—Maria de Lopez, for example, belonged to at least six, even though she worked full-time as a teacher.[18] The vast array of cultural, social, and educational opportunities women's clubs offered was unquestionably a key part of female life across Southern California.

The members of these women's clubs chose to devote themselves to various kinds of civic activism because, while they themselves did not work outside the home for wages, they still wished to make meaningful, useful contributions to society. To this end a group of local women organized the Woman's Parliament of Southern California in late 1892. Designed to bring all of the women's groups in the region together, the Woman's Parliament believed this was the best way for women to further their common goals of reform. It soon came to focus most of its attention on achieving women's suffrage.[19] The Los Angeles Civic League, founded by the Ebell Club and several other local women's groups, followed in 1899. This, too, was designed to be a vehicle of reform in the city. A similar development occurred on the state level with the creation of the California Federation of Women's Clubs (CFWC) in 1900.[20]

The "Race Question" in Southern California Clubs

While these groups purported to speak for the women of the city and the state, they simultaneously excluded most women of color from their networks. The California Federation of Women's Clubs, for instance, voted in 1902 to refuse African American women membership. In part this could be done because the number of African Americans within the state remained small: by 1900 there were only eleven thousand in California and twenty-eight hundred in Los Angeles. Undeterred by such treatment, in 1906 black women created the California State Federation of Colored Women's Clubs, and in 1908 this organization joined the National Association of Colored Women.[21]

When the California Federation of Women's Clubs refused African American women membership, it also spurred a public debate in Los Angeles over what role, if any, American-born women of Spanish or Mexican descent should play in Anglo clubs. A group of elite *Californianas* had long been the center of the city's social life and charitable work. While some of them were by now quite elderly and not very active in the new clubs, they remained a key source of funds, in-kind donations, and society support for club causes. The most formidable of all was Arcadia Bandini Stearns de Baker, who had ruled Los Angeles society in the 1850s and 1860s. The deaths of de Baker's two husbands had made her the richest woman in the city. There were, of course, other notable women whose wealth, lineage, and social standing placed them in the top tier of Spanish-Mexican society. They included Rudecinda Sepulveda Dodson and her daughter, Florence Sepulveda (Dodson) de Schoneman, and Ysabel Varela del Valle and her Anglo-American (but apparently Catholic) daughter-in-law, Mrs. R. F. del Valle.[22] Women like de Baker cooperated with club women on a variety of city events, most notably the annual Fiesta de las Flores. This tourist attraction always drew heavily on the perceived romance of the area's *Californio* past.[23]

In 1902 the issue of where Spanish-Mexican women might fit into organized womanhood came to a head. That year planning for the Fiesta coincided with planning for the biennial convention of the General Federation of Women's Clubs (GFWC). That organization was to meet for the first time in Los Angeles, and its members would attend Fiesta activities. As part of that year's Fiesta, the city's "Spanish American ladies" were to contribute an "exact representation of the gay wedding journey which followed Spanish marriage under the old regimes." To make sure everything was as authentic as possible, Arcadia de Baker planned to loan historic wedding apparel from her own family.[24]

But there was trouble on the horizon. The General Federation had been embroiled in a debate over what role, if any, race should play in club membership. At the Los Angeles meeting, it ultimately voted to institute new membership policies explicitly excluding African American women.[25] In an interview about the new whites-only policy, Caroline Severance, still the most prominent club woman in the city, halfheartedly defended the decision. She argued that until white women were willing to forgo making racial distinctions between people, it would be unfair and unwise for the clubs to practice racial equality. She then pointed out that she did not understand the philosophy that "causes Americans to receive with honors Italians, Spaniards, and representatives of other dark-skinned races, while the natives of Africa are debarred socially."[26]

Severance thus challenged one of the most dearly held privileges of "Spanish American ladies"—that of being white. John Nieto-Phillips notes that asserting "Spanish" blood had been critical for families laying "claim to a European (read: racially white) heritage." Claiming "Spanish" ancestry had also been one of the key mechanisms *Californios* used to distinguish themselves from Indians, Anglo-Americans, and more recent Mexican immigrants.[27]

Severance's categorization of them as part of a "dark-skinned" race thus struck at the very heart of *Californianas'* racial identity. Arcadia de Baker was so angry she withdrew both her participation and her fifty-dollar donation to the Fiesta fund, and several other prominent Spanish-Mexican women evidently followed suit. Although the Fiesta went ahead as scheduled without their participation, a minor social debate ensued. The *Los Angeles Times* called Severance's remarks "an absurd blunder," noting, "If there is a difference between the Anglo-Saxon and the Negro then there is manifestly a similar difference between the Spaniard and the Negro. As a matter of fact, those whom Mrs. Severance denominated the 'dark-skinned races' are often as light skinned as Americans or Englishmen when it comes to considering the varying shades of the human cuticle."[28]

One woman wrote to the *Times* defending Severance and suggesting that the ladies were just being too sensitive about the issue. "Undoubtedly," Helen Densmore protested, "Mrs. Severance thought that the Spanish-American ladies' position is so well-assured that the possibility never occurred to her that they could take umbrage at what she said, or that they could be placed in the same class as the Negroes."[29]

People on both sides of the debate finally seemed to agree that the descendants of the Spanish-Mexican elite were in an intermediate racial position.

They were not white in the same way that Anglo-Americans were white, but they were not "dark" like African Americans or even their working-class Mexican counterparts. As they had during the American conquest of California, Anglos chose to continue to consider Spanish-Mexican elites as "Spanish," and therefore members of the white European family. It is important to note that the line being drawn was about class as well race: *Californianas* were white Spanish American *ladies,* and not Mexican *women.* In the eyes of Anglo-American ladies, that was what made them socially acceptable.[30]

Club women's orientation to middle-class Anglo-American Protestant values can perhaps best be seen in the work of the Los Angeles branch of the YWCA. The YWCA worked to solve some of the worst of the city's social ills through employment agencies, boardinghouses, and educational classes, with both the blessings and the financial support of the Merchants and Manufacturers Association and local employers. This enabled employers to compliment themselves on how much they did for working women without forcing them to confront how their employment practices might contribute to their female employees' woes. But the YWCA initially reached out to only one type of Los Angeles worker: the Anglo-American one.

The Working Girl and the YWCA

By 1890 social commentators had recognized that Los Angeles's reputation as the "Land of Sunshine" had proved just as attractive to women as to men and that many of these women now lived on their own in the city. One investigator found some one thousand women employed at night as cashiers, candy girls, and cabaret singers between Temple and Tenth and Main and Olive downtown. Half of those women lived away from home. Vulnerable, underpaid, and often away from home for the first time, it was these "women adrift" who first attracted the attention of the YWCA of Los Angeles, founded in May 1893.[31]

The YWCA had been founded to encourage the spiritual development of young women. But in the years after the turn of the century the YWCA increasingly devoted itself to the improvement of the social and economic conditions of wage-earning women across the nation. With a history of cooperation with local businesses and politicians, the YWCA proved particularly well suited to the task. In Los Angeles it gained the support of even conservative city organizations like the M&M, which viewed private charities as an alternative to the unionization of female workers.[32]

In 1903 the YWCA of Los Angeles opened its own Employment Bureau (later the Vocational Department) to help the city's women find employment.

The bureau put a woman in search of work in direct contact with a potential employer whenever possible. If it could not find her a position, it referred her to other reputable employment agencies in the city. The YWCA provided all of this as a free service to YWCA members. Nonmembers paid twenty-five cents for each position secured, while day workers paid ten cents for each day's work obtained. In its first year the YWCA's Employment Bureau received ninety-nine inquiries about employment and managed to place forty-six women. The demand for domestic help in the city remained especially high. Interviewed in 1907, Mrs. T. G. King, then head of the Employment Bureau, observed that "the domestic help problem is more difficult than ever before to solve in Los Angeles. . . . I have positions waiting at $35 and $40 a month with board and room. I can't fill them. [Meanwhile] commercial and clerical departments are badly overdone." King argued that there were too many elderly women, unskilled in and unsuited for the demands of household work, in such jobs. "If we could have young women who understood their work and looked upon it as a profession, the 'domestic help' enigma would vanish." To this end King advocated the establishment of a school to train young women in domestic service. But other than some "opportunities" provided by Los Angeles Polytechnic High School such formal training remained unavailable in the city.[33]

In spite of a demand for female employees that skewed toward domestic service, the YWCA continued to do its best to find work for any woman who applied for help. In fiscal year 1910–1911 alone, 3,711 women applied for employment through the YWCA, and 2,320 positions were filled. The bureau also offered what it called "emergency service," short-term jobs paid by the hour, day, or week. A family that needed someone to pack a trunk, mend clothes, tend children, or cater a party could locate help through the YWCA. To encourage city residents to trust the bureau's recommendations, the YWCA provided job seekers with an official card of introduction that bore the organization's name to show she was a suitable job candidate.[34]

The bureau's female managers recognized the special circumstances that women faced while in search of employment. Interviewed for a story on age discrimination in women's employment, Miss Achenbach, who ran the Employment Bureau's business department, observed that businessmen only wanted stenographers under the age of thirty. As she observed, "As a rule [he] wants a stenographer who can adapt herself to the position and many of them think that after thirty a women is not so adaptable." On the bright side, she told the Los Angeles Herald, potential employers actually looked for older, more experienced women when they filled bookkeeping positions. For domestic workers, however, no such bias existed. "I believe there is work for everyone who can and will do it," Mrs. R. Planette, in charge of domestic help, said. "This month I placed three deaf-mutes and they are doing well as domestic servants and are happy. If they can get work, it makes me think anyone can." The YWCA's Employment Bureau did its best to find work for everyone but acknowledged that it had not always been successful: "The list of furnished employment during the last fiscal year included all forms of household help, clerical and stenographic positions, bookkeepers, collectors, demonstrators, dressmakers, nurses, caterers, candy-makers, tutors, kinder-gartners, photographers, interior decorators—forty occupations in all were represented in the classifications. While the majority of those who make application are efficient, there is always a proportion of unskilled workers who are doomed to disappointment. The secretaries in charge find opportunities for true Christian work in helping the unsuccessful to meet the situation bravely."[35]

By 1908 the Los Angeles YWCA had raised enough money to build and dedicate its own building downtown. By the fall of that year the YWCA offered educational classes in its new building. The program eventually expanded to offer everything from arithmetic and English to shorthand, millinery, and "selling experience as well as shop training." In 1912 it charged ten dollars for a series of courses in millinery work taught through its trade school. Leoria Duia, brought from the East to teach the classes, argued that the city held more openings for skilled milliners than there were women to fill them and that a hatmaker or trimmer could make anywhere from five to forty dollars a week, depending on specialty and skill. A skilled designer, she reported, could "get almost any [salary] she demands."[36]

The YWCA's particular orientation can be seen in how it chose to address the most basic needs of working women. It opened a cafeteria downtown that served some 1,000 women a day at affordable rates. However, it also policed the diets of the women it fed: when cafeteria managers discovered young girls spent their hard-earned pennies on ice cream instead on more nourishing fare, the treat promptly dropped from the menu. Clearly, the YWCA felt itself to be a better judge of what women should eat than the women themselves. In 1905 the YWCA also opened a boarding home at 1951 Grand Avenue, housing some 40 "minimum wage girls." Demand for this safe, affordable housing soon outstripped availability: in its 1910–1911 annual report the YWCA observed that it had accommodated 595 women but had to refer 2,306 elsewhere. In 1913 the YWCA opened the Clark Memorial Home at 336 Loma Drive, which filled immediately. California senator William A.

Clark donated the money for the building to the YWCA with the provision that it serve as a home for the city's working women. Designed to accommodate 200, the Clark Home appears to have been a far cry from the often-bleak accommodations working women could afford. As a YWCA brochure enthused, "French Chateau is the style of architecture followed; the material is concrete, faced with gray tapestry brick. The basement, largely above ground, contains ice and heating plants, storerooms, sewing-rooms, laundry with electric dryers, gymnasium and bowling alley, eighteen bedrooms, and a completely equipped hospital suite. Each of the three upper floors, at the rear of which extends a wide porch, has forty-four bedrooms. A closet and lavatory adjoins each. Circassian walnut is the furniture used on these floors."[37]

Because Senator Clark expected the Clark Home to be self-supporting, it did charge its residents rent. However, it operated on a sliding-scale fee designed to make its accommodations affordable to all. Rents ranged from $4.00 to $7.50 a week, including three meals a day. The home also accepted "transient" guests when it had space, charging them by the day or week. One brochure noted the female residents belonged to eighteen different church affiliations and thirty-three vocations. Celebrating the opening of the Clark Home, the Los Angeles Herald newspaper attempted to break down the budget of the city's average working girl. It concluded that if she lived at Clark, she could be "not only comfortable but happy" in Los Angeles on $8.50 a week. The Herald calculated $4.00 for room and board (including meals), $0.90 for lunches, $0.15 for laundry, $0.30 for carfare, $0.15 for the church collection plate, $2.00 for clothes, and $1.00 for incidentals. Obviously, such a budget made no provision for unemployment, illness, or savings.[38]

Ethnicity and class played a role even in the Clark Memorial Home. A study of the women who stayed there confirms that the YWCA served only a segment of Los Angeles's female population. Sixty-seven percent of the women who checked into the Clark Home between February 1913 and January 1915 worked in clerical and sales positions. Just 15 percent held professional and white-collar jobs, making such work a distant second. Only one woman, Thelma Saunders, worked in service, and she carefully noted that she worked as a "companion for child," not a maid-of-all-work. Clark Home management did not keep track of the ethnicity of the residents, but none of the women who checked in during this period had Spanish surnames. Nor did the home reflect the ethnic composition of the city's recent immigrants: the one woman who indicated she had arrived directly from Europe came from England. Residents also earned more than many other working women in the city. On average a woman at Clark made $14 a week and stayed for just over five months before moving to more permanent housing or to another city.[39] Saunders may have been the only domestic worker to check into Clark because wage-earning women had their own class-based hierarchies of desirable occupations, and domestic service continued to be at the bottom of the list, or because most servants lived with their employers.[40]

Segregated from its beginning, the YWCA in Los Angeles did nothing to reach out to African American women. This was a policy that the city's main African American newspaper, the *Eagle,* sharply criticized. Although surviving brochures are silent on the subject, it seems extremely unlikely any non-white women would have been allowed to stay at either the Clark residence or any of the YWCA's other boarding homes. Fortunately, young African American women in the city found a home at the African Methodist Church's Sojourner Truth Industrial Home, opened in 1904. Working mothers also benefited when, in 1908, a group of civic-minded black women formed the Woman's Day Nursery Association. They opened a nursery facility to care for the children of working mothers and women who were unemployed. Recognizing the needs of African American women working as servants in the city, the Woman's Day Nursery Association also provided homes for children whose mothers had to live with their employers. The class and occupational status of these women is unknown, but, like their white counterparts, African American female reformers tended to be middle or upper class.[41]

The YWCA also organized what it called "self-help" clubs for working women. One, the Adelphian Club, organized in April 1899 with the motto "Mutual helpfulness among self-supporting women." Like the Hermosa Club (see chapter 2), the Adelphians funded the construction of a cottage for the members' use, this one in Venice Beach. The club rented out the cottage to members free of charge in the off-season, and for $4.50 a week for full board during peak times of the year. Fifty cents of this fee went into a collection fund used to give other needy women a vacation. The club also funded a room at the Southern Pacific train depot for use by travelers in distress.[42]

The Los Angeles YWCA did little to redress the fundamental inequities in women's economic opportunities in the city. Groups like the YWCA were ambivalent about unions even though they had observed firsthand the poor working conditions of women. Los Angeles's reform women tended to dislike and distrust the radical labor movement. This may have been a function of class status (many of these women had no experience of or contact with unions and union members). This may also have been an expression of the distrust of trade unions common among some Anglo-Americans in this era. The YWCA steered clear of any political or ideological stance that might have helped improve the material conditions of working women. At its 1911 national convention, for example, the organization announced that it supported the idea of a "living wage" for women, but then failed to say what that wage should be or even how many hours a woman should be employed. When three girls in one week working in department stores had to be aided by the YWCA because they did not earn enough money to pay rent, the organization placed all three in domestic service, where employers provided room and board. Although it recognized that the wages of women in department stores were abysmally low, the YWCA argued that this was due to inexperience and that enrollment in its courses it salesmanship (under the slogan "Greater efficiency means more money") would lead to higher wages. Occasionally, the YWCA Vocational Department pressured employers to offer more money than originally listed for the open job, although it also often chastised women who refused to switch to better-paid vocations. By 1913 the YWCA had added a "Dead Center Loan Fund" to its offerings. Organizers intended the program for those women in straits so dire that "the loan of $5 might save her from taking the downward step" (that is, into prostitution). The YWCA asked only that the woman repay the money when she could.[43]

Unlike many private charities, the YWCA of Los Angeles recognized its limitations. After more than a decade studying and attempting to improve women's work in the city, a 1914 board meeting acknowledged, "There is little change in business conditions, that is, in the matter of receiving better class positions—salaries continue low."[44]

Conclusion

Greater Los Angeles's club women clearly believed they had the best interests of working women at heart. By providing a range of recreational options, safe housing, and career guidance, club women hoped that they were sparing working women from the abuses that had become commonplace in other cities. But although there was some overlap between the two groups, the cooperation between working women and club women was always tenuous at best. Female workers often expressed resentment at the level of control that often went hand in hand with accepting aid from these organizations. The YWCA, for example, clearly wanted to reshape women's social and personal lives to reflect middle-class morality. For their part club women brought their own class and ethnic biases to the table. Working women in nonwhite ethnic and racial groups, and women in certain occupations, were never factored into the club's outreach efforts.

The biggest supporters of club women's work appear to have been Los Angeles's male establishment rather than working women themselves. Male business owners allowed private organizations like the YWCA to deal with working women rather than addressing the women's concerns directly. They could then continue to ignore Los Angeles's working class. This left many of the city's working women still searching for ways to obtain better pay, better working conditions, and better organization. The answer, at least for some women, was to pursue unionization, a strategy made all the more difficult by Los Angeles's gender, class, political, and ethnic divisions.

4

Race, Class, and Gender in Los Angeles's Unions

"MAN'S COMPETITORS"

During a meeting in November 1913, the Los Angeles Business Woman's Civic Club appointed a special committee to investigate conditions facing unemployed women in the city. Worried about finding work for all the new arrivals, Jane Neil Scott, head of the Vocational Department of the YWCA, told a reporter, "The only way I can sleep at night is to stop thinking. I have been connected with this business for years and have never seen more tragedy than I have witnessed since coming to Los Angeles to take charge of this employment bureau. Understand I most emphatically wish it made clear that I am not knocking Los Angeles. I love the place and enjoy living here. But this office is daily embarrassed beyond words by hordes of women who have come here from the east without money or friends, expecting to find fine positions the moment they stepped off the train." Scott pointed out that many women who arrived from the eastern United States had trained for jobs that did not yet exist in Los Angeles.[1]

Sue Brobst, president of the Business Woman's Club, reserved her vitriol for the city's boosters, particularly the railroads and the Chamber of Commerce. She argued that most women could not find work because city boosters continued to advertise that the city offered well-paid, plentiful jobs. "Those organizations represent the employing class and put out literature representing the employers' side of the question. I know women who earned a hundred and fifty dollars a month back east who are toiling here for five dollars a week," she complained. Although concerned about what would happen to the women themselves, Brobst also pointed out that such recruitment was "unfair to California, to the working people and philanthropic societies to have constantly to struggle to secure work for untrained women, or those whose sole training or experience has been in factories, of which we have none. If the Chamber of Commerce insists that there is plenty of work here it should boost not only for workers, but for industries that can give them something to do."[2] Brobst's and Scott's comments reflected a new awareness in Los Angeles that, in spite of the best efforts of women's clubs and the YWCA, Angelenos still needed to confront the conditions affecting the female workforce.

For many working women, particularly in new industrial and semi-industrial lines of work, organization into unions seemed to be their best option. The power of collective bargaining, they hoped, would win better hours, better conditions, and higher pay. Unions also filled an important need for working women, becoming a "crucial 'social space' necessary to assert their independence and display their talents." As Vicki Ruiz explains, union participation allowed women to demonstrate that "they were not rote operatives numbed by repetition, but women with dreams, goals, tenacity, and intellect."[3] This chapter provides a brief history of unionization in Southern California and case studies of unionization in two heavily female professions: waitressing and laundry work. In pre–World War I Los Angeles, both racism and gender segregation kept prounion forces divided. As noted in the previous chapter, such problems were hardly unusual given Greater Los Angeles's tremendous ethnic, racial, and class diversity. But the difficulty working women had in speaking with one voice often had dire consequences for unions. It prevented them from forming a coherent stance on the need for and benefits of organizing female workers in the city, and therefore often limited their effectiveness.

The Challenges to Unionization in Los Angeles

Los Angeles's population growth continued to accelerate as the city moved into the twentieth century. But jobs for both sexes remained scarce. In spite of boosters' hopes that Los Angeles would develop an industrial economy along the lines of San Francisco or Chicago (but with more docile labor), it remained overstocked with professionals and semiprofessionals. After all, city boosters had long focused their promotional efforts on well-off farmers and sickly bankers. City residents were only just becoming aware of the long-term economic problems such an imbalance might cause. One pamphlet described the city as "probably the least promising city of the size in the United States for persons who are seeking light employment, in the shape of clerks, or bookkeepers, or anything of the kind, as well as lawyers, and doctors, and parsons, and other professional men, or for people who desire to run a small store of some kind. . . . On the other hand, there is an active demand for mechanics of all kinds." Crowded out of the fields they had trained in, men and women who had been professional or skilled workers elsewhere often took any job they could get in Los Angeles.[4]

Large numbers of women (and men) entered into a form of work relatively new to the city: manufacturing. Prior to 1900 Los Angeles's manufacturing concerns processed raw materials and did small-scale fabrication for local markets, including California, the Pacific Northwest, and the Southwest. Both light and heavy manufacturing continued to lag behind the rest of the country, however. This was due primarily to fierce competition with eastern manufacturers. Competition, combined with the expense involved in shipping finished products to the rest of the country, made many potential investors shy away from sinking money into such concerns. By the turn of the twentieth century, however, the population of Los Angeles itself, combined with the growing pool of skilled and unskilled labor available, made manufacturing an increasingly viable economic sector. California's manufacturing output doubled between 1900 and 1914, with the largest growth occurring between 1900 and 1909. The damage wrought by the San Francisco earthquake of 1906 also allowed Los Angeles to make a play for an increased share of such businesses.[5] However, manufacturing remained focused on nondurable goods (clothing, foodstuffs, and the like) for local consumption.[6] The construction of the Panama Canal and the completion of the Owens Valley Aqueduct seemed to be just the boon the city needed to become a first-rate manufacturing power. The canal promised to substantially cut the time needed to ship manufactured goods to and from the eastern United States. Angelenos hoped the aqueduct would ensure a steady supply of water for Los Angeles's consumption and thus enable sustained growth in the region.[7]

But who would work in these new factories, and who would speak for them? The people who took an active interest in the city's tight labor market—business owners and union organizers—coexisted uneasily in Los Angeles, and neither spared any attention for the city's women or minorities. The impasse between capital and labor became embodied in two organizations: the Merchants and Manufacturers Association and the Los Angeles Council of Labor. Union members across the city had, by 1890, recognized Harrison Gray Otis, editor of the virulently antiunion *Los Angeles Times,* as the greatest obstacle to transforming Los Angeles into a city of closed (union member–only) shops. Loyal unionists, male and female, then refused to shop in stores that advertised in the *Times.* Increasingly angry at such behavior, Otis retaliated and formed the Merchants and Manufacturers Association in 1896. He combined the existing Merchants Association, which had been formed in 1894 to promote La Fiesta de Los Angeles, with a new organization, the Manufacturers Association. Under the direction of Felix J. Zeehandelaar, the M&M took on the task of stimulating the local economy. The M&M echoed the Chamber of Commerce's sentiment that more industry needed to move into the city to achieve stable economic growth. Called by its proponents "balanced prosperity," this new vision saw manufacturing as an essential part of expansion. Under the guidance of the Chamber of Commerce and the M&M, the city embarked on a program to attract as much business as it could. Area businessmen recognized that San Francisco already had a fifty-year head start in terms of both population and industrial development and searched for ways to attract eastern capital. As one inducement, local leaders wanted to offer potential investors plentiful, docile labor, something largely unavailable in heavily unionized San Francisco. They thus actively opposed any and all union activities. Merchants had no choice but to join the Merchants and Manufacturers Association if they wanted to survive in the city. While it did not have the power to intervene directly in labor disputes, the M&M used guards, spies, police protection, and strikebreakers to intimidate labor and refused bank loans, diverted orders, and denied advertising space to nonmember businesses. An estimated 80 percent of business firms in the city eventually joined the M&M.[8]

Largely due to these efforts, Los Angeles quickly became the most anti-union city on the West Coast. However, its stance was hardly atypical for the day. Business owners across the country in the 1890s generally resisted employees' attempts to unionize. For men like Otis, the issue was much more than the expense and inconvenience of unionized employees. Union opponents argued that the material benefits provided by organization would breed dependence in the citizenry, and thus undermine American democracy itself.[9]

While the M&M presented very real difficulties for area businessmen, it also radicalized Socialists and labor organizers. The two movements had been intertwined in Los Angeles since the 1880s, drawing from the same pool of radicals and reformers.[10] The creation of the M&M thus served as a catalyst that pushed these two groups into better organization and cooperation. In September 1890 labor in the city began to benefit from the regular meetings of a new central body, first called the Council of Federated Trades, and later the Council of Labor. In October it formally joined the San Francisco Federated Trades Council. Hoping to counterbalance the influence of the M&M, in 1893 the Central Labor Council of Los Angeles established the Free

Employment Bureau, which it maintained jointly with the city and county of Los Angeles. Designed to save the unemployed from the often excessive fees charged by private employment agencies, in its first two years the bureau managed to place 5,068 of its 10,000 applicants. Los Angeles's Council of Labor paid little or no attention to working women's needs, even though several unions did admit women into their ranks. Unfortunately, an economic slump and widespread unemployment in the late 1890s dampened enthusiasm for labor organization. Still largely independent from the national economy and buoyed by a good wheat crop in 1893 and a growing export trade with the Pacific Rim, Los Angeles did not begin to feel the effects of the panic of 1893 until 1897. By early that year, however, an estimated 2,000 to 5,000 Angelenos had been thrown out of work, and wages had sunk to the lowest level ever known in the city.[11]

However, renewed interest in unionization swept across the United States in the first decade of the twentieth century. The increasing concentration of production in the hands of powerful corporations, the perceived threat of immigration, and increasing mechanization led many workers to view unions as their best hope for preserving jobs and wages. Daisy Houck, a garment worker and one of the leaders of Los Angeles Local 125 of the United Garment Workers of America (see chapter 6), pointed out that Los Angeles women faced unique challenges both within and without the labor movement. "Women's work has been taken for granted all through the centuries," Houck argued, "and only through organization can women hope to impress upon their employers that 'equal pay for equal work' should be the norm."[12]

Throughout the 1890s and the early 1900s unions across the country affiliated with the American Federation of Labor (AFL), which provided the centralized authority and direction many unions needed. The AFL focused most of its attention on the unionization of skilled craftsmen and some semiskilled workers, leaving many employees in large-scale unskilled industries out in the cold. Because they were fixated on the potential of cheap immigrant labor to undercut wages, most unions refused to recognize their common bond with other exploited wage earners. The AFL leadership was neglectful of and often openly hostile to women, immigrants, and unskilled workers.[13]

Following the example set by the AFL, labor in California tightened its own ranks, forming both the California State Federation of Labor and the State Building Trades Council in 1901. By 1900 workers had founded twenty-nine identifiable unions within the Los Angeles labor movement. Organizing drives led by the California State Federation of Labor between 1901 and 1905 added several more to that number. The city's Council of Labor also worked hard to cultivate goodwill in the community, most notably by sponsoring public celebrations of Labor Day. Between 1901 and 1903 the council held public parades complete with floats celebrating various trades and banners proclaiming union principles. Thousands of workers marched through the streets of Los Angeles to demonstrate their support. In 1904, when the organizing drives began to slacken, the council substituted a picnic and labor rally for the parade. But in spite of all this activity, neither the Los Angeles Council of Labor nor the California State Federation of Labor initially put much effort into organizing Los Angeles's female workers. They preferred instead to focus their organizing drives on men.[14] Frances Nacke Noel, a German-born wife and mother active in the Los Angeles branch of the Woman's International Union Label League, perhaps best articulated the reservations that male trade unionists often had about female workers. "It would surprise you how often there arises the opportunity to stand up for womanhood even in our labor conventions," she wrote to a fellow WIULL local president. "You see, women in the field of labor are really man's competitors, men know it directly or indirectly and our interests will clash in spite of good intentions."[15]

With male unionists unwilling or unable to take up their cause, local women had two choices: push for inclusion and participation in male unions or create gender-separate unions. Los Angeles's female waitresses turned to gender-separate locals in keeping with how the industry had organized in other cities. Female laundry workers, on the other hand, joined mixed-sex unions where men assumed the leadership roles. In both industries, however, ethnicity and gender divisions between white and nonwhite, male and female, limited the development of unions strong enough to take on Los Angeles's antiunion foes or make real gains in wages or hours for female workers.

The Gender-Separate Union in Los Angeles: Waitresses

Women employed in Los Angeles's food service industry attempted to unionize earlier than most other workers in the city. This was because they faced some of the worst working conditions in the city, as well as competition from Asian workers. Their struggle to form a gender-separate union and to bar Asian workers from Los Angeles's restaurant industry reveals how ethnicity and gender combined to shape a union and drive its goals.

Greater Los Angeles's waitresses worked very long hours. Those working in hotels and boardinghouses could, like domestic servants, be "on call" twenty-four hours a day. Those employed in restaurants and cafés usually worked split shifts that resulted in ten to fourteen hours of work a day. Before World War I most worked seven days a week. Pay was also low: nationally, waitresses took home an average wage of four to five dollars a week, exclusive of tips. Part-time waitresses in Los Angeles made just thirty-five to fifty cents for three hours' work, plus lunch. Even when these women were not working, conditions were poor. Many women had to share their dressing rooms with male waiters.[16]

From the beginning race and ethnicity divided the organization of California's food service workers. In California many Anglo-Americans held long-standing resentments against Asians and Asian Americans. This usually resulted in Asians being excluded from unions. Resentment was particularly fierce in the food service industry. In other parts of the United States such enmity was usually reserved for African Americans, but in California it focused on the Chinese and, later, the Japanese. In part this was because the food service and laundry businesses were among the few economic niches that employed large numbers of Asians.[17]

Los Angeles's first food service union, the Cooks' and Waiters' Union, formed in 1886 and became Branch no. 3 of the San Francisco–based White Cooks', Waiters' and Employes' [sic] Protective Union of the Pacific Coast in the fall of that year. The union did accept white American women as members, and several founders of the union's southern branch were female.[18] In 1887 the union joined the Los Angeles Trades Council, and in May established an employment agency for its members. Instead of pushing for shorter hours or higher wages, Branch no. 3 devoted much of its energy to ensuring that only white labor worked in Los Angeles's restaurants. The local boycotted employers who hired Chinese cooks and waiters. In spite of Anglo-American fears about being undercut by Asian labor, demand for union (and therefore white) cooks, waiters, and waitresses in the city generally outstripped the supply.

The American Federation of Labor founded the first national waiters union, the Waiters and Bartenders National Union (later the Hotel Employees and Restaurant Employees International Union, or HERE), in 1891. Perhaps because of this development, in 1893 Los Angeles's Branch no. 3 split into the Cooks' and Pastry Cooks' Union no. 5 and Local 48 of the Waiters' International Union. Most of these early unions were affiliated with the Knights of Labor, but by the 1890s surviving unions increasingly affiliated with the AFL.[19]

But racial homogeneity did not ensure cooperation between waiters and waitresses in these unions. The unionization of waitresses lagged behind compared to that of waiters. Only 5 percent of the estimated forty-one thousand waitresses in the country belonged to a union in 1900, compared to

58 percent of waiters. Part of this may have been due to discrimination from male union members. HERE's constitution took an officially neutral position on admitting female members. It did allow for the creation of separate but subordinate race- or gender-based locals. But waitresses across the United States generally preferred separate-gender organizations whenever possible.

Dorothy Sue Cobble has argued that waitresses in other American cities, working in a female-dominated profession with its own unique culture, may have seen separate organizations as the ideal solution for organization. Cobble suggests that historians have misunderstood the impetus for women-only unions in the United States. While she admits that many unions did indeed bar female members, separate-gender organizations were not merely reactions to male discrimination. They emerged instead from a complex combination of community and class ties, feminism rooted in "separate spheres" ideology, and a desire to have gender-specific concerns addressed.[20]

The first such women-only HERE-affiliated organization appeared in Seattle in 1900. San Francisco waitresses, with the support and encouragement of female organizers like Maud Younger, did the same in 1906. Butte, Montana, waitresses followed in 1907. By 1909 the waitresses of Los Angeles had their own women-only local, no. 98. The members of Local 98 knew that Los Angeles's open-shop philosophy put them in a particularly vulnerable position. Their counterparts in Seattle and Butte used protest and publicity to advance their cause. But in the antiunion atmosphere of Los Angeles, waitresses adopted subtler methods of persuasion. Representatives of Local 98 encouraged Angelenos to look for the small green union button worn by members when eating in restaurants, and told members to quietly make nonmembers "wise" to the benefits of unionization. In 1910 the Cooks and Waitresses Union no. 27 absorbed this gender-separate local, but the result appears to have been unsatisfactory. The following year the union split again, and Waitresses Union no. 98 reemerged from the Cooks Union. Union no. 98, now with forty-seven members and only female officers, paid burial and sick benefits and planned to start an employment agency for its members. Whether this agency ever actually opened is unknown.[21]

But while more than happy to promote the rights of Anglo-American female workers, Local 98 also made discrimination against Asians a key part of its activities. In 1912, for example, members argued that unionists could support them by "keeping away from the Jap restaurants and patronizing houses where the green button is displayed by the waitresses." Instead of incorporating Asian food service workers into the union (thus creating an organized opposition against employers), members of the local refused to regard Asian waiters and bartenders as anything other than a threat to their jobs. Ironically, even when racism worked against some Anglo-American waitresses, Local 98 did not rush to their defense. In 1914, for example, the Los Angeles City Council bowed to public pressure and passed an ordinance prohibiting white women from working in cafés owned by the Chinese or Japanese. The public evidently believed that such work was a path to white slavery. The ordinance threw a dozen or so women out of work, with no protest from the union.[22]

In an era that saw supporters of the open shop defeat union after union, Los Angeles's waitresses remained steadfastly committed to unionization. In 1917 the Los Angeles Waitresses Union became Local 639 of HERE, which would organize the city's waitresses until 1974. Whether the union lapsed between 1912 and 1917 or if this was simply a renaming of Local 98 is unknown.[23] But with only part of the workforce (the Anglo-American female part) organized, waitresses' unions had little real leverage to force changes in either wages or working hours across the city. By and large they remained at the mercy of their employers until the passage of statewide legislation establishing a minimum wage and limiting women's working hours.

The Mixed-Gender Union in Los Angeles: Laundries

While waitresses turned to gender-separate locals for organization, women employed in Los Angeles's steam laundries proved one of the richest fields for local mixed-gender union organizers. But allowing men and women into the same union did not produce instant successes, either. Racism directed at Asians again prevented any industry-wide organizing. But gender discrimination also became a problem. Female laundry workers and their male leaders struggled, and often failed, to forge lasting alliances even with each other.

The need to organize the laundry industry became acute after the turn of the century because it employed so many people. By 1909, 124,214 people worked in American laundries, 71 percent of whom were women. The boom in laundry work can be attributed to three key social changes across the United States. First, rising standards of cleanliness demanded that housewives wash both clothes and household linens more frequently. Second, air pollution, soot, and the limited water supplies of nineteenth-century American cities made doing laundry at home increasingly impractical at exactly the same time there was more washing to be done. Third, housewives turned away from using traditional washerwomen. American wives increasingly feared washerwomen (who were often either immigrants or African American) spread diseases and were a negative influence on other servants.

Entrepreneurs and machinery manufacturers rose to the challenge and transformed laundry work into an industrial process in the 1880s. The new "steam laundries" introduced large washing machines and steam-heated mangles in the 1880s and 1890s, followed by ironing and starching machines. These machines reduced the work required for the most unskilled and demanding tasks and cut the overall time required to wash and dry laundry. The transition, of course, was a gradual one, based on the size of a laundry and the capital an owner had available to invest in machinery. Consumers who had the option increasingly chose to send their washing out to one of the new steam laundries springing up across the United States. Because urban populations demanded the convenience of having someone else do the laundry, those states with large urban populations had the most steam laundries. New York had 508 steam laundries by 1910, with 126 in New York City alone; Illinois had 448. California, although only ranked twelfth in the nation in terms of population, ranked third in the number of steam laundries, with 321. The popularity of steam laundries in California can probably be attributed, at least in part, to both the difficulty in finding servants and the tourist industry.[24]

Steam laundries separated work by gender. Women worked as checkers (tracking the incoming laundry), markers, and sorters; washed delicate garments by hand; shook out laundry as it emerged from the washing machines; operated the mangles that pressed and dried fabric simultaneously; starched items like shirts and collars; and ironed. Men tended the large washing machines, maintained the boilers, and delivered the finished laundry to customers. Pay varied tremendously by task. Nationally in 1911, a skilled ironer could earn fifteen dollars a week, but many other employees earned as little as six dollars a week. As mechanization increased, the best-paid jobs in a laundry increasingly became the clerical ones, such as checking and marking incoming clothing. Men occupied most managerial positions.[25]

This gendered division of labor, and the resulting inequalities in pay, meant that female laundry workers faced considerable challenges. A study of Los Angeles's Excelsior Laundry found that fifty-one of the eighty-nine women employed there made eight dollars or less a week. The very lowest-paid female employees there worked at the tables shaking out laundry as it came from the washing machines. All of these women came from immigrant families and lived at home. Hours remained long: before unionization Los Angeles laundry workers worked from twelve to sixteen hours a day. Unfortunately, this study did not distinguish between white and nonwhite immigrants.[26]

Regardless of location, laundry work was not for the faint of heart. Arwen

Mohun, in her magisterial study of steam laundries in the United States and Great Britain, notes that the workday usually began between six and eight in the morning. The heat and steam generated by the washing machines required most female workers to go without corsets, something no "respectable" woman, regardless of social class, was supposed to do in this era. Some women resorted to wearing a larger pair of shoes to work to accommodate feet that swelled over the course of the day.[27]

Other states took steps to limit the toll such a job might take on a woman's health. The State of Oregon, for example, in 1903 passed a law that barred the employment of women in factories and laundries for more than ten hours a day. That law was ultimately upheld by the U.S. Supreme Court in the landmark 1908 case *Muller v. Oregon. Muller v. Oregon* paved the way for a raft of new protective labor legislation for women across the country.[28] But in California such legislation would be passed only after women's suffrage was won in 1911. Even then the effectiveness of legislation regulating women's working hours and pay was still quite limited (see chapter 5).

Laundry work attracted women in large part because paying by the piece allowed for some flexibility. By 1914 just over half of Los Angeles's laundry workers were twenty-five years of age or older, and most were either single or widowed. Of the female laundry workers interviewed that year, 78.4 percent lived at home, usually as close to the cluster of steam laundries downtown as possible. But it must be remembered that many of these women worked sixty-hour weeks and then returned home for a second shift of child care or housework or both. Investigators noted that female laundry workers returned home at night too exhausted to cook or eat dinner. These women used Sunday, their only day of rest, to perform a week's worth of household chores.[29] One investigator, Helen V. Bary, noted a general air of hopelessness among the laundry workers she interviewed: "The majority of the women said they could not save a penny, and that they simply existed. The older women all had a dread of the future." Bary worked for California's Industrial Welfare Commission. (For more on the IWC, see chapter 5.) She found that single women made up just over 45 percent of those in the study; widows made up 33 percent.[30]

Laundry workers in Los Angeles first attempted to unionize in 1896. Laundry owners across the city retaliated with a combination of price and wage cutting that finished off the union in March 1897. In 1901, with the support of Los Angeles's organized labor behind them, the laundry workers again attempted to organize. Local 52 of the Shirt Waist and Laundry Workers' International Union formed in April 1901. This union had started in Troy,

New York, in 1898, and had become an international in 1900. From its beginning it tended to focus more on the needs of male workers than those of female workers. But in Local 52 unskilled female workers outnumbered the men. It soon had more than three hundred members. The union did not, however, hire its first female organizer, a Mrs. Walden, until 1911.[31]

Mixed-gender Local 52 launched immediately into action. Most notably, the union appealed directly to Los Angeles's Council of Labor for help pursuing better conditions and pay. This alliance dramatically increased the union's leverage. In May 1901 the union, with the backing of the Council of Labor, presented the Steam Laundry Proprietors' Association with a list of demands. These included a ten-hour day, equal pay for women, and the closed (union-only) shop. On June 29 J. Bonfilio, owner of the Excelsior Laundry and president of the Steam Laundry Proprietors' Association, told his employees that no union member should show up for work on Monday. When other employers began adopting Bonfilio's stance, the union threatened to strike. The union gave the proprietors until June 25 to respond to its demands. On June 22 the owner of Cleaver's Laundry gave his workers an ultimatum: renounce the union or quit. Seven girls walked out. The Council of Labor dubbed this a lockout and instituted a boycott against Cleaver's. The union extended the grace period but resolved to strike on July 1 if it didn't have a favorable answer by then. On July 1, 1901, 500 employees of seven Greater Los Angeles laundries walked out of their jobs. An estimated 1,000 other nonunion workers also struck in solidarity with the laundry employees. In contrast, while the Council of Labor was certainly supportive of Waitresses Union no. 98, I found no evidence of this body ever directly intervening on its behalf in a labor dispute with employers. Whether the waitresses chose to keep the largely male council at arm's length or there was some other dynamic at work is unknown. Most laundry owners indicated they were willing to recognize the limitations on hours, but not the unions.[32]

Pro–open shop forces rallied to defeat the strike. The *Times* attacked the moral character of the striking women. Several smaller establishments stood by their workers, but most refused to recognize the union. Financial support from other unions, as well as benefits held in their name, helped support the workers as the strike dragged on through the rest of 1901. Several strikers gave up their union membership and went back to work in association laundries, but most found work either in friendlier laundries or in other lines of work. In September 1901 a cooperative union laundry, the New Method Laundry Company, opened, providing employment for some 100 strikers.[33]

The laundry unions made several real gains for both male and female workers, but fierce opposition from open-shop forces limited their long-term success. Although the 1901 strike fizzled out without reaching a settlement, in 1903 the laundry workers union managed to sign contracts with four of the biggest laundries in the city. The agreement ensured higher wages, better hours, and a closed shop for laundry workers, drivers, and steam engineers. Now at the peak of its power, Local 52 boasted some 750 members across the city. But although most workers were women, the union still had no female officers. In 1905 laundry workers struck again for better hours and a pay increase of one dollar a week. Now in private hands, even the New Method Laundry refused to recognize these worker demands. Some 200 workers struck, but the union proved unable to institute the shorter hours in all the city's laundries.[34]

These failures proved particularly galling for Los Angeles's laundry unions because of successes in its rival city to the north, San Francisco. There union activity soon produced a gradual shift to the eight-hour day, a fixed scale of minimum wages, and the negotiation of closed-shop agreements for laundries. But there was more to the San Francisco victories than meets the eye. San Francisco's laundry owners tolerated the union in large part because it had agreed to help drive Asian and French competitors out of business. Moreover, the new minimum-wage scale placed the markers and washers at the top of the scale, and men increasingly dominated both of those jobs in the city.[35] In Los Angeles no such entente cordiale existed between capital and labor.

According to the *Los Angeles Union Labor News,* in 1906 Los Angeles had only five strictly union laundries: the Magnet, Sanitary, Central, Overall, and Puritas. With their opposition well organized and well funded, union power in Los Angeles's laundries began to slip. Part of the problem in maintaining Local 52's strength may have come from differences between male leadership and female members over strategy, organization, and even the benefits of unionization itself. Evidence suggests that laundry unions across the country did not have as much success in retaining female members as in recruiting them. A 1908 U.S. Department of Labor study of laundry unions found that although women did turn out for strikes, they were far less likely to remain in unions than men. Even after the victories in San Francisco, only 21 percent of female laundry workers in California belonged to unions. In fact, female membership in San Francisco's laundry unions may have been high only because it was a closed-shop system. Women had to join or lose their jobs.[36]

Friction with male union members may explain low female enrollment; certainly, the continued male dominance of union leadership would have made it easy for them to marginalize female members. It is possible some women feared that male union leaders in Los Angeles's laundry industry might make decisions that favored the male worker over the female, as had occurred in San Francisco. There is no evidence that male laundry workers in Los Angeles tried to deliberately sabotage their female members, as often happened in other mixed-gender unions. But they never directly addressed the gendered division of labor in laundries that ensured that women almost always earned less than men, union or no union. The wage gap between men and women in Los Angeles's laundries remained particularly wide. As late as 1916 a female laundry worker in Los Angeles earned an average of $8.36 a week compared to $14.89 for a man. Those women employed in Japanese-owned laundries earned less than those in the larger steam laundries. Investigator Bary found that Japanese laundry owners sometimes hired Anglo-American women to work as ironers; Chinese laundry owners did not. Bary argued that in both cases standards of cleanliness lagged behind those of American-owned laundries. She was particularly horrified to find that Japanese families often ate and slept in the workroom.[37]

The competing demands of work and family probably also limited female participation in laundry unions. Given the other pressing demands on their time, workers may have been understandably reluctant to give up their evenings and Saturdays to union activities unless there seemed to be a good chance for real gains. A strike or the implementation of the closed shop would thus have drawn more women into laundry unions, while losses and periods of inactivity would have pushed them out again. In Los Angeles's case the local's failure to make any permanent changes in the structure of the industry caused some women to turn their backs on the laundry unions.

As the union's strength declined, it increasingly played the race card in an attempt to mobilize public sentiment. The biggest competitors to the state's steam laundries remained the so-called Chinese laundries. Owned by Asian entrepreneurs pushed out of most other small businesses and staffed by relatives who worked for room and board, Chinese laundries undercut the prices of steam laundries. Although such businesses often advertised that they did all work by hand, by the turn of the century machinery and mechanization increasingly became a fixture of both Chinese and steam laundries. Labor organizers and state investigators fed Anglo-American fears about the dangers of patronizing Chinese- and Japanese-owned laundries. Such laundries were dirty, and some, they warned, even had the gall to employ white women at pay rates below the standards of steam laundries.[38] Patronizing an Asian-owned laundry, such arguments suggested, not only undermined white women's opportunities to earn a living but also could potentially damage human health.

Many Los Angeles–area laundries who abandoned their closed-shop policies to stay financially competitive in the face of competition from Asian-owned laundries echoed these same arguments but deployed them differently. In 1910, for example, the Sanitary Laundry Company gave its workers thirty days' notice before switching to the open shop. The laundry's owners argued that they had to drop the union in order to stay economically competitive. Laundry owners also fought against the passage of a statewide minimum wage for women by arguing that if such legislation passed, they would only be able to hire Asian workers. In response to such complaints the prounion newspaper the *Los Angeles Citizen* scoffed, "What a calamity! The laundries threaten to abandon the field to Chinese and Japanese. Well, if the laundry business depends upon the heathenish practices of its present managers, the sooner it is turned over to the heathen Orientals the better!" Such rhetoric failed to significantly lower the numbers of Asian-owned laundries, however. As late as 1911 "Chinese" laundries continued to outnumber steam laundries in the city, although the gap was slowly closing. In 1901 Los Angeles's *City Directory* advertised forty-three "Chinese laundries" and twenty-seven "laundries." In 1911 there were listings for fifty-seven "Oriental laundries" and forty-three "laundries."[39]

Unions across Los Angeles mirrored the problems encountered by female service workers in restaurants and laundries. Certainly, the presence of the Merchants and Manufacturers Association and the *Los Angeles Times* had a corrosive influence on the unions. Joining the M&M and the *Times* in their antiunion stance was the new Los Angeles Citizens' Alliance, formed in 1904 with Zeehandelaar as secretary and Otis as chairman of the executive board. Like other alliances across the country, the Los Angeles Citizens' Alliance developed elaborate procedures to support members whose employees were out on strike. Disgusted by these tactics, organized labor responded by organizing the Anti-Citizens' Alliance, whose four thousand members refused to do business with or support candidates connected to the Citizens' Alliance.[40]

Neither the M&M nor the Citizens' Alliance ever focused much of their attention on unions or industries where most of the members were female. Aside from the occasional editorial in the *Times,* even Otis reserved most of his vitriol for male unions. Of the fifty-one strikes occurring between 1905 and 1906, for example, forty-two were failures, and only five were outright victories for the unions. By 1907 Otis and the *Times* had claimed total victory for the open shop. That year the American Federation of Labor singled out Los Angeles as a site for intensive unionization. As the city was flooded with migrants seeking relief from the financial panic of 1907, employers easily withstood the push for unionization by firing troublesome workers and hiring new ones.[41]

But it would be oversimplistic to argue that the power of Los Angeles's antishop forces made all union organizing futile. Unions that were women run or women dominated may, in fact, have had better chances for success than those of men precisely because they attracted little attention from the M&M and the *Times*. This may help explain the relative success of Local 98 and Local 52 compared to other unions in the city. But if unions in both the food service and the laundries had not remained divided along the lines of race and gender, their impact and effectiveness would likely have been much greater.

Showdown: The Times *Bombing and* *Its Consequences for Working Women*

Relations between capital and labor grew increasingly strained over the next several years, and by 1910 San Francisco labor organizers decided to launch a major organizing drive in Los Angeles. Labor in San Francisco had grown increasingly entrenched after helping to rebuild the city after the earthquake of 1906. With wages anywhere from 30 to 40 percent lower in Los Angeles than in San Francisco, unionists recognized that unless Los Angeles's workers organized, employers might begin abandoning San Francisco in favor of cheaper labor in Southern California. In 1910 union leaders in that city met and resolved to break the open-shop rule in Los Angeles, sending ten skilled organizers to begin the campaign.[42]

Yet labor again targeted primarily white male workers in the skilled and semiskilled trades. The organization campaign of 1910–1911 reached workers in a variety of different occupations across the city: in that year butchers, trolley car operators, painters, printers, brewers, and workers in the metal trades all struck for better pay and for recognition of their unions. On a smaller scale the drive even managed to reach some unskilled and minority workers. Largely through the work of organizer Juan Ramirez from the State Federation of Labor, Laborers' Union no. 13097, for Mexican workers, and the Laborer's Protective Union no. 13149, for Russians, Slovenians, and other eastern Europeans, joined the city's Central Labor Council. By and large, however, organized labor in the city not only refused to work with minorities but often exacerbated dislike and distrust between white workers and their minority counterparts. In 1908, for example, when a wave of anti-Japanese sentiment swept though the country over Japan's imperial ambitions abroad, labor groups convinced local employers to fire several hundred Japanese workers. The Central Labor Council even purchased 25,000 "Fire the Jap" stickers for distribution by union members. Although it reached only a fraction of the city's workers, the strategy paid off: by 1910–1911 some 7,000 new members had joined local Los Angeles unions, an average weekly increase of about 115. Workers themselves formed twenty-five new unions.[43]

Responding to this activity, and particularly to the metal-trades lockout, the city council passed an antipicketing ordinance on June 1, 1910. The ordinance only increased labor's resolution to break the hold of antiunion forces. In the midst of the increasing enmity on both sides came a seminal event in Los Angeles labor history: on October 1, 1910, an explosion at the *Los Angeles Times* building in downtown Los Angeles killed twenty men. The next day investigators found explosive devices outside both Otis's home and the home of Felix J. Zeehandelaar of the Merchants and Manufacturers Association. Socialists and labor supporters claimed to be victims of an antilabor conspiracy, but to no avail. On the contrary, fearful Angelenos viewed the bombing as evidence of a vast prolabor conspiracy at work in the city. The bombing unleashed a reign of political terror across the city. The M&M sought to use the event as the means of breaking any remaining popular support for labor. Anyone supporting a union seemed to be a potentially dangerous radical. With both employers and ordinary citizens now determined to stamp out prolabor sentiment once and for all, the bombing dealt a near-fatal blow to the nascent labor movement in Los Angeles.[44]

Women who still wished to pursue unionization now had an even greater hurdle to overcome: that of negative public opinion. "As women of the Labor Movement," Frances Nacke Noel told a joint meeting of club women and working women, "we want to let the world know that we are minus hoofs, horns, and dynamite bombs."[45]

Conclusion

In the years after the turn of the century both male and female workers in Los Angeles turned to organization in the hopes of improving wages, hours, and working conditions. Women, particularly those in the service industries, initially made some gains by working in gender-separate unions or in female-dominated unions under male leadership. However, racial and gender divisions combined with the open-shop stance of the Los Angeles City Council, the Merchants and Manufacturers Association, and numerous employer organizations to make long-term change difficult to maintain. The *Times* bombing in 1910 only hardened employer resolve not to deal with unions. The city's laundry unions, for example, never regained their former strength after 1910. Unfortunately, organization would probably not have been enough to save the laundry industry. Technological innovations after World War I, most notably the introduction of home electric washing machines, led to the hasty decline of the steam laundry.[46]

Against the background of these events, the creation of both gender-separate and mixed-gender unions must be seen as different manifestations of female workers' desire to materially improve their situations. Although their tactics differed, both Waitresses Union no. 98 and Local 52 of the Shirt Waist and Laundry Workers' International Union failed to forge lasting racial and gender alliances, even when it would have been in their own best interest to do so. With the open-shop ascendant in Los Angeles after 1910 and capital and labor more at odds than ever, working women turned to reform legislation in the hopes of achieving real changes in wages, hours, and gender segregation in the workforce. This would provide the first real intervention by the State of California in women's working lives. But while much of the discourse surrounding female suffrage and a minimum-wage law for women involved working women, the polarization of city politics between a Socialist-labor coalition and Progressive reformers often marginalized them further.

5

Suffrage and Politics in Los Angeles

"THE SAFE, MIDDLE GROUND"

In 1911 California prepared for local and statewide elections. Even to those individuals with a great deal of political experience, there seemed to be something different in the air that autumn. In Southern California women were suddenly everywhere in the political process because two of those elections dealt with issues near and dear to their hearts. The first election, scheduled for October, would grant or deny California's women the right to vote. The second, the election for Los Angeles's mayor, to be held in early December, would determine whether a Socialist-labor coalition or Progressives would gain control of the city. From handing out free doughnuts tagged with "Votes for Women" ribbons to stumping for one mayoral candidate or the other, women of every political stripe seemed to be on the campaign trail. The results of those two elections, many women seemed to recognize, would have direct consequences not only for women who worked but for every woman in the region.[1]

With unions producing at best mixed results for female industrial workers, it is hardly surprising that some women, particularly white-collar workers and those who did not have access to unions, put their faith in political reform. Across Southern California working women of all classes gave their voices to the fight for statewide suffrage. In so doing they carved out surprisingly effective but short-lived cross-class, cross-racial, and cross-gender alliances. The suffrage victory was followed by a wave of new organizations and investigations, including the California Bureau of Labor Statistics, California Industrial Welfare Commission, Los Angeles National Women's Trade Union League (LANWTUL), and Los Angeles meetings of the United States Commission on Industrial Relations. With the Progressives triumphant in the city after 1912, the focus shifted to bringing the power of government to bear to solve the "working woman problem."[2]

The suffrage fight and subsequent events illustrate that the difficulty reformers faced was not a lack of awareness about the problems working women faced. Rather, it was that reformers themselves, male and female, had such diverse opinions about how to improve conditions that it was difficult to agree on and stick with a consistent approach. Would gaining the right to vote be enough? Did Los Angeles perhaps need a new kind of government? Should that government be Progressive or Socialist? Did the State of California or the federal government need to intervene in the local economy, or would that be too much government intrusion?

This chapter considers how women forged coalitions, particularly around the issue of suffrage, but also how quickly those coalitions dissolved in the face of political differences. Like the industrial unions, both the fight for suffrage and the subsequent organizations became mired in political differences between male and female, labor and capital, organized and unorganized workers, and white and nonwhite workers.

Women and Politics in Turn-of-the-Century Los Angeles

Los Angeles early on captured the Progressive spirit that swept across the United States between 1896 and 1914. On December 1, 1902, Los Angeles became one of the first American cities to officially approve the initiative, referendum, and recall, as well as civil service reform, for the city. Other organizations took up the call for reform. At its first meeting in May 1907, the local Lincoln-Roosevelt Republican League, at the urging of Katherine Phillips Edson, endorsed female suffrage as part of its new platform. Edson, a prominent local club woman, argued that with so many women now working outside the home, only equal suffrage would give women a voice in policy making. The LRRL's platform also called for the direct primary; a statewide initiative, referendum, and recall; regulation of utility rates; a minimum wage for women and children; and worker's compensation laws.[3]

In 1909, when Los Angeles Mayor Harper resigned in the face of corruption charges, advocates of reform, or "Good Government," ran George Alexander as their candidate. Alexander managed to narrowly beat the Socialist candidate to become mayor. This success, however, left male reformers in an awkward position. Angry conservative Republicans recognized that the election had nearly gone to the Socialists. Led by Harrison Gray Otis of the *Los Angeles Times*, these Republicans took to mockingly calling the Good Governments the "goo goos."[4]

Fearing for its own political survival, the Good Government movement now expressed interest in enfranchising women to counteract the male Socialist vote. Club members and other reform-minded women already had a history of cooperating with male reformers. They now capitalized on those connections. They helped persuade the new "Goo Goo" city government to crack down on prostitution, burlesque houses, gambling, and saloons. Los Angeles even hired its first female police officer, reformer Alice Stebben Wells, specifically to work with "wayward" women and girls. Such moves endeared the city government to reform-minded women. Other women who supported the Good Government movement did so because they expected that social reform would also include female suffrage.[5]

The Los Angeles Consumers' League perhaps best exemplifies the alliance between Good Government and organized womanhood. Organized in 1902 at the urging of Florence Kelley and Jane Addams, the Los Angeles chapter of the league investigated labor conditions for the city's women and children. Like the YWCA, the Consumers' League did not try to directly intervene on behalf of these workers. Rather, if the league found conditions acceptable, the factories received permission to use their "Consumer's White Label." Dominated by club women, the league also worked hard for the support of women in the local branch of the WCTU. In 1911 members announced their support for the eight-hour day for women workers, suggesting that legislation, not organization, would finally ensure the safety of female workers.[6]

At the other end of the political spectrum, the Socialist Party also tried to gain the support of working men and women. Many city residents had been part of the Populist movement of the 1880s and 1890s and had found themselves without a political party after 1900. The Socialist Labor Party, the most outspoken of the city's three Socialist groups when in came to workers and politics, allied with the Council of Labor in the city elections of 1898. Although Socialist candidates drew less than a tenth of the popular vote in that election, both sides were pleased enough with the outcome to continue the alliance when the city's Socialists consolidated into a Los Angeles branch of the newly organized Socialist Party of the United States in 1901.[7]

The Socialists advocated pro–working class policies such as unions and workers' rights. The party seems to have held limited appeal for ethnic minorities in the city, however: whether intentional or not, white Angelenos made up most of its membership. Socialism attracted the city's skilled and semi-skilled Anglo- and Euro-American workers, those who felt most vulnerable to exploitation and who most feared competition from unskilled immigrants.[8] The party confined its work among immigrant populations to

European immigrants: Mexicans immigrants and Asian Americans, who by and large were not citizens, had no place in Socialist plans for the city. Recognizing the pool of untapped potential voters among the city's African American population, however, the Socialists did organize a special chapter of the party to work with them.[9] Socialists held regular outdoor meetings at the busy intersections of Second and Los Angeles, Fourth and Los Angeles, and Seventh and Main and along Market Street and distributed its free newspaper, the *Los Angeles Socialist* (later *Common Sense*). Annoyed at these tactics, the city government used a 1901 ordinance requiring police permits to speak in public parks to arrest Socialists and anyone else speaking in Pershing Square. In 1903 the ordinance was expanded to include public streets, and in 1908 the police revoked the Socialists' permits for the street-corner meetings. In the face of free-speech protests led by the Socialists, the city abolished its permit requirement for public speaking, but also set aside a no-speech zone around the downtown white-collar districts west of Main Street between Commercial and Ninth, including Pershing Square. The Socialists, however, regarded this as a victory, for they regained the right to speak at the Plaza. The new antipicketing ordinance, passed in 1910, prohibited both picketing and simply standing in front of a business in hopes of influencing public sentiment. Violators faced fines of up to one hundred dollars, up to fifty days in jail, or both. Angered by such tactics, union supporters turned away from the city's Good Government movement (which had passed the hated ordinance) and turned increasingly to socialism. In July 1910 the Socialist Party moved its headquarters into the Labor Temple, making the alliance between the two movements clear to all observers.[10]

While many Socialist women participated in more mainstream clubs and in the suffrage movement, in 1901 they also created their own organization, the Woman's Socialist League of Los Angeles. In September 1902 the Woman's Socialist Union of California (wsu) became an umbrella organization for the state's autonomous Socialist women's clubs. Socialist women articulated what Sherry Jeanne Katz has called a "dual political identity," considering themselves "both socialists and feminists, committed to ending the oppression of women as a group and to abolishing class society." They advocated women-only Socialist groups, arguing that they could better develop political skills and methods of educating women in a single-sex environment. Moreover, they believed female political autonomy was a necessity because women's struggle for freedom could be won only if they worked together as a group. Unlike women's Socialist clubs in the rest of the country, which were relatively short-lived, California's wsu activists found a receptive audience for their messages both in the California Socialist Party and among organized womanhood. The Los Angeles WSU committed itself to the study of economics generally and economic conditions for women and children in Los Angeles in particular. To further this goal it created a committee of four to study the conditions of female and child workers in the city.[11]

Although economic independence for women formed a fundamental part of its political platform, the WSU's political agenda appeared similar to that of the larger late-nineteenth- and early-twentieth-century women's movement. Suffrage became the cornerstone of the WSU's movement, and it failed to develop any lasting ties to female trade unionists in the state. The Los Angeles club consisted primarily of professionals with flexible schedules, retired professionals, and housewives, and met on weekday afternoons, not a time conducive to the participation of most working women.

Southern California WSUS did meet sporadically with locals of the Woman's International Union Label League. The local branch of the WIULL had its roots in a 1901 protest against the People's Store, owned by the pro–open shop A. Hamburger and Sons. In protest of Hamburger's support of antiunion activity, the wives and daughters of union men had used tactics like flooding into the store on a Saturday just before Christmas to examine merchandise they had no intention of buying, keeping store staff so busy other patrons gave up and went elsewhere to shop. Some WSU chapters periodically distributed leaflets to wage-earning women at offices, factories, and stores. Affiliated with the American Federation of Labor, the WIULL consisted not of wage-earning women but of working-class housewives who advocated the consumption of only union-made goods. In 1907 the Los Angeles WSU also launched an investigation of California laws pertaining to the status of women and raised money for striking telegraphers. In 1908 members went before the Los Angeles City Council to advocate offering public-works jobs to male heads of households in an attempt to ease unemployment. They also supported the free-speech fight being waged by the Socialist Party, the Socialist Labor Party, and the Industrial Workers of the World.[12]

After 1909, however, Socialist Party member Frances Nacke Noel helped strengthen ties among suffragists, organized womanhood, and the WIULL. Noel transformed the local branch of the Woman's International Union Label League into an advocate for the eight-hour day for women and for suffrage. The Label League put pressure on the California State Federation of Labor, which in 1909 added female suffrage to a list of demands it submitted to the state legislature. Noel not only pushed the State Federation of Labor for support but also pressured local women's clubs to become involved in the labor cause. In November 1910, for example, Noel set up a meeting between the Votes for Women Club and Local 36 of the WIULL to discuss the relationship between suffrage and current social problems. A month later the groups joined forces to finance a Christmas benefit for the wives and children of striking workers.[13]

Noel stressed the need for a broad, inclusive female movement in the city. In January 1911 she persuaded representatives of Local 36 and five women's unions (garment workers, laundry workers, waitresses, saleswomen, and stenographers) to meet for the purposes of creating a permanent cross-class organization to discuss and help enact laws protecting women and home life. She also invited 150 local women's organizations, and some 100 delegates attended. The organization born from this meeting, the Woman's Conference of Los Angeles County, met on Saturdays to facilitate the participation of wage-earning women. The new organization vowed in its mission statement to "secure all data that is of importance to the welfare of the home and family, and particularly to women employed in gainful occupations." One local newspaper lauded the creation of the Woman's Conference, arguing that "there are many women in the average clubs who are sick and tired of just working in their own little groups." Unfortunately, the conference lasted only a few months, as many of its constituent groups soon splintered to work on the 1911 suffrage campaign. Undaunted, both the Socialist-Labor coalition and the Good Governments continued to look hopefully toward enfranchising women as the way to finally defeat their opponents and gain control of Los Angeles.[14]

The 1911 Battle for Suffrage

Given the pervasive interest in social reform, Southern California's women early on expressed an interest in gaining suffrage. As early as 1888 Los Angeles had a Woman's Suffrage Club that met semimonthly at the Women's Exchange.[15]

The first real chance to extend the franchise to California's women had come in 1896. Then, recognizing the uphill battle before them, Southern California suffragists had made a concerted effort to include women from both ends of the political spectrum. Populists and Socialists had joined with club members and temperance women. Organizers had also tried to reach across class lines. Speakers had presented noontime meetings to working-class men in factories, workshop, and railroad stations. The wives of these men were also invited to hear the presentations. One woman involved in this campaign remembered that a "large proportion of foreign citizens were thus reached in a quiet, educational manner." However, these presentations seem to have been confined to industrial laborers. Suffrage advocates thus probably ignored Mexican Americans and other racial minorities in the city, who would have been found in lower-paid service jobs and doing manual labor. Immigrant men who were naturalized would, of course, have been eligible to vote. But suffrage supporters may have assumed that for cultural reasons these individuals would not support giving women the vote. However, the Afro-American Congress, meeting in Los Angeles, did hear a speech by a suffragist, and members of the Colored Woman's Club had worked to convert black men to the suffrage cause. In spite of the bitter opposition of the *Los Angeles Times,* suffrage had won a majority of forty-six hundred votes in the city.[16] Ultimately, however, suffrage had lost because it lost in San Francisco. Since that city still had the majority of the state's population in 1896, this was enough to defeat the measure.

But now, under pressure from both the Right and the Left, the California state legislature in February 1911 again announced it would put suffrage on the fall ballot. Suffragists launched a new campaign to win the franchise, and the place of women in the workforce became a key issue in prosuffrage arguments.[17] Proponents seized on giving the ballot to women as the best way to end low pay, long hours, and gender discrimination on the job once and for all.

With an election scheduled, Central Suffrage Committees formed in both Los Angeles and San Francisco to organize and coordinate the campaigns. Perhaps recognizing the divisions already present in the community, Los Angeles's organizers focused on identifying and lobbying particular groups. Socialist women organized the Los Angeles Wage Earners' Suffrage League (LAWESL) to attract both Socialist women and the wives of trade union men. Working women affiliated with this group organized the city's first open-air suffrage meetings in July 1911. Because city ordinances forbade giving political speeches in public parks, these savvy women instead sang suffrage songs and passed out doughnuts tagged with the slogan "Votes for Women." Antisuffrage women appealed to the deputy district attorney to stop the distribution of the delicious dunkers, but to no avail. The city evidently found cooking for the suffrage cause perfectly acceptable. After all, handing out doughnuts must have seemed much less threatening than picketing. Although at first put off by such public displays, more elite women within the suffrage movement soon began passing out doughnuts in the park, too.[18]

An examination of statements by prosuffrage, prolabor forces in Los Angeles makes the connection between gender, class, and the ballot blatant.

Such groups failed to develop a consistent stand on exactly why working-class women needed the vote. Instead, gender and class shaped their arguments in different ways. Trade unionists viewed the ballot as a way to protect their wives and daughters on the job and to increase Socialist power in the city. Good Governments and reform women viewed suffrage as a way to place one more tool of reform in women's hands.

The Los Angeles Wage Earner's Suffrage League, a Socialist organization that one expects might have advocated suffrage for women as a political right, often relied on gender stereotypes when making its case. "Our daughters must go to the stores and factory to work," one of its appeals read, "and the mothers need to have a voice in making these places safe and sanitary, with healthful hours and such wages as do not make our girls a prey to immoral tempters. . . . Most of all, the woman who is forced to work outside the home needs the ballot with which to protect herself."[19] The LAWESL may have calculated this approach as the best way to gain the ear of Los Angeles's working-class men.

With their sketchy record of supporting female workers, it is hardly surprising that the Los Angeles Central Labor Council took a similar tack. They, too, supported suffrage not as a workers' right but as a way to protect frail women and vulnerable girls. As Brother Misner, president of the Central Labor Council, explained at one meeting, "Our women in industry, we murder them by inches. . . . [W]e rob them of the crown of womanhood; we wreck them morally and physically. The daughters of the rich are well cared for; the ballot in the hands of women means more to the women of the working class than to the women of wealth." Many labor leaders also hoped suffrage would lead to equal pay for equal work, and thus prevent low-paid female work from undercutting male jobs.[20]

But evident in Misner's statement is awareness that female suffrage was also a class issue. He seems to suggest that working women had more to lose socially, politically, and economically than their wealthier counterparts and thus needed the ballot more. The labor newspaper the *Los Angeles Citizen* took the argument one step further. An editorial argued that women owed no obeisance at all to upper-class women in the pursuit of the vote: "You cannot prevail upon Mrs. John Smith who works for a living, or Mrs. Tom Brown, who has to cook and wash for her husband and children, that women suffrage would be a good thing because Mrs. Algernon Vere de Vere says it is; or because Mrs. Chauncey Smythe Robbynson wears a suffragist badge as she rushes past in her magnificent automobile. . . . [T]he battle must be won through the efforts of the working women of California."[21] If women were going to get the vote, this article suggested, it could not be through pressure from the upper classes. Working women and the wives of working men needed to believe in the value of the vote, mobilize, and send their men to the polls to vote "yes."

For her part Frances Nacke Noel urged a rapprochement between club women and more politically radical suffrage advocates, particularly the Socialists. As an experienced organizer, Noel recognized that male Socialists' gender biases, if not addressed, might lead some to vote against suffrage as a way to keep women out of direct economic competition with men. "Stop saying women's place is in the home," she wrote in a newspaper article aimed at Socialist voters. "We know our place and always will, but it all depends on the economic status of affairs. . . . [Y]ou need not fear that great army of club women. They have studied, they know our cause better than you think."[22] She thus reassured them in print that, even if enfranchised, Socialist women would remember their "place" in the Socialist vision for Los Angeles.

Unlike in the failed 1896 suffrage campaign, this time some suffragists focused on reaching immigrant voters. Maria de Lopez, then teaching at Los Angeles High School and serving as president of the local chapter of the College Equal Suffrage League, spoke in favor of suffrage to Mexicans in the Los Angeles Plaza. She also frequently translated speeches into Spanish at suffrage campaign meetings. Pershing Square and the Plaza, which bracketed the most crowded working-class section of the city in the period, were frequent sites for political actions of all varieties. On October 3, 1911, for instance, the Votes for Women Club held a large rally at the Plaza that featured de Lopez giving a speech in Spanish. The prosuffrage, prolabor newspaper the *Citizen* cheered, "There is no way of estimating exactly how much she has accomplished with the vote."[23]

On the more conservative end of the female political spectrum, the Southern California Political Equity League went door-to-door distributing leaflets, stressing the need for the ballot so mothers could have a say in local government. Katherine Phillips Edson and John H. Braly had founded the Southern California Political Equality League in 1910. A retired millionaire and equal-suffrage supporter, Braly had recruited a hundred of the area's leading citizens into the organization, which dedicated itself to the achievement of suffrage through political pressure and endorsing prosuffrage candidates for office. The league also argued that enfranchising women would help curb the profit taking of big business and enable daughters to have the same opportunity to make a living as sons. Organizations such as the California Federation of Women's Clubs, the Teachers' Club of Los Angeles, the

Woman's Parliament, the Mother's Congress, and the Southern California and Redlands Ministerial Union also publicly endorsed suffrage.[24]

Racist sentiment against Asians also played a key role in the suffrage campaign. Ignoring the reality of ethnic discrimination in the state, some California suffragists argued that it was unfair that some Asian men (at least in theory) could vote when native-born women could not, and that such inequalities led working women to "maintain a constant struggle to maintain wages and conditions under which white women can work and live." Without the vote, they suggested, white women's economic status in the state would continue to decline. Like the LAWESL casting the vote in gendered terms, this appeal to racism may have spurred white men to the voting booth. Given the long-standing antagonisms in the state, pure racism and fears about a declining standard of living for their wives and daughters may have swayed some men to the prosuffrage camp. Some may have even assumed that giving white women the vote would help the state pass stricter immigration laws.[25]

Antisuffrage arguments centered on undermining the case that female suffrage would or could produce social, economic, or political reforms. The antisuffrage campaign found a mouthpiece in the Los Angeles Times, which frequently ran editorials against suffrage and reported on the activities of local antisuffrage groups. The Times took particular pains to point out that, in states like Colorado and Utah that already had female suffrage, neither the conditions of women wage earners nor political morality had noticeably improved.[26]

Most of the city's women, however, took heart at how well the disparate prosuffrage groups worked together. As one woman reported, "Wage earning women and the wives and daughters of workingmen have worked side by side with their more fortunately situated sisters, and there has developed a mutual understanding that will result in splendid achievements for the many objects, aims, purposes, and reasons for which the ballot is sought if the spirit of unity and sisterhood is carried into the greater task that awaits womankind when the boon of equal suffrage is actually and permanently in their possession."[27] Both sides, radical and conservative, expressed hopes for a continued alliance.

On October 10, 1911, a narrow margin granted the vote to California's women. While the amendment lost in San Francisco and Oakland, it carried in Los Angeles by more than five thousand votes.[28] Observers on both sides agreed that the precincts where working men lived gave women the largest number of votes: in the precinct around the Labor Temple, for example, suffrage carried by a two-to-one margin. The wealthier westside and the poorest sections of the city voted against extending the franchise to women. When a postelection analysis confirmed these findings, the Los Angeles Socialist-labor coalition claimed credit for winning women's suffrage in the city.[29]

After Suffrage: The Election of 1911

The first challenge to sustaining the new cross-class coalition of women in Los Angeles came with the city election of December 1911. Less than a month after the passage of female suffrage, the fissures between women who were working or nonworking, rich or poor, and Socialist or Good Government erupted into enormous fault lines that reshaped hopes for a female-led reform revolution in Southern California.

In Los Angeles the most contested race that election cycle was for mayor: incumbent Good Government mayor George Alexander faced Socialist Job Harriman in a runoff election. Still angry over the handling of the 1910 *Times* bombing, and over the arrest of John and James McNamara for the crime, union supporters gave Harriman a plurality in the November primary, 44 percent of the vote. Both sides now looked to newly enfranchised women for their votes. Even the antisuffrage *Times* pleaded with conservative women to get out and vote.[30] Socialist and Progressive women, who had allied so effectively in the pursuit of suffrage, now competed directly with one another to court this new electorate.

Elite women organized the Woman's Progressive League, a nonpartisan group that nonetheless registered women only in the wards that had given Alexander a majority in the primary. They went door-to-door, spoke to working women during noon talks, and registered thousands of women in just a few days.[31]

Female Alexander supporters tailored their message so they would connect with women voters. While male supporters of Alexander argued that a Harriman victory would destroy the city, female supporters instead focused on the morality of Good Government and the benefits Alexander could bring to all classes in the city. They also appear to have successfully tapped into women's economic anxieties. The Alexander campaign argued that women who voted Socialist in the hope it would raise women's wages would be sorely disappointed. In fact, the *Times* wrote, a Harriman victory would actually endanger jobs. "Credit will be paralyzed, and without credit, and large credit at that, hundreds of the stores, offices, and factories of Los Angeles will have to close up, and thousands upon thousands of our male and female workers will be walking the streets, vainly looking for a job," the newspaper editorialized. Two Alexander supporters spoke to the women employed at the Brownstein-Louis garment factory on Los Angeles Street, and reported that they had converted some thirty women from the Socialist ticket to that of Alexander. The switch in allegiance may have had something to do with the fact that the company suggested that if Alexander were elected it would increase its employment to one thousand factory hands.[32]

To stem female support for Harriman, the Women Wage-Earner's Alexander Club formed, with workers from Coulter's Department Store, and the Crown, Munger, Troy, American, Western Angelus, and Hygienic laundries represented. This club went so far as to organize mock voting demonstrations to teach the city's working women how to cast their ballots. Interestingly, representatives of other women's groups, such as the Progressive Women's League, usually led meetings of the Women Wage-Earner's Alexander Club. Perhaps working women's support for Alexander was not as strong as press coverage suggested, or perhaps this arrangement may have simply reflected how little free time working women had to devote to such voluntary associations.[33]

The Socialist-labor coalition, on the other hand, assumed women's votes would be for Harriman. Local Socialist women scrambled to register women in the working-class districts of the city. At a meeting of the Women's City Club, held in an unnamed hotel downtown, an observer noted that the waitresses who had served the luncheon then gathered in the back of the room to hear pro-Socialist speeches and that they "vigorously applauded" throughout. But once again gender and ethnicity complicated the situation. Not only were many Mexican and Asian men and women unable to vote, but many white immigrant women in Los Angeles had never bothered to obtain U.S. citizenship even when their husbands, brothers, and sons had. This can be easily understood, since before the October election the chief benefit of citizenship, the vote, would have been withheld from them anyway. With the mayoral election following so close on the heels of the passage of female suffrage, there was little the Socialists could do to remedy the situation. To make matters worse, the Alexander campaign knew of the Socialists' problems registering Los Angeles's immigrant population. Organized special police squads and private detectives, hired with financial help from both the Women's Progressive League and the city, sought out and removed from registration lists men and women without proper proof of citizenship and residency. Daniel J. Johnson estimates that some twelve hundred voters, largely from the working-class east side of the city, were removed from voter registration rolls.[34]

Compounding the situation, on December 1, 1911, John and James

McNamara, labor organizers who had been on trial in the city for the 1910 *Times* bombing, abruptly pleaded guilty to all charges. Socialists had been using the highly publicized trial as their best example of capital oppression and the need for labor-relations reform. Debate over the guilt or innocence of the McNamara brothers had polarized pro- and antilabor sentiment and turned Angeleno against Angeleno for months. Coming only four days before the municipal election, the confessions shook the Socialist camp to its core.[35]

Alexander won a second-term as mayor in a sweeping victory on December 5, and Los Angeles's female voters helped him win. Although just 43 percent of the city's eligible voters, women cast approximately 55 percent of the total vote that put Alexander in office.[36] Although there are no exact numbers for how the election broke down among female voters, both sides agreed that newly enfranchised women had given the election to the Good Governments.

Why? The answer appears to be that social class mattered as much as gender in predicting the behavior of the city's new female electorate. James P. Kraft's skillful election analysis reveals that female voter turnout in working neighborhoods lagged behind that in middling and elite ones. Men and women in the traditionally blue-collar east side of the city who did vote voted for Harriman and the Socialists—almost 92 percent. It does not thus seem likely that the McNamara confessions kept committed Socialists away from the polls. Overall voter turnout may have been the bigger factor behind the Socialists' defeat. Historians of American voting patterns have long noted that voter turnout in working-class neighborhoods consistently lags behind that of middle- and upper-class areas.[37] The failure of so many Los Angeles residents to vote at all in this hotly contested election seems to indicate two things. First, some of those struggling to make ends meet, male or female, who might have otherwise tipped the election in Harriman's favor were ineligible to vote. Second, those who were eligible to vote who did not do so evidently saw little potential for change regardless of who gained control of City Hall.

Elite women simply were more likely to be registered and more likely to vote than their working-class counterparts. These women, from the beginning, had backed Alexander. Failing to see the significance of class in the election results among women, however, the Goo Goos viewed Alexander's victory as a repudiation of the idea that female voters would be radical, headstrong, or even dangerous. This argument pleased Los Angeles's leading female reformer, Katherine Phillips Edson. She argued that the city's women well understood that the current political climate of the city was no place to experiment with socialism. "Women," she wrote, "have declared in favor of Progressivism, the safe, middle ground."[38]

Relations between the Socialists and the Good Governments quickly soured. Angry over their loss and outraged that the national Progressive Party had adopted national women's suffrage as part of its political platform, Socialists and local labor leaders quickly pointed out that the Socialists had advocated women's suffrage since before the creation of their rival party. The Progressives retaliated by reexamining election data and suggesting (falsely) that Socialists in some precincts had actually voted heavily against suffrage in the 1911 election.[39]

Not only did the 1911 mayoral election damage relations between Socialist and Good Government women, but the old alliance between working women and the Socialist Party also began to break down. In part this can be attributed to changes within the party itself. Socialist women became convinced that they now needed to work from within the party. To this end in 1911 WSU leaders abandoned their state union and instead devoted themselves to building a State Woman's Committee within the Socialist Party.[40]

Leaders of the SWC tended to have experience working for feminist and humanitarian reform within nonpartisan women's clubs. This may explain why they advised their organizers to focus primarily on women's concerns for home and children and municipal housekeeping rather than an overtly feminist agenda. Some of these leaders, such as Pasadena's Marion L. Israel, who served as "woman's correspondent," did work for a living. But Israel's status as a single woman and a white-collar worker (she was a stenographer at the time of her election, and later a teacher and author of children's books) put her in a more privileged class position than the bulk of Southern California's working women. The party advised Socialist women to join women's clubs, trade unions, and parent-teacher associations to expose people there to the Socialist message. Otherwise, it expected them to shoulder the same burdens as their male comrades, such as raising money for the party, staffing polls on election days, and running for elective offices. All of this diverted Socialist women from pursing workplace reform.[41]

In a last-gasp effort to reach out to working women, Los Angeles's Socialist women founded the semiautonomous Woman's Socialist Federation of Los Angeles County in early 1912. The WSF intended to sustain both the woman's committee and what remained of the old WSU. The WSF organized party propaganda meetings on the conditions of female department store workers, women's economic independence, and the new "progressive" woman. Party members hoped that the suffrage victory would lead more women to join, and this seems to have been true. By 1914 the Los Angeles County locals were 30 percent female. Hoping to continue to build on the cross-class alliance, both Noel and Edson advocated the admission of female trade unions to the California Federation of Women's Clubs. For her part, Daisy Houck, a Socialist Party supporter and a member of the United Garment Workers Union, agreed that wage-earning women wanted to join the club women, but she wondered how far the club women themselves would be willing to go to help the wage earners. While leaders on both sides such as Noel, Edson, and Houck favored the move, there remained the problem of overcoming long-standing distrust among the rank and file of the two classes of women. This may explain why the much anticipated union between female unionists and the CFWC never took place.[42]

But club women remained suffused with a spirit of nonpartisan cooperation, at least when it came to politics. Wanting to coordinate and consolidate the gains made by women in the state, the CFWC created the Women's Legislative Council in the fall of 1912. Fifty-three women's organizations, ranging from the Women's Christian Temperance Union to the women's committees of the Democratic, Progressive, and Socialist parties, signed on. On the first day of the 1913 legislative session, each California assemblyman and senator found on his desk a list of seventeen bills on a card entitled the "First Legislative Platform of the Women's Legislative Council of California." The proposals included bills for red-light abatement, mothers' pensions, equal guardianship of women over their children, and the establishment of a commission to study the possibility of instituting a minimum wage for women.[43]

The *Los Angeles Citizen* pleaded with women to maintain solidarity, arguing that a new woman, the "feminist," needed to take the place of the suffragist and battle on for women's economic equality with men.[44] But in spite of working together so effectively in pursuit of suffrage, California's women again fragmented into smaller groups. Each pursued a different agenda. These differences came to a head in the debate over a statewide eight-hour day for women and in the California Bureau of Labor Statistics' investigations of women's work.

The Eight-Hour Day, the Minimum Wage, and the Industrial Welfare Commission

Now in control of Los Angeles's city government and feeling that female suffrage had been a mandate from California voters, Progressives and other reformers in Los Angeles turned their attention back to the issue of women's work. Casting their proposed reforms in terms of protecting women and children allowed them to raise these issues without reopening the old wounds of the 1910 *Times* bombing. Progressives argued that statewide industrial reform would finally solve the bitter standoff between capital and labor. Appalled by what she had seen in her city, Katherine Phillips Edson later told a reporter, "None could have gone through the McNamara trial in Southern California and remained uninterested in industrial problems."[45] The argument for statewide labor reform thus resonated with those who desperately wanted to avoid a repeat of the ugly events of 1910–1911.

Having been reintegrated into the Socialist Party, Socialist women continued to push for legislation to protect wage-earning women. They advocated a combination of protective labor legislation and unionization as the best way to promote women's economic independence. Frances Nacke Noel pointed out that the California State Federation of Labor had failed to target women workers in their campaigns, and that few women served as delegates to the organization's conferences. Local organized labor leaders did support an eight-hour bill for women, but only as the first step to achieving a universal eight-hour day for all workers. On April 15, 1911, the Central Labor Council held a parade to advocate for the eight-hour law through downtown Los Angeles. There had been a similar push to establish an eight-hour day for women in 1907; although the bill passed both the house and senate, then-Governor Gillette had vetoed it.[46]

With the backing of both Progressives and Socialists, an eight-hour bill for women became law in 1911 in spite of opposition from the owners of department stores, laundries, hotels, and confection, cotton goods, and cracker factories. It called for an eight-hour workday and a forty-eight-hour workweek for women employed in manufacturing, mechanical and mercantile establishments, laundries, hotels, restaurants, telegraph or telephone establishments, and express or transportation companies. It excluded women working in the production and canning of fruits and vegetables because many canneries had to process produce as quickly as possible before it spoiled. This often demanded long working hours from everyone on the production line.[47]

The first local test case of the law, brought by the State of California against the owner of Los Angeles's Anchor Laundry, came in the spring of 1912. The owner argued that the law did not apply because the women had voluntarily worked overtime for extra pay, but a local judge upheld the right of the state to determine the maximum hours a woman could work. The owner paid a fifty-dollar fine. The laundry owner, A. E. Messerly, had paid some of his employees a dollar extra to volunteer to work more than eight hours; they ultimately worked twelve and a half. Such arrangements became commonplace as employers tried to circumvent the new law. The California Supreme Court upheld the new law again two months later in a case involving house-maids at a Riverside hotel.[48]

Hoping to make the California Bureau of Labor Statistics more respon-sive to the needs of women, California's governor, Hiram Johnson, appointed Katherine Phillips Edson to the bureau in September 1912, making her the first woman to receive a political appointment in the state of California. The bureau took responsibility for monitoring women's hours, wages, cost of liv-ing, and unemployment. It also enforced new labor laws such as those on child labor, factory inspection, and the eight-hour workday for women and children. Edson turned the bureau's attention to the ever-growing numbers of working women in the state. Working with labor commissioner John P. McLaughlin to gather statistics, Edson found the largest numbers of women statewide employed in the seasonal canning industry. Like many reformers of the day, male and female, Edson believed protective legislation would be necessary to protect women on the job. Appalled at the poor conditions and low pay of female workers in the canneries and other industries, Edson also worked to enlighten her fellow club women about these issues.[49]

Some segments of California society, particularly conservative ones, found the new legislation threatening. While opponents remained concerned about the economic impact of the eight-hour law, some also believed such laws would damage the very fabric of society. The debate over extending the eight-hour law to nurses demonstrates how such arguments worked. Since women employed in public lodging houses, apartment houses, hospitals, and places of amusement had not been specifically included in the original eight-hour law, in 1913 state lawmakers proposed amending the law to include such workers. The proposal to limit nurses' hours drew particular ire from some quarters. Overworked nurses were a very real problem across Southern Cali-fornia. Those at the Los Angeles County Hospital, for example, worked at least fifty-eight hours a week. The *Los Angeles Times* argued that an eight-hour day for nurses would force them to leave in the middle of childbirths and other hospital emergencies and result in substandard patient care. The *Times* flipped gender stereotypes on their head and argued that male union-ists were jealous of women's success "in the higher lines of employment." The *Times,* which had never been a supporter of working women, now told its readers that union men wanted the eight-hour law because it would pre-vent women from succeeding in their chosen professions. Only people who sought to "turn society upside down" supported such a law. White-collar women forced to bend to laws written by blue-collar men, nurses (who as women were supposed to be naturally nurturing) walking out on patients, laboring women left alone to suffer—the *Times* clearly hoped to convince readers that the eight-hour law would disrupt social order and women's place in it. This time, however, few Californians believed the newspaper. In spite of such dire warnings, the amendment became law later that year.[50]

During Edson's tenure in office the bureau also extended the state's eight-hour laws to cover student nurses, arguing that private, for-profit hospitals took advantage of their student nurses by forcing them to work long hours. These hospitals bitterly opposed the move, and the battle ultimately ended up in the U.S. Circuit Court of Appeals, which ruled in the state's favor. Enlightened by the experience, Edson also began to advocate the public training of nurses, arguing that training provided by state or municipal institutions would produce better-qualified nurses than those coming out of private training.[51]

But the eight-hour law did not make all of the state's women happy. Socialist women, in particular, believed the failure of the law to actually set minimum-wage rates for women made it a failure. In Los Angeles leaders of the Woman's Socialist Federation, female party members, and union women took matters into their own hands. They founded the nonpartisan Women's Wage League in April 1913, demanding that the City of Los Angeles pass an ordinance establishing a Woman's Living Wage Investigation Board. The proposed board would collect and publicize the names of businesses paying women less than eight dollars a week. The ordinance never passed, but Los Angeles's city council, dominated by reform-minded members of the Good Government movement, did launch an investigation of women's wages in the city.[52] The city council created a committee and charged it with determining what a living wage in the city might be. Councilmen chose four men and two women, among them Frances Nacke Noel, to investigate the issue. All had previous experience with and interest in social reform. The other female appointee, Mrs. M. E. Johnson, had already investigated the wages paid to nurses. She reported that she had found all but two hospitals paying seven dollars a month plus room and board for the first three years of nurses' training. The other two paid only five dollars a month for the first two years. A male member with experience investigating labor problems, the Reverend George A. Henry, told the city council that so many women feared for their jobs that they often failed to speak the truth to investigators. Women working in department stores, in particular, refused to report violations of state laws, such as not allowing salesgirls to sit down between serving customers, out of fear they would be fired. In response to such concerns city councilmen

advised the committee to gather data as quietly as possible, lest any attempts
to hold public meetings on the issue cost workers their jobs. Noel, ever the
diplomat, made the case for the investigation in terms easily understood by
every turn-of-the-century Angeleno, no matter where he or she might stand
on organized labor. "The conditions of working women especially is of tremendous importance, not alone to this municipality, but to the whole nation,
for if the women are not taken care of the whole race goes down," she told a
local newspaper.[53]

In June 1913 the committee made its report to the city council. It had
determined a subsistence wage in the city of Los Angeles to be not less than
two dollars a day, and a living wage for a person with one dependent to be
not less than four dollars a day. Noel in particular expressed dissatisfaction
with what the committee had been able to accomplish, and complained that
a lack of publicity and resistance from employers had hampered investigators
from the start.[54]

Nonetheless, Noel and Johnson also submitted a supplementary report
focusing specifically on the conditions of working women. The two women
estimated that one-quarter of the women and children employed in Los
Angeles worked for "starvation wages" (that is, less than two dollars a day).
They had found the lowest wages in the canneries, clothing factories, laundries, restaurants, department stores, dry-goods shops, and groceries, all of
which depended heavily on cheap female labor. Seventy percent of women
employed in laundries and 64 percent of those working in department stores
earned less than two dollars a day. Women employed in the canneries, which
were exempt from the new eight-hour law, complained to investigators of
poor conditions and abusive foremen. Women employed in cracker bakeries and manufacturing industries reported that frequent speed increases on
the line had resulted in more injuries and greater fatigue on the job. Noel
and Johnson blamed these conditions in part on the oversupply of labor in
the city, as the attractive power of Los Angeles's climate ensured fierce competition for the few available jobs. This competition kept wages down. The
two investigators also blamed greedy and inefficient employers for refusing
to raise the wages of female employees. Noel and Johnson also pointed out
the dangers to white female workers presented by the eminent opening of
the Panama Canal. The resulting influx of cheap foreign labor, they warned,
would make women's labor situation worse. The authors ended by pleading for the help of the city's women's organizations to ameliorate the worst
abuses. Indeed, much of the statewide rhetoric surrounding the need for a
women's minimum wage in California was tinged with racism. White Cali-

fornians feared an influx of cheap labor due to the opening of the Panama Canal might lower the standard of living across the state unless some preventive measures were in place.[55]

In response to such dire warnings, Katherine Phillips Edson, still an official of the Bureau of Labor Statistics, raised the possibility of establishing a statewide women's minimum wage. Edson collaborated with Helen Todd of the National Consumers' League to draft a bill providing a minimum wage for California's women and children. Massachusetts had become the first state to pass such legislation in 1912, and by 1913 seven more states had some kind of minimum-wage law on their books. Reformers considered these laws a vital step in protecting working women and children from exploitation. As Katherine Phillips Edson explained, minimum-wage legislation was based on the economic theory that "the basis of competition must be fixed, and it must not go below the weakest members of society, and they are the women and the children. It fixes a basis for competition, so that under it none can go; and therefore, women and children are protected from exploitation by society." Minimum-wage legislation also received support from such diverse groups as the state and national consumer leagues, the National Conference of Charities and Corrections, the California Federation of Women's Clubs, the Women's Christian Temperance Union, the Socialist Party, and Progressives across the country.[56]

In 1913 Governor Johnson signed the minimum-wage bill into law. To determine what the new wage should be, Californians voted in favor of an amendment to the state constitution authorizing the creation of the Industrial Welfare Commission in November 1914. The new IWC consisted of five members, one of whom always had to be female. One commissioner represented organized labor, one unorganized labor, two represented business, and one would be a neutral state representative. Each would be paid ten dollars per day while meeting and receive full powers to fix wages for women and children, enforce maximum hours and laws, and oversee working conditions. Governor Johnson appointed Edson to the board as the sole female, and established IWC offices in San Francisco and Los Angeles.[57]

Edson spoke to women's clubs several times a month trying to gain support for the work of the IWC. In her speeches on such occasions, Edson made it clear that she felt the best place for wives and children was in the home. However, she did not approve of discriminating against either group: "A woman has every right to express herself ... but that is a different matter from being forced out into life and to work, just to add to the family income, whether she is fitted for it or not and at great cost to herself and her family.

I think industry today is absolutely wrong for women. Women were made long before industry, so we have got to make industry to suit women."[58]

Edson also gained the support of some employers, most notably the dry-goods industry, which recognized that more money in employee pockets would mean more money to spend at local stores. In 1914–1915 the IWC studied the cost of living for a single woman across the state and determined it to be no less than $9.63 a week. It found that almost half of the female workers in the state made less than that a week.[59]

The IWC directed its first order, issued in early 1916, solely at the canning industry. It had been exempted from the eight-hour law, and its pay scale lagged furthest behind other industries. The IWC established a minimum-piece rate for canneries, developed sanitary standards, and limited hours to ten per day (sixty hours a week), with provisions for overtime. The order had an immediate impact on cannery workers. Edson inspected five canneries in the spring and summer of 1916 and found that while women in the canneries had formerly made ten to twelve and a half cents per hour, they now made fifteen to sixteen cents. Where workers had received five, six, or seven cents per forty-pound box of fruits, they now received nine cents. On July 6, 1917, following the decision of the U.S. Supreme Court to uphold the constitution-ality of Oregon's minimum-wage law, Edson and her fellow commissioners approved a minimum wage for women in other California industries of $10 a week, or $43.44 a month.[60]

From its very beginning, the IWC bogged down in controversy. Nothing it could do made both organized labor and opponents of a minimum wage happy. Even how the IWC settled on the minimum wage sparked considerable debate. They had mandated a minimum wage of $10 a week, for example, but their own studies showed that between 1914 and 1917 the minimum cost of living statewide had already risen to $14 a week. When criticized by her peers for neglecting to take this factor into account, Edson argued that it was better to introduce a wage that did not hurt employers and get them used to the idea slowly than to set the wage higher and have it promptly overturned.[61]

In another point of contention, the IWC chose to base its new wage standard on a single woman living alone, or in a boardinghouse, and not on a woman with dependents. In doing so the IWC was in line with contemporary thought about women's wages, which refused to recognize dependents or the need to help families as a factor in their wage calculations. It was not until 1927 that all states establishing minimum-wage guidelines factored dependents into their calculations.[62]

The limitations of the commission itself also hampered the IWC. They had to set a minimum wage, not a maximum or a wage they felt a woman deserved. The commissioners recognized that the minimum wage could not be fair to everyone, but hoped that it would still make a substantial difference in most women's earnings. The IWC also agreed to set a special minimum wage for the "physically defective" on a case-by-case basis; to punish employers in violation of its orders with a fine of not less than $50, imprisonment up to thirty days, or both; and to fine any employer $300 for demanding gifts or other "remuneration" from employees.[63]

Even after the establishment of the minimum wage, the IWC struggled to gather the data it needed to analyze women's work in the state. Manufacturers often did everything they could do to thwart investigators. "You would suppose," Edson wrote with a remarkable mixture of optimism and naïveté, "that Californian manufacturers particularly would be interested in seeing that any unfair discrimination in the way of longer hours and cheaper labor was removed—not by bringing California women down to the conditions existing in the Eastern states but by seeing that the Eastern women workers are raised to decent conditions of livelihood and therefore such differences in competitive standards would be equalized." Over the course of an investigation commissioners usually tried to visit several employers and gain insights into the type of work, conditions, and pay. If they found salaries to be inadequate, the IWC commissioners established a wage board to examine the issue. The commission had to hold public hearings before it could issue any orders. With offices and employees in only Los Angeles and San Francisco, however, it lacked the means and manpower to consistently implement and enforce those orders statewide.[64]

Edson remained a staunch defender of the IWC to the end. She argued that, in spite of initial resistance to the new laws, most employers had voluntarily raised wages to comply with the new regulations. In 1917 the IWC issued orders establishing either the minimum wage or a piecework standard to the vinegar, preserving, and olive industries; the mercantile industry; the fish-canning industry; office workers; commercial packing establishments; and laundry workers. In 1918 it took similar actions for the fruit and vegetable canning industry, telephone and telegraph workers, hotel and restaurant employees, and the skilled trades.[65] It did not investigate the film industry at all because the daily earnings of the lowest-paid extra always exceeded the established daily minimum wage of $1.67. While the motion picture industry was seasonal, neither reformers nor the IWC tried to argue that it was identical to other seasonal industries like fruit packing. Film work remained exempt from most of the commission's special orders (see chapter 6).[66]

Organized labor in general remained antagonistic toward the IWC, believing the state would inevitably set wages too low and that such commissions hampered unionization. Moreover, union members argued, the IWC placed women at the mercy of a government body not responsible to the electorate. Among working women, resistance to the establishment of a minimum wage was highest in the already-organized garment industry. Garment workers feared the IWC's actions might overturn the advances they had already made in their industry. Even the legislation's supporters within the unions remained suspicious of the IWC's motivations. In 1917 the *Los Angeles Citizen* sniffed at its efforts. "Isn't it a pity that the labor union is THE ONLY AGENCY IN ALL THE WORLD that demands economic justice for women? Women, why do you look to your employers and to the State and to fakers for help? Why don't you help YOURSELVES?"[67]

For her part, Frances Nacke Noel remained philosophical about the impact of the minimum-wage law on women's union activity. "We may grant that the eight-hour and minimum-wage laws, in a measure and for the time being, have lessened the desire on the part [of] women to organize," she admitted. "On the other hand, what had Organized Labor done to bring women in industry into its fold? Look at Labor's conventions. How many women delegates are there?" Sentiment also varied with geography. In closed-shop San Francisco trade unionists bitterly opposed the legislation, fearing that IWC orders would both lower unionized women's wages and set a precedent for state intervention in labor disputes. In Los Angeles union supporters called for its creation as one of the few potential sources of leverage against the city's militant open-shop policy.[68]

Women in the state's organized trades, such as garment and some laundry workers, did actually experience a drop in wages because the new IWC statues forbade overtime work.[69] But overall the benefits of minimum-wage legislation accrued most to those women living in cities that already had a strong union presence. After the introduction of the minimum wage to the laundry industry in 1917, for example, salaries rose most dramatically in already unionized San Francisco and Oakland. The IWC attributed this to high rates of voluntary compliance by local employers. These men, accustomed to periodic wage negotiations with unions, may have indeed accepted IWC orders with little resistance. But in Los Angeles, which had no such history of peaceful negotiations between labor and capital, owners often tried to manipulate IWC policies to their advantage. In spite of IWC regulations, by 1917, 21.3 percent of women working in Los Angeles's laundries, for example, still earned less than $10 a week. Rebecca Mead argues this was done largely through the manipulation of apprenticeship regulations.[70]

Other professions, however, found that the IWC policies did work to their advantage. Waitresses' unions, in particular, used the discovery that union employers were less likely to violate IWC orders as another argument in favor of unionization. In this case the IWC provided waitresses with the best of both worlds: the power of collective bargaining through a union but also an outside organization that created and enforced protective legislation.[71]

As far as the *Los Angeles Times* was concerned, however, even a minimum wage of $10 was too high. "Two successive legislatures have declined to pass a minimum wage law for women," it complained, "yet an Industrial Welfare Commission had issued from its offices in San Francisco an executive order.... [T]his 'Industrial Welfare Commission' is one of the numerous Progressive parasites that is fattening off the labor and industry of California." Clearly, the paper wrote, such a law would be a wedge to open Los Angeles to the union wage scales of cities like San Francisco and Sacramento. The newspaper also warned that the IWC's decision would raise prices on goods and throw women working part-time as department store clerks out of work. The *Times* argued that since the minimum wage was based on a full-time workweek, part-time workers would be let go.[72] This did not happen.

The IWC received criticism from both unions and women's groups for being too slow to recalculate their standards to reflect economic conditions. When the cost of living rose, the commissioners often had to compromise their principles in order to keep the statewide minimum wage from rising too quickly and hurting business owners. In 1919, for example, the commission set its estimate for clothing at $18.18 per year, a number it regarded as too high. The commissioners thus changed the clothing allowance to allow for only one suit, one coat, and one dress every two years instead of every year. Women and union representatives up and down the state complained bitterly about such estimates, arguing IWC data gathering was at best perfunctory and at worst biased in favor of employers.[73] The divide between those who supported the IWC and those who did not again illustrates the ideological gulf between Progressive women and their counterparts in organized labor. Even though both desired the same outcome—better pay and conditions for California's working women—they could not form a consensus on how to go about it. This gulf also undermined what might have been a significant force for reform in Southern California: the Los Angeles National Women's Trade Union League.

The Los Angeles National Women's Trade Union League

The short life span of the Los Angeles National Women's Trade Union League illustrates the challenges inherent in cross-class alliances in Los Angeles. In other American cities the National Women's Trade Union League was a powerful and influential force for the rights of working women. In Boston, New York, and Chicago, branches of the NWTUL tapped into existing settlement-house networks to help organize female workers and to advocate protective labor legislation at the state level. But in Los Angeles the NWTUL had a short and troubled life. In part as a response to the perceived failures of minimum-wage legislation and the IWC, in 1914 Socialist women, again led by Frances Nacke Noel, founded a Los Angeles branch of the NWTUL. The LANWTUL became the latest attempt to create a cross-class women's movement in the city, and for a time was a vocal champion of wage-earning women. A seven-person committee, consisting of four trade union members and three at-large NWTUL members, held educational meetings across Los Angeles to drum up support for the league. But it still took more than a year for the committee to become a regular local of the NWTUL, and membership remained small, with only ten to twenty active members at any one time. Of the local unions, only Local 125 of the United Garment Workers Union stayed continuously involved with the committee. Local 125 already had a long tradition of collaborating with both Socialists and organized women's groups (see chapter 5). Henrietta Hasselberger, a department store worker, and Helen Zuhlke, the head of a small domestic workers' union, also played leadership roles in the NWTUL, but for the most part participation of wage-earning women remained sporadic. Working women's more precarious economic situation as well as constantly changing workplace and union demands simply limited the time available for work with the league. "The strong depression in industry and in consequence closed factories for months at a time in the needle trades to which a number of our workers belong had much to do with preventing us from developing from a mere national committee into a full fledged league," Noel wrote in 1915. The Los Angeles Central Labor Council supported the LANWTUL but continued to do little to organize women in the city. The league nonetheless offered its moral and financial support to both new unions and to striking women. In 1914 and 1915 female cannery, bindery, domestic, and boot and shoe workers benefited from league funds. The LANWTUL also sponsored mass meetings in both English and Spanish to educate voters about labor-related initiatives on the 1914 ballot. Maria de Lopez, so vital in the 1911 suffrage campaign, again served as a translator at these meetings. In 1915 the league pushed the city government to create a committee to investigate the unemployment problem in Los Angeles. It also founded a recreational camp for wage-earning women, Camp Aliso, in the hills above Los Angeles, one of the first recreational facilities in the United States designed to serve this population. Unfortunately, the hard winter of 1915 damaged the facilities, and though the league rebuilt them, it could not maintain the camp. Camp Aliso was leased to the City of Los Angeles in 1917, and the demoralized LANWTUL disbanded in June of that year.[74] It is possible that the LANWTUL ultimately failed because there were already other organizations working toward similar goals, most notably the IWC. That may have limited the number of members the LANWTUL could attract. But in any case its failure contributed to Los Angeles's inability to develop powerful women's groups that could lobby for statewide industrial reform yet still connect with female workers and union members.

But the troubles in Los Angeles had not gone unnoticed on the national stage. In 1914 the United States Commission on Industrial Relations chose Los Angeles as a site to investigate labor unrest, and many key players on both sides of the debate appeared to offer testimony about Los Angeles's ongoing problems.

The United States Commission on Industrial Relations in Los Angeles

Attracted by the work of the IWC, the newly created United States Commission on Industrial Relations held hearings in Los Angeles in 1914. The commission called a variety of local pro- and antiunionists, civic leaders, and reformers to testify. Felix J. Zeehandelaar, secretary of the Merchants and Manufacturers Association, argued that Los Angeles's "open shop" remained the city's most valuable economic asset. He insisted that the M&M had never distributed any literature on the local job market, let alone attempted to lure workers to the city under false pretenses.[75]

The commission called on both Frances Nacke Noel and Katherine Phillips Edson to testify about the conditions of working women the area. Their testimony illustrates the fundamental difference of opinion that remained between women on the Progressive end of the political spectrum and those on the Socialist-labor end. While their testimony certainly represents only two women's personal opinions, both had enough experience in reform that it is worth examining their statements in greater depth.

As a representative of the Industrial Welfare Commission, Edson reported that she believed conditions for women employed in stores had improved due to welfare work. She also told the commission that she believed most mem-

bers of the garment workers' unions belonged only because their jobs were at
stake. Otherwise, she said, "there seems to be absolutely no sense of solidarity
or of the fact that they are being benefited personally by their membership."
Edson had a very different understanding of local union sentiment than did
Noel. Before the committee Edson argued that workers in Los Angeles actually harbored more antiunion sentiment than the employers themselves. As
proof she cited the fact that workers often refused to speak with her until she
assured them she worked for the government, not the unions. She advocated
a better understanding between employers and employees, but admitted she
had no idea how to foster it. Edson also drew the committee's attention to the
increase in the numbers of married women employed in the city.[76]

Edson tried to explain to the commission the impact working wives had
on the city:

I find the women working, the women themselves, all complaining about the great
number of married women that are engaged in this city. Women who have come
from other parts of the country say that they never have worked in any community
where there were as many married women employed as there are in Los Angeles. . . .
[W]e do not believe that the married women are working in Los Angeles because
of a so-called desire for independence, but we believe that most of them are working because they actually must work. . . . We hear a good deal about the workingmen
of this city buying their own homes, and we know it is true. But the fearfulness with
which these women—under which these women work—is great. They are so afraid
that they are not going to be able to meet the payments. And I think that a large number of the women who work in this city, work to help pay for their homes. They fear
the irregular employment of their men folks.[77]

The logical solution, Edson told the commission, would be to pay men a
living wage so their wives could stay home. She also blamed minorities for
keeping wages down for local women: Mexican women, she said, accepted
unskilled, low-wage jobs. Even so, she suggested, both the Russians and the
Italians made better workers than Mexicans. Edson admitted that she had no
figures to support her contention.[78]

Frances Nacke Noel, testifying as a member of both the National Women's
Trade Union League and the Central Labor Council, offered more direct
criticism of labor conditions in the city. Like Edson, she fingered the high rate
of home ownership as a burden on both male and female workers. Install-
ment payments on their little cottages, she argued, just "produced more out-
and-out slaves in the labor world" of Los Angeles. Noel complained that it
had proved impossible to organize the city's Mexican workers and that, next

to the underpaid department store girl, competition from Mexican labor remained the greatest problem facing the city. Noel spoke of the fierce battles waged by the M&M and other open-shop forces, as well as their political control of city government. She also expressed her belief that her work in organized labor had cost her husband his job as a bank teller. Noel remained justifiably skeptical about the ability of government, and the IWC in particular, to secure better pay and conditions for workers. In perhaps a subtle jab at Edson, Noel testified, "The woman you had on the witness stand this morning was a true example as to what that labor commission does in securing justice to the workers at the present time. . . . [W]hen we did go there all we did get in answer to any difficulty was that they could not attend to it because they were just gathering statistics. We were always controlled by statistics. We could never figure out what statistics could do for us in case of trouble." Nor did she hold out much hope for voluntary women's groups to solve local labor woes. Why did Angelenos pump thousands of dollars into the YWCA, she asked, when such organizations could not reach the root of the problem? For her own part, Noel proposed a statewide eight-hour law for both sexes as the first step in solving labor problems in Los Angeles.[79]

The commission recommended that Los Angeles establish a permanent industrial fact-finding and mediation board, pass an ordinance prohibiting the employment of children under twelve in the sale of newspapers or merchandise on the street, and adopt the provisions of California's Workmen's Compensation Act.[80] But while both labor and open-shop forces in the city lauded the work of the commission, neither side liked the recommendations enough to follow up on them. Labor conflicts in the city would continue to flare up for the rest of the decade.

Conclusion

By 1910 the demand for reform in the city increasingly centered on women's suffrage, and in 1911 women from every walk of Los Angeles life combined their efforts to successfully win the vote for the state's women. Quickly, however, class divisions between women who worked and those who did not, and between politically radical and politically conservative women, fragmented this coalition. Even such legislation as an eight-hour day for the state's working women became embroiled in controversy. In the next decade, as Progressive reforms failed to bring dramatic changes in the city, working women would turn away from women's groups and Progressivism to focus again on collective action and unionization. Their more conservative allies fared little better. Organized women's close ties to the Progressive Republicans, who suffered many defeats in California's 1914 elections, hampered progress. Male party leaders increasingly concluded they no longer could or would push for reform.[81]

As if to confirm the warnings of the IWC and the LANWTUL, in 1914–1915 a business slump marked the low point for the city's workers. So many had been thrown out of work, in fact, that the Friday Morning Club organized a meeting to discuss the problem. The club recommended that the city stop advertising across the Midwest and Southwest, because promises of abundant work in Los Angeles drew too many people to the area. It also advised that local, state, and federal relief agencies should step in and help but that local aid should be restricted to city residents. Unemployed immigrants, the club argued, should be sent elsewhere. Although the Friday Morning Club meant well, both city government and employers sharply rebuked it for trying to interfere.[82]

The population of women looking for work in the state continued to outstrip available jobs, and even in closed-shop, industrialized San Francisco unemployment rates for women remained high. The Bureau of Labor Statistics noted the same conditions across the western United States, and estimated that one-third of all workers in the Pacific Coast and mountain states had lost their jobs. With the closing of San Francisco's Panama Pacific Exposition, another twelve to fourteen hundred female employees joined the ranks of the state's unemployed.[83]

Back in Los Angeles on Christmas Day, the city's unemployed gathered at the Plaza, but the gathering turned into a riot when the police arrived to dispel the crowd. Unemployed women, angry that none of the city's proposals took their needs into account, held a rally at the Polytechnic High School to draw attention to their plight. The City of Los Angeles finally resorted to opening a Women's Municipal Employment Bureau, a free service that tried to find women work. It was part of the larger Municipal Free Employment Bureau and operated under the management of chief clerk Isabel Daugherty.[84]

In early 1915 female members of the garment workers' and bakers' unions conducted a house-to-house publicity campaign to remind city housewives of the importance of buying only from closed-shop manufacturers. Closed-shop businesses received a large placard to place in their windows, advertising their employment of union labor to consumers.[85]

State organizations responsible for monitoring women's pay and working conditions, like the Industrial Welfare Commission, struggled to survive in the face of continued criticism from both sides of the political spectrum.

When the United States entered World War I, many employers began to call for an end to any restrictions on hours, arguing that such laws hampered the war effort. Union organizers increasingly questioned whether the IWC ultimately benefited female employees at all.[86] There seems little doubt, however, that the IWC did make a difference for some of the state's working women and children. By 1918 the Industrial Welfare Commission estimated that it had added $1.14 million to the wages of women in the state of California.[87]

Although these activities benefited some female workers, none of them reached perhaps the most needy female workers in the city—minority and immigrant women. While social reformers and union organizers debated about the rights and needs of industrial workers, they continued to focus most of their attention on white American-born female workers. In the meantime immigrant working women faced new challenges. The development of manufacturing in the city, most notably the garment and food-processing industries, created new jobs. But many unions and charitable organizations alike remained more interested in assimilation and Americanization than speaking out for the rights of workers. The white women who worked with the city's immigrant populations brought to their work a distinctly white middle-class American orientation and sought to "teach" their values to minority women. But in reality most of these groups had already developed their own survival strategies based on cultural values and family needs. The next chapter considers how trade unions, Anglo-American reformers, and minority women struggled to understand each other, their different needs, and the meanings of ethnic and gender identity in Los Angeles.

6

Immigrant Women, Work, and Americanization

"YOU DON'T KNOW WHAT HARD WORK IS"

In the 1920s sociologist Pauline Young interviewed Los Angeles resident Cora Jackson. Jackson was a Molokan, part of a reclusive religious sect that had fled Russia. Jackson had arrived in the city at the turn of the century. She told Young about her work history:

We came to America on a Saturday, and I went to work in an American home on Monday. I was servant girl and nurse for small babies. I was only ten years old. I was never sent to school. I never could play. I work and give all my money to father. They tell me: "We poor and you must help." I stayed in that place a year, then I went to work in a laundry. Ever worked in a laundry? No? Then you don't know what hard work is. I too sick to work there ten hours a day. I find another home with Jewish people, eight dollars a month. Nice people, and no children. I wash dishes, clean house, and stay there three years. I give all my wages to father, and he give me a dime on Sunday. I ask what could I do with a dime? No nice clothes, no time for friends, nobody be nice to you and visit with you. I can't live like stone.[1]

In her story, Jackson touched upon many of the same difficulties expressed by female workers anywhere in the United States. The pressure to help support her family, the low pay and long hours, and the conflict between her personal desires and what was expected of her are common concerns whether one is listening to a nineteenth-century woman or a twenty-first-century one.

But Jackson's story is particularly significant for the light it sheds on immigrant women's work in turn-of-the-century Los Angeles. True, Los Angeles was far removed from the waves of immigrants arriving from Europe through Ellis Island. But employers in Southern California were every bit as dependent on immigrant women's labor as industry was in the East. In Los Angeles, Mexican women, Russian women, Italian women, and others supplied the region's new businesses with labor. The bakeries, canneries, candy factories, and sweatshops established in or near immigrant neighborhoods needed these women's labor to keep costs down and business competitive. However, their overall numbers were smaller, and therefore these women often worked alongside native-born Anglo-American women. This created conflicts, but also interesting opportunities for alliances. This chapter explores the interplay between immigrant geography and industrialization in Los Angeles, the challenges these women faced in the workforce, their struggles to balance work and home life, and finally their conflicts and cooperation with union organizers, Progressive reformers, and white American-born women.

Women in the Garment Industry

As difficult as finding work could be for an Anglo-American woman, it remained even harder for non-Anglos. Most eastern and midwestern cities of the day were divided between native-born white Americans and European immigrants; southern cities were divided between whites and African Americans. But Los Angeles became divided between a "white" American-born majority and a large "colored" minority that often lumped together Mexicans, African Americans, Asians, and European immigrants. Even when compared to San Francisco, the City of Angels contained more people from more nations than anywhere else on the Pacific Coast. This "colored" minority became the base of the city's economic structure, working in the unskilled and service jobs that helped drive Los Angeles's economic expansion. Such a structure underwrote most late-nineteenth- and early-twentieth-century industrial capitalism in the United States. Minority and immigrant women in Los Angeles occupied the very bottom of the city's occupational ladder behind white men, white women, and (in some but not all cases) minority and immigrant men. This resulted in part from fierce competition for jobs. Los Angeles's location on the Pacific Coast, as well as its use as a railroad terminus, made it a popular destination for Mexicans emigrating from south of the border, for Asians crossing the Pacific, and, eventually, for Europeans traveling through the Panama Canal. But it was also the result of occupational segregation in the female workforce. As in the case of retail work discussed previously, many employers consciously chose Anglo-American women over those in other ethnic groups, and some white women fiercely protected their racial privileges on the job.[2] Although unable to compete with the industrial output of New York, or even San Francisco, Los Angeles nonetheless increasingly offered new opportunities to young women in need of paid employment. By 1910 a women could find work in one of the city's new garment factories; in a cannery processing fruit, vegetables, or fish; or in a commercial bakery.

The garment industry perhaps best exemplified the promise and pitfalls of women's industrial work in Los Angeles. Nationally between 1910 and 1920, opportunities in semiskilled manufacturing and mechanical industries increased 33.4 percent, while numbers of women working in dressmaking and millinery outside of factories declined. The shift from garment making outside of factories to inside of factories produced a corresponding loss in status and pay for women in the industry. Before 1880 women had worked in all aspects of garment making. But with industrialization, and particularly the introduction of cutting knives at the turn of the century, the most skilled and prestigious jobs in the garment trade (cutting, sampling, and pressing) increasingly went to men. Although a few women worked as samplers and pressers, most found work as sewing machine operators. These divisions of labor often presented formidable barriers to organization, and the largely male well-paid cutters paid little attention to the needs or demands of other garment workers. "Inside" and "outside" shops further divided the industry. "Inside" shops employed up to three hundred people and produced entire garments from start to finish. "Outside" shops, in contrast, operated under a contractor or subcontractor and often focused only on garment assembly. The notorious sweatshops of American history, "outside" shops earned the moniker because such arrangements encouraged piecework, long hours, low wages, and labor exploitation. This same arrangement also drove many garment workers into labor activity, most notably in the New York City shirt-waist strike of 1910.[3]

Los Angeles's garment manufacturers occupied a unique niche in the national clothing industry. Most of the ready-made clothing worn by Californians continued to be made in the eastern or midwestern United States, so local firms instead specialized in producing men's work clothes (aprons, overalls, and coats) and medium-grade shirts. Clothing produced in Los Angeles sold in markets west of the Rockies, but also in Alaska, Mexico, the Hawaiian Islands, and Central and South America. Los Angeles also had a custom trade that produced suits for both men and women. Because of the geographical distance separating Los Angeles from eastern clothing manufacturers, some local garment factories also specialized in "fill-in business." They produced particular kinds or sizes of garments to order for a retailer whose stock of such models or sizes was low and who could not wait for delivery from the East.[4]

Shirt, overall, and other work-clothes garment manufacturing paid by the piece. Men's and women's suit and coat production paid on a time basis. By 1916 three thousand women worked in California's garment factories, making the industry second only to canning in the numbers of women it employed. Centered on a small district of downtown Los Angeles, small garment factories and sweatshops worked on a seasonal schedule, with peak demand for workers coming in spring and fall. The rest of the year work, if a female garment worker could find it, tended to be part-time only. By the 1920s the city's garment district was located between Seventh and Tenth and Broadway and San Pedro streets.[5]

Los Angeles's garment industry faced its fiercest competition not from eastern manufacturers but from prison-made garments that sold for below the union price. In 1915 twenty penal institutions in fourteen states held contracts to manufacture men's work shirts, overalls, pants, and jumpers.[6]

The organization of work within Los Angeles's garment industry also limited how much a worker could earn. Like their counterparts in New York's garment district, all of California's wholesale clothing manufacturers used the "string system." Each operator made only one part of the garment at a time, with no one producing one entire item of clothing. Men worked as cutters, considered a skilled job; women operated the sewing machines. Since such work paid by the piece, how much or how little a woman earned depended on the particular task she performed. Women hemming, sewing box pleats, and piecing the sleeves together could easily earn twenty-five cents an hour, considered by employers to be the industry norm. If she worked on a more difficult stage of garment production such as attaching and sewing cuffs and collars, however, her earnings would be closer to twenty cents an hour. Of those women who specialized in producing only one part of the garment, an estimated 60 percent worked on fronts, cuffs, and collars. Thus, many women never earned enough to produce what even employers considered adequate pay. Moreover, employers tended to shift workers from one machine to another, so no sooner had a women "gotten up to speed" on one stage of the process than she would have to learn another. Workers and union organizers suspected (but could not prove) that this occurred so employers could keep women on the low end of the pay scale.[7]

Unionization seemed to many garment workers the best hope for solving such problems, but the geographic, ethnic, and gender segregation of the

Los Angeles garment trade presented formidable barriers to effective organization. Jewish and Italian garment workers, who occupied the most skilled
positions in the trade, lived in Boyle Heights and Lincoln Heights, to the east
of the garment district. Mexican and Mexican American workers, however,
remained centered around the Plaza, near the Jewish neighborhood in Boyle
Heights, or in the east-side community of Belvedere. As the garment trade
grew, women from these communities increasingly supplied the unskilled
labor needed in factories and outside shops. Garment work attracted Mexican women, in particular, because its seasonal nature allowed them to work
only when they needed to supplement the family income. The most comprehensive study of Los Angeles's Mexican and Mexican American women
workers, done in 1928, found that 62 percent of them entered employment
only out of necessity. A Mexican garment worker would often enter and
leave the trade several times over the course of her life.[8] Nonetheless, with
both Anglo-American and minority women and immigrant men facing low
pay and poor conditions, both genders increasingly turned to unionization to pursue better conditions in their industry. Examining the activities
of the unions these men and women created reveals how gender and race
dynamics often influenced each organization's strategies as well as its chances
for success.

Unionization in garment manufacturing made more advances in the post-
1911 closed-shop atmosphere of the city than perhaps any other industry. The
city's first International Ladies' Garment Workers' Union (ILGWU) local,
formed in 1907, attracted only twenty members and lasted for three months.
In 1910 or 1911, Ladies' Tailors Local 52, of the International Ladies' Garment
Workers Union, formed. The union consisted mainly of skilled Jewish and
Italian cloak makers, fitters, and tailors who had moved from the East to the
West Coast of the United States, as well as a handful of skilled women.[9]

Blessed with strong local leadership, the Ladies' Tailors Local 52 struck
several times, hoping to gain concessions from individual factory owners. In
1911, for example, the union initiated a general strike against all firms manufacturing women's garments. Owners, however, retaliated by blacklisting the
strikers. But members of Local 52 did not remain cowed for long. In July
1914 the Central Labor Council launched an investigation of sweatshop conditions in Los Angeles's cloak- and suit-making firms. An anonymous union
member singled out the firm of Hackel and Gutterman at 751 South Broadway as the grossest example of such conditions. Women workers there never
made more than six dollars a week, and men who had made thirty dollars a

week in the East made only twelve dollars a week in Los Angeles. Female tailors also targeted the store's poor working conditions: "offensive language" from foremen, having to share a restroom with men, and dirty and unsanitary conditions. All the workers at Hackel and Gutterman quit and refused to return to work until conditions improved. By August the strike had spread to four more garment firms, all of which shared one building at 347 South Spring Street. With the help of an organizer from the American Federation of Labor, that year members of the Ladies' Tailors no. 52 gained an eight-hour day, no Sunday work, and the elimination of piecework.[10]

Local 52 also targeted the firm of Max Marks, where women produced silk shirtwaists. When the workers complained about continuous speedups, management told them to leave if they did not like it. The women walked out and went straight to the Labor Temple, now the official headquarters of the city's organized labor movement. The building, funded by local unions and private donations, had opened on February 22, 1910. There the Central Labor Council agreed to take up their cause. The Max Marks strike lasted less than two weeks. In the end the Ladies' Tailors Union secured all of its demands, including an eight-hour day and a revised wage scale.[11]

Max Marks's employees walked out over wages for a second time in June 1915. Max Marks shirtwaists, which retailed for $1.50 to $5.00 each, had grown more complicated to construct. Each now took longer to make, but the women in the factory still made only $0.15 to $0.20 per garment. The firm's workers thus faced a loss of income. Again, Max Marks employees appealed to the Labor Temple for help. Daisy Houck of Local 125 of the United Garment Workers of America, along with two other male unionists, visited Mr. Marks to plead the workers' case. Marks argued he paid the best wages he could. When asked if "he considered that a woman or girl could get along properly on a wage of from $5 to $6 per week ... [he] replied that he did not believe it could be done, but when asked what a poor girl was to do if not receiving enough to live decently on, he had no solution to offer." Houck responded to this impasse by enrolling the striking women in Local 125 of the United Garment Workers. Each striker found a well-paid job in a union garment factory.[12]

Los Angeles's garment manufacturers, in an attempt to counter these union victories, organized into the Cloak and Suit Manufacturers' Protective Association in 1917. That year the manufacturers rejected an agreement with Local 52. The manufacturers instead submitted their own version of the agreement. The proposed agreement refused to recognize that women working as fellers (hemming garments) were skilled, thus denying them equal pay with men. It also refused to discontinue the practice of blacklisting workers who tried to switch from one shop to another. The local refused the agreement and threatened to strike. An organizer from the California State Federation of Labor hastily intervened, pleading with both sides to reach an agreement. The local did ultimately resort to a strike, but won it in a few days and successfully negotiated a wage increase for all of Los Angeles's closed shops.[13]

Local 125 of the United Garment Workers of America

While Local 52 did improve conditions and pay for some Angelenos, the union's orientation toward the skilled worker meant that most of the city's female garment workers could not and did not belong to it. Instead, the bulk of the women in the garment industry who were unionized belonged to Garment Workers no. 125 of the United Garment Workers of America, created in 1901.[14] Through a series of effective alliances, Local 125 achieved more real change for its members than perhaps any other union in open-shop pre–World War I Los Angeles.

In contrast to the largely skilled and male workers of Ladies' Tailors, members of Local 125 of the United Garment Workers manufactured work clothing. Under the able leadership of Daisy Houck and Jennie Haisch, Local 125 became a vocal advocate of both women's rights and workers' rights in the city. Although, sadly, the names of most of the city's female garment workers have been lost to history, both women were so visible in local newspaper coverage and union records that they can be traced with relative ease. Haisch was an Iowa-born widow whose work as a seamstress in an overall factory allowed her to support her young daughter. Houck had been born in Illinois and worked as a "boss" in a shirtwaist factory.[15]

It was common in other cities for labor leaders to criticize club women who "failed to expand their activity and truly help the city's workers."[16] But Houck had a particular genius for skillfully tailoring her union's message to appeal to more elite women as well as to other garment workers. In urging local women's groups to support the union, Houck spoke the language of Progressive Era reform. She argued that the city's elite and middle-class women had an obligation to help workers and their families, not to create any sort of worker's paradise but to create happy, secure American homes.[17] However, Local 125 also supported union activity across the city and the country. It publicly expressed its support for 1910's massive and controversial shirtwaist strike in New York City. Members of the local who did not participate in Los Angeles's union events often faced fines: those women who did not attend the city's annual Labor Day parade, for example, had to pay the union fifty cents each.[18]

Local 125 also wielded some power through the use of its union label. It allowed those companies with union agreements to place a special "union-made" label on each garment produced. The local kept close tabs on those manufacturers using the union label, and did not hesitate to revoke it when companies violated union agreements. The popularity of the union label on clothing led three large Los Angeles garment manufacturers—Brownstein-Louis, the Myers Company, and Peerless—to voluntarily adopt the closed shop. The largest of these, the Brownstein-Louis Company, founded in 1895, specialized in the production of "Stronghold" overalls, a staple among working men up and down the Pacific Coast. Knowing that many of their consumers belonged to unions themselves, Brownstein-Louis proudly played up its closed-shop policies in advertisements. The company touted its well-lit new factory and safety record, as well as the library and dining room that served its seven hundred employees. Advertisements also declared that although Brownstein-Louis paid women by the piece, they could earn twelve to eighteen dollars a week working eight hours a day in its factory. By 1915 a forth closed garment factory—Cohn-Goldwater and Company, makers of white coats and aprons for barbers, butchers, and dentists—also carried the union label. Cohn-Goldwater took employee relations to a new level in 1919 by offering a free day nursery for employees. While garment manufacturers found ways to profit from using the union label, Local 125 hoped that consumers recognized the label's larger significance. If consumers would purchase only goods bearing the union label, Local 125 argued, women working in union factories would not face the prospect of being let go during the slack winter season.[19]

With the help of organizer Margaret Daily, membership in Local 125 grew steadily through 1911 and 1912. In 1913 the union launched its most audacious action: a seventeen-month strike against local manufacturer P. A. Newmark and Company. Most of Los Angeles's manufacturers recognized the power of Local 125, and in 1913 all but one of the companies that employed union members signed voluntary agreements with the local. The one holdout, P.A. Newmark and Company, refused on the grounds that any negotiations should be a personal matter between the company and its employees. Seventy-five of Newmark's three hundred garment workers struck, charging that the company did not pay its workers a living wage. One former employee gave her pay stub to the *Los Angeles Citizen,* which published it in its March 7, 1913, edition:

Many of the Garment Workers state that under present conditions it is impossible to make a decent living. As an evidence of this fact Ester Frendenando, who worked as a Garment Maker in Newark, N.J., for three or four years, has in her possession her tickets for the last four days' work before the strike at Newmark's. These tickets are O.K'd by the head of the department in which she was working and show that Miss Frendenando earned 17 cents the first day, the next 48 cents, the third 32 cents and the fourth 70 cents, giving her, with extras, $2.84 for the four days' work. Others show similar earnings.[20]

Newmark retaliated by arguing that the union lied to its members about what a strike could accomplish and that the company already paid the best wages it could.[21]

The *Los Angeles Times* leaped into the fray and charged strike leaders with lying to the public about the size and scope of the strike. The Garment Workers Local 125 was so desperate for attention, the *Times* said, that it had placed a fake advertisement in a local paper, luring five hundred men to the Newmark factory at the corner of Fourth and Los Angeles with a false promise of motion-picture work. The union, said the *Times,* had been trying to provoke a riot to gain public sympathy for its cause. Moreover, the strike itself was baseless, the *Times* wrote, because Newmark already paid better than scale and the union had unfairly demanded a wage increase based on Los Angeles's high cost of living. "P. A. Newmark, the head of the company, is confident that the advertisement was inserted by union sympathizers in the hope that the 'demonstration' would intimidate his workers, who have cut loose from the union and are now enjoying the free and unrestricted right to think for themselves."[22]

By the second week of the strike the city's Building Trades Council had pledged its support. Committees of female strikers visited cities across Southern California to publicize the strike. Merchants from as far away as Phoenix agreed to stop handling Newmark merchandise. Local 125 remained steadfast in its demand for an 8 percent wage increase, arguing that all the other manufacturers in town already paid the new scale and had not complained. Led by Daisy Houck, some women took to the streets, selling a special edition of the *Los Angeles Citizen* to raise money for the strike fund. The women did so, however, under the watchful eyes of police and detectives, who often followed the strikers home in an attempt to intimidate them. But the boycott of Newmark shirts and the local support buoyed the spirits of striking garment workers. "Our girls are in better spirits now than the first day we went out," strike leader Edith Sutor reported. "We realize that this is a fight against the entire organized labor movement. . . . [S]ome of the girls who have scabbed on us now see the difference in the Newmark factory. They are hoping and praying that the union will be successful."[23]

To their chagrin, however, union members found that popular support for the strike could erode quickly in the face of pressure from the Merchants and Manufacturers Association. As the strike lasted through the summer of 1913, Local 125 found out that several local merchants, in spite of promises to the contrary, had resumed carrying Newmark's shirts. The local suspected that the m&m had pressured the stores to keep Newmark products on their shelves. One business owner told the union that the m&m had threatened to blacklist him if he canceled his Newmark order. This powerful opposition notwithstanding, the Newmark strike dragged on for a total of seventeen months. Local 125 ultimately emerged victorious. In July 1914 Newmark management, just as worn down by the long strike as their former workers, gave in and granted the union its demands. In the wake of the strike the union inducted 81 new members into the union. That September a chastened P. A. Newmark and Company took out space in the *Citizen* to send a special Labor Day greeting to its employees, and said it was misunderstanding, and not any animosity on the part of ownership toward workers, that had produced the strike.[24]

By 1915 the Los Angeles's garment unions had reached peak strength. The largest union, Local 125 of the United Garment Workers, now had 650 members in the city. To celebrate Labor Day, the local took out an advertisement in the *Citizen*. "We are working in the best equipped and most modern factories west of St. Louis," they told readers, "and through our organization we are receiving the best wages and conditions prevailing in the garment-making industry."[25]

The struggle between capital and labor also affected the shoe industry. After the metal-trades strike of 1910, several manufacturers had moved to Torrance, just outside of Los Angeles, hoping the eight miles separating the city from Los Angeles would spare them any labor unrest. But in 1914 Frances Noel and Daisy Houck helped employees of the California Shoe Manufacturing Company in Torrance organize a chapter of the Boot and Shoe Workers International Union, a first for Southern California.[26]

Outreach efforts to minority workers became a cornerstone of the garment workers' unions in Los Angeles. Such unions made more progress in reaching out to workers of all ethnic backgrounds than did any other industry in the city. Letters urging organization for both men and women in the tailoring industry circulated in English, Hebrew, and Italian, and garment workers increasingly translated speeches into Spanish and Italian for the benefit of their audiences. One industry organizer noted about the foreign-born workers that "while they are all of the first water as far as union principles are concerned, many of them do not thoroughly understand the English language and consequently often miss much of the good things said." Such efforts remained as much a survival strategy for the union as a gesture of goodwill. Leaders recognized that any garment worker who remained outside of a union could endanger union advances. Local 125 estimated that by 1916 the three remaining closed-shop garment factories in Los Angeles employed some 150 foreign-born workers, most of them women and teenage girls with little or no English skills. The local began subsidizing night-school English classes at the Labor Temple to both educate and, more important, organize these workers. As Daisy Houck argued, "Coming from countries where, in many instances, they have been unthinkably poor and oppressed, we could secure the loyal support of these people by giving them education in our language, in our standards of living, and in practical lines along the occupation they have chosen." Soon, however, native-born workers showed an interest in attending night school as well, and this program eventually expanded to include classes in cooking, millinery, music, and even Spanish for English speakers. The local paid teachers from the Los Angeles Normal School to teach these classes.[27]

Ethno-Gender Conflict in Los Angeles's Food-Processing Industries

Developments in the city's growing food-processing industry offer a marked contrast to the successes in the garment industry. More and more women found work canning tomatoes and baking crackers, but ethnicity and gender so deeply divided these workers that union proponents had an extremely difficult time organizing them.

Like the garment industry, the food-processing industry provided employment for growing numbers of area residents. As commercially produced foods became a staple in the American diet, the numbers of women employed in such work nationally jumped from 1 woman per every 16,000 people in 1870 to 1 out of every 1,116 people at the end of World War I. California's food-processing industries grew rapidly, spurred on by both international and domestic demand. Between 1914 and 1917 alone California farmers virtually doubled their output of fruit, vegetables, and grain. Initially, factory owners built their facilities on the edges of Los Angeles, close to orchards and farmlands. The same women who picked the produce during the day packed it in the evenings. But increasingly packing plants appeared within the city as well. Most female cannery workers were between sixteen and twenty years old. Gender divided labor, with men cooking the produce and women preparing raw fruits and vegetables as well as filling and labeling the bottles and cans. By the second decade of the twentieth century Los Angeles also had several fish canneries centered on Terminal Island and in San Pedro. Tuna, in particular, proved "a new sensation for the jaded palate." However, producers initially had so much trouble getting local consumers to eat canned tuna that most cans were shipped to New York. Tuna canneries employed women to separate the white meat from dark meat and to pack the meat into sterilized cans. By 1914 eleven Los Angeles–area fish-packing companies produced 115,000 cans of tuna a year.[28]

When unions and women's organizations periodically tried to focus their attention on female cannery workers, they found that the seasonal nature of canning made organization difficult. Some canneries operated only as long as a particular product remained in season; others adapted their machinery to pack different products at different times of the year. Even so, the labor market fluctuated considerably, with the greatest demand for workers coming in spring and early fall and the lowest in winter. The large numbers of foreign-born women employed in canneries created another problem for male union organizers. By 1908 54 percent of women employed in California canneries were foreign born. Unlike their counterparts in the garment industry, male union organizers showed little interest in the needs of foreign female workers. Nor is there any evidence that Anglo-American women in the canneries found common ground with immigrant workers, as they would in later decades. However, in 1915 the Los Angeles branch of the Woman's International Union Label League worked with women employed in the San Pedro fish canneries to create the San Pedro Fish Cannery Women's Union. The women who produced the cans for such companies did not fare so well. The Los Angeles Can Company summarily fired twenty female employees who had had the gall to complain when the pay they received for working on dangerous machinery nine hours a day dropped. There would not be a national union focused on the needs of cannery workers until the creation of the United Cannery, Agricultural, Packing, and Allied Workers of America in 1937.[29]

Workers in other forms of food production also remained unorganized. Los Angeles had several large commercial bakeries that specialized in making crackers and candy. As in produce packing, men held the better-paid and more skilled jobs, in this case mixing the dough. Women tended the machines, iced cookies, and packed and labeled the boxes. Bakery owners also considered tending the ovens a woman's job. Though this position paid reasonably well, due to daylong exposure to intense heat few women lasted in the job for more than a few weeks.[30]

Bishop Candy and Cracker Company, Los Angeles's largest bakery and confectionery company, took a particularly hard line on union activity. In early 1911 it fired twenty men and seven women workers who had attended meetings at the Labor Temple. In response, Los Angeles's bakers organized their first union, Local 37, in February 1911. Bishop promptly locked out all union members. Local 37 retaliated with a strike and a boycott of Bishop products.[31] The strike led to a jump in Local 37's membership, as did news that Bishop had imported two strikebreakers from Kansas City. But the company continued to fire anyone with connections to organized labor. In one case it fired eleven female cracker packers just for attending a dance at the Labor Temple. By August the cracker bakers had run out of money to continue their boycott, and the Los Angeles Central Labor Council stepped into the fray. The council organized the female strikers into committees. These women visited more than a thousand local stores that sold Bishop-produced goods, and some supportive owners actually returned shipments of crackers, cookies, and candy to the company. In September these women proudly marched in the city's annual Labor Day parade at the head of their union. They "made a natty appearance ... with smart walking sticks and soft gray hats, shirt waists, and black skirts," the *Citizen* reported. "They made a decided hit with spectators and were cheered repeatedly." For its part Bishop and Company received the support of the Merchants and Manufacturers Association, which refused to allow the company to settle the strike. Although the prolonged boycott did have some negative impact on Bishop's business, with the formidable M&M supporting the company the strike dragged on into 1912. As employees found work at other bakeries, the strike lost momentum. The union ultimately proved unable to combat Bishop's lockout.[32]

In open-shop Los Angeles, the relative success of female garment workers in their pursuit of better wages and working conditions is remarkable. It is even more so when one considers the inherent difficulties in organizing a multiethnic, polyglot workforce. Yet some garment unions had an uncanny ability to speak the language of Progressive reform, on the one hand, and to mobilize their largely immigrant rank and file for labor actions, on the other. True, surviving records of pre–1920 Los Angeles's garment unions indicate that the leadership still tended to be native-born Anglo-American women. But without female immigrant workers' willingness to put their jobs on the line in labor actions, that leadership would not have been able to produce any real results. Indeed, the repeated failures of unions for cannery and bakery workers are evidence that many organizers could not overcome the hurdles in their way. By the 1930s more and more immigrant women would themselves step into leadership positions in garment unions and lead waves of labor activity in Greater Los Angeles.

With their jobs often tenuous and underpaid, minority and immigrant women understandably attracted attention from Progressives and other social reformers. But here again, they asserted their prerogative to meet their own and their families' needs on their own terms.

Minority Life in Greater Los Angeles

Historical research has focused on how definitions of "white" and "nonwhite" came to be used to separate those entitled to full participation in American society from those subject to racial and ethnic segregation. Thus, "whiteness" increasingly defined "Americanness," although the line was a fine and shifting one. Under such a system, however, African American, Asian American, and Mexican American women who had been born in the United States, as well as some European immigrant groups, could not claim American identity. These issues hardened the ethnic divisions among Los Angeles's wage-earning women.[33]

Social service agencies reinforced these divisions by offering aid through different, often racially segregated, channels than those used to reach white working women. Settlement houses and the Los Angeles Young Women's Christian Association's International Institutes, in particular, focused on the role of the immigrant woman as both the center of the immigrant family and a potential worker in Los Angeles's economy. Reformers, male and female, focused most of their attention on "Americanizing" European immigrants. Anglo-Americans expected to be able to assimilate these men and women into local society. However, immigrants such as the Russian Molokans, while phenotypically "white," resisted these attempts in favor of maintaining their traditional way of life. The same reformers largely ignored the needs of the city's nonwhites, its Asian American, African American, and Mexican American populations. Only with the entry of the United States into World War I did civic leaders and Progressives take an interest in Mexican American and Mexican immigrant women. However, decades of such neglect spurred some Angeleno immigrants and minorities to create their own networks of social support and mutual aid, networks they refused to surrender to Anglo-American social workers and politicians. Repeated attempts and failures by

Progressives to transform Mexican women and their offspring into perfect "American" workers, and mutual misunderstandings on both sides, illustrate the gulf between Anglo-Americans and minorities in the city.[34]

Racism and residential segregation limited minority and some immigrant groups from advancing either economically or socially in Los Angeles. Early-twentieth-century Los Angeles's economic structure promoted residential segregation, and Anglo-Americans accelerated this trend by increasingly abandoning downtown and the east side for the westside and white-collar suburbs. As the number of non-Anglo residents grew, working-class, immigrant, and nonwhite Angelenos began to cluster in several neighborhoods across the city. These included the densely populated areas around Chinatown and the Plaza, but also suburban areas like Watts and Chavez Ravine. By 1910 the Plaza and Sonoratown, while historically Mexican, were also home to African Americans, Italians, Asians, and poor Anglos. Chavez Ravine, just north of Sonoratown, sheltered the three racially mixed neighborhoods of Palo Verde, La Loma, and Bishop. Lincoln Heights, northeast of downtown across the Los Angeles River, was populated largely by native-born skilled white workers at the turn of the century, but also saw growing numbers of Mexicans and Mexican Americans move into the area as the decade progressed. While racial covenants and other exclusionary practices kept non-Anglos from settling in some parts of Los Angeles, these neighborhoods either lacked such covenants or were in areas where they were not enforced.[35]

Immigrants and nonwhite Angelenos chose these neighborhoods due largely to their proximity to places of employment. The growing industrial and commercial nature of downtown Los Angeles and on both sides of the river required large numbers of employees. The railroads, for example, built storage yards and other facilities north and south of the main passenger and freight stations downtown, with some going so far as to house Mexican employees in abandoned boxcars nearby. Boxcar settlements sparked the growth of immigrant communities east of the river in "Dogtown" near Lincoln Heights and in an area known as the Flats, a small area on the east side of the river below the bluffs and south of the Macy Street bridge. The pollution of these areas repelled Anglos who could afford to live elsewhere. Both industrial waste and sewage discharged directly into the Los Angeles River, which still flooded periodically. The Flats became increasingly multiethnic as the decade wore on, with Mexicans, Russian Molokans, Armenians, Japanese, and Jews populating the area. On the west side of the river the area around the railroad stations made those neighborhoods a "port of entry" for many new arrivals in the city. Centered on the "Skid Row" running along Fifth Street east of Main to the railroad yards, Jewish, African American, Italian, Mexican, Chinese, and Japanese Angelenos all made homes here. The produce-market district of the area, centered on Ninth and San Pedro streets, both served minorities excluded from the Central Market downtown and provided employment for local residents. In 1918 a nearby Methodist church, noting the area's diversity, renamed the area the "All Nations District."[36]

Boyle Heights, once a fashionable Anglo residential district on the east side of the river providing views of downtown, became the center of another new immigrant community. In 1905 it became home to the Russian Molokans, peasant pacifists who had fled Russia with the onset of the Sino-Japanese War and the Russian Revolution. Pegged by area social workers as the most reclusive and clannish of all the city's ethnic communities, some three to five thousand Molokans settled in the area, particularly in a ravine known as Fickett's Hollow.[37] Mexicans also lived in Fickett's Hollow, as well as another ravine in Boyle Heights known as Bernal Gully (or, to its inhabitants, as "La Barria"). African Americans lived west of the Evergreen Cemetery in a neighborhood called "Pecktown" by area whites. The area of Boyle Heights north of Brooklyn Avenue became a residential and commercial center for Jewish Angelenos, with smaller numbers of Armenians and Japanese also living nearby.[38]

The changing face of the city did not please many of its Anglo-American residents, who increasingly moved away from the city center. The "westside" neighborhoods of Bunker Hill, Echo Park, and the area around Temple Street north of downtown had originally been settled by middle-class Anglos, but increasingly attracted the more wealthy and socially prominent immigrant and non-Anglo city residents. Some elite Angelenos increasingly looked to neighborhoods even farther from downtown for their homes.[39] With many Anglos increasingly abandoning downtown and the east side, Asian and African Americans carved out their own communities in sections of the city. However, these two groups, though relatively small, remained outside the purview of Anglo-American social reformers. Instead, Asian American and African American women relied on their own communities to provide both employment and aid in times of need.

Americans Denied: Asian American
and African American Women in Los Angeles

In spite of Los Angeles's economic and geographic growth, in many ways it remained an insular town. The racial attitudes of Anglo-Americans had changed little in the previous thirty years. Asians and Asian Americans remained at the very bottom of Los Angeles society, and blatant racism directed at those of Chinese or Japanese descent kept them there. The city's small population of African Americans also continued to maintain a life largely separate from that of Anglo Angelenos.

Anglo-Americans tended to regard Asian immigrants as "sojourners," a temporary workforce that would eventually return to Asia. Ronald Takaki points out the irony of this charge—in fact, many immigrants from Europe had also originally intended to stay only temporarily in the United States. White workers opposed large-scale immigration from Asia, seeing these newcomers as potential competitors for jobs. Ineligible for citizenship, both Chinese and Japanese immigrants remained marginalized in Los Angeles. As discussed in previous chapters, many Asian men worked as domestic servants because the local demand for servants remained high. For turn-of-the-century Angelenos, even outdoor recreational activities like camping required servants. As one publication advised, "Delicate women are likely to come back worse than they were when they started out . . . unless they can afford to have a Chinaman with them, or some other kind of servant, thus giving them the chance to rest and get the good from the open air." Due to immigration policies, most Asian women arrived in the city as part of a family, and cultural mores for both Chinese and Japanese immigrants did not support women working outside the home. But discrimination against Asian men in all but the most menial employment may explain why some women sought out paid employment they could integrate into the demands of family life. But they usually found work only in family businesses and in home work, such as rolling cigars, sewing, and sorting vegetables. Census reporters, however, did not record such work because it was usually performed in the home, and the census did not yet recognize this kind of work. As a result the official numbers of Los Angeles's Asian women who were gainfully employed are probably far too low. According to the 1880 census, for example, only 3 percent of Chinese women in the city worked for wages.[40]

The numbers of Chinese residents of the city had been steadily declining since the passage of the Chinese Exclusion Act in 1882, although loopholes in the laws allowed a few Chinese women and children to enter the country. Prostitution, which had brought many Chinese women to California in the decades following the Gold Rush and kept them in virtual slavery, declined sharply after 1870. Throughout the state most Chinese women in the census of 1880 listed their only occupation as "housekeeper." Between 1900 and 1910 the area's total Chinese population dropped from 3,089 to 2,455, although the numbers of Chinese women and Chinese American women grew slightly, from 120 to 147 individuals. In Los Angeles, for instance, 99 of the 147 Chinese women recorded in the 1910 census had been born in the United States. Given the difficulty in bringing Chinese women into the United States in this period, Chinese American women soon outnumbered Chinese women in Chinatowns across the United States. It should be noted that being born in the United States did not ensure that these women were treated as U.S. citizens. A series of laws made their status, and that of all Chinese in the United States, ambiguous, a situation that would not be resolved until after World War II.[41]

Chinese American women found few opportunities for advancement in the city. Educational and workforce discrimination continued to limit their employment options well into the mid-twentieth century.[42]

But while the Chinese population of Los Angeles declined, the Japanese population increased. Unlike the Chinese, the Japanese preferred Los Angeles to San Francisco. Between 1900 and 1915, due to a new Japanese imperial policy permitting its citizens to emigrate, large numbers of Japanese relocated to the United States. Largely the sons of farmers with few employment options in Japan, Japanese men found an economic niche on the West Coast. Unlike the Chinese, the Japanese benefited from entering California later in the nineteenth century when the state had developed both economically and socially. Between 1900 and 1909 urban Japanese communities appeared in western states. In Los Angeles the number of Japanese-owned and operated businesses jumped from 56 to 473 in those nine years. Anglo Angelenos initially tolerated the Japanese because they believed the Japanese to be more adaptable and easier to Americanize than the Chinese. The Japanese also had more success in establishing families because the Japanese government actively promoted the emigration of women. Between 1911 and 1920 women made up 39 percent of all Japanese immigrants to the United States.[43]

Japanese residents of the city took particular interest in developing their own small businesses because discrimination prevented them from entering other professions. Farmers rented small parcels of land within the city limits from whites. In the hands of a skilled farmer such plots could produce quality fruits and vegetables. With the help of ethnic solidarity and mutual-support systems developed in the United States, the Japanese soon had a virtual monopoly on the retail and wholesale trade in produce like lettuce, celery, and berries. By 1909 Japanese or Japanese Americans owned 120 of the 180 produce stands in the Los Angeles City Market. Many Japanese settled near Little Tokyo downtown. Dubbed "Five Points," this area was notably multiethnic.

Others moved into neighborhoods recently "opened" to integration by African Americans, including parts of south-central Los Angeles and Boyle
Heights. No studies of Japanese and Japanese American women's work
in Los Angeles from this period exist, but many no doubt worked alongside husbands and sons on farms and in small businesses.[44] Both Jennifer
Koslow's and Natalia Molina's work also uncovered Japanese women working as midwives in Los Angeles during this period, but their exact numbers
are unknown.[45]

In part due to fear over economic competition with whites, xenophobic
hysteria halted immigration from Japan to the United States in 1907. Under
the agreement Japan promised not to issue passports to laborers, whether
skilled or unskilled. This prevented laborers from entering the United States.
However, parents, wives, and children of Japanese already resident in the
United States were not included in the ban. Due to natural increase and
migration from other parts of the United States and Hawaii, by 1910 four
thousand Japanese lived in Los Angeles, and eight thousand lived in Los
Angeles County.[46]

Because the city had gained a reputation as being relatively friendly to
African Americans, between 1900 and 1910 the African American population of Los Angeles grew from two thousand to seventy-six hundred. During a visit to the city in 1913, W. E. B. DuBois declared that Los Angeles,
while not free from prejudice, was still one of the best locations for African
Americans to settle. This perceived air of tolerance may have existed largely
because Anglos directed most of their racial hostility at the city's Japanese
and Mexican residents instead. Migrants from rural southern states like Mississippi, Georgia, and Alabama tended to live in Mud Town, or Watts, on the
outskirts of Los Angeles, while those from Tennessee and Georgia preferred
an area near Temple Street. The center of African American Los Angeles,
pushed south by white encroachment, became Central Avenue.[47]

As the population increased, so too did the number of African American
women working outside the home. By 1920 50 percent of African American
women in Los Angeles worked outside the home, compared to just under 30
percent for native-born whites.[48]

Anglo-Americans, secure in their hegemonic control of the city, had no
qualms about neglecting these two segments of the local population. But in
the face of increasing immigration from Europe and Mexico they became
concerned about how best to assimilate European immigrants and about
where Mexican immigrants could or should fit into the racial hierarchy. In

attempting to solve these problems Los Angeles's social reformers developed a system of settlement houses and agencies that tried to intervene directly in immigrant life.

Immigrant Communities, Social Reform, and Women's Work

After 1900 organized welfare programs in Los Angeles, hoping to create both better citizens and better workers, increasingly focused their attention on recent immigrants. Housing in immigrant communities became one of the first issues to attract the attention of Anglo-Americans in the city. One of the most characteristic forms of residences for poor Angelenos was the "house court," sometimes called "cholo courts" in reference both to the ethnicity of large numbers of their inhabitants and to the perceived Mexican roots of the design. House courts consisted of a number of small houses joined together and sharing an open courtyard. The single water supply was usually located in the center of this courtyard, leading residents to use the space as "kitchen space, laundry, garden, animal pen, and washing area." Hemmed in by both industrial development and the Los Angeles River, these neighborhoods suffered from poor ventilation, industrial pollution, and an appalling lack of basic sanitation. In 1905 the overcrowding and poor sanitary conditions of these areas attracted the attention of Jacob Riis, who had reported on the living conditions in New York City's tenements. After touring downtown Los Angeles, Riis reported that he had seen slums "of greater area, but never any which were worse than those in Los Angeles." Chastened and angered by Riis's criticism, city boosters called for the creation of a municipal agency to address these problems. The city created the Los Angeles Housing Commission the following year. The Reverend Dana Bartlett, a local reformer, also took umbrage with Jacob Riis's observations about city housing conditions. Barlett argued, "There are no slums in Los Angeles in the sense that a slum is a vicious congested district, for one must always distinguish between districts filled with working men and their families, and those filled with vicious immoral characters. There are slum people in Los Angeles, but no one district where they are centered."[49] Obviously, Barlett believed there should be clear distinctions made between deserving immigrants and those unworthy of reformers' concern.

Los Angeles's organized womanhood had initially focused its attention on Anglo-American working women, but by the turn of the century club women increasingly sought to reach out to European and Mexican immigrant women as well. The YWCA estimated that some eight hundred immi-

grant women had arrived in the Los Angeles in 1913–1914 alone. These
women believed that immigrants should be Americanized, but they rejected
demands for immediate assimilation in favor of a more gradual approach.
They recognized the social and economic difficulties new immigrants often
faced, and worked to ameliorate the worst effects of immigration. Remaining sensitive to the immigrants' historical and cultural traditions, however,
was a struggle. To do so they tapped into a new development in social reform
in the United States: the settlement house. Settlement work called for educated women to relocate to poor and immigrant neighborhoods. There these
women performed charitable service but also gained experience that could
springboard into careers. Because most clients could not afford to pay for
services, settlement workers depended on charitable donations from wealthy
women. This dependency created a uniquely symbiotic relationship between
reform-minded professionals and elite laypeople.[50]

Just as the women's club movement had spread from the East to the West,
so too did interest in settlement houses and other social reforms. In the more
flexible social structures of western cities, settlement and other charity work
allowed many women to establish themselves as community leaders. In cities
like Denver and San Francisco, where men continued to outnumber women,
reform tended to focus on morality. But in Los Angeles immigration became
the key issue. Several settlement houses served Los Angeles's immigrant
populations. In such houses, Dana Bartlett, wrote, "the settlement workers
are not missionaries going down to the people to lift them up, but rather
being just 'folks,' living the simple life of friendship and neighborliness." The
Los Angeles Branch of the Association of Collegiate Alumnae operated the
city's oldest secular settlement house, the College Settlement. It opened in
1894 on Alpine Street and was managed entirely by women. The College
Settlement organized children's activities and investigated conditions among
the city's Mexican immigrants. It later changed its name to Casa de Castelar,
named after its new location on Castelar Street. The Catholic church opened
El Hogar Feliz (The Happy Home) in 1897. Located in the Plaza district, El
Hogar Feliz served the area's Mexican population, providing primary school
classes, classes in Catholic doctrine, and youth activities. Female volunteers
managed most of the day-to-day management of the settlement, while a
priest from a nearby church served as spiritual director.[51]

The city also had the Catholic church's Brownson House on Jackson Street
and the Stinson Memorial Industrial School on Amelia Street, run by the
Council of Jewish Women. The Congregational church funded Bartlett's own

Bethlehem Institute on Vignes Street as well as the Congregational Chinese Mission on North Los Angeles Street. The sponsoring institutions depended on volunteers to keep the houses operating. Settlement work in Los Angeles thus seldom became the path to professional careers in reform that it was in eastern cities like New York and Chicago.[52]

Not to be outdone when it came to charitable work, the Los Angeles branch of the YWCA also leaped into the fray. In 1913, the same year it opened the Clark Home, the YWCA founded the International Institute for foreign-born women on Utah Street. Originally developed in New York City by Edith Terry Bremer, a veteran of the Chicago network of social workers and reformers, the International Institutes were expected to serve functions similar to those of the settlement houses. Unlike the settlements, however, the institutes tried to hire foreign-born and first-generation American women as case workers whenever possible.[53]

Recognizing that immigrant women remained the least-likely members of families to interact with American society on a daily basis, the International Institutes offered these women formal and informal classes in English, American history, government, child care, and homemaking. In 1913 the Los Angeles Institute operated a special summer school to teach English to Dutch-, German-, Swedish-, Russian-, Italian-, French-, and Yiddish-speaking Angelenos.[54]

The institute operated its own employment bureau for immigrant women. The YWCA clearly hoped to steer these women into domestic work or other kinds of manual labor the city needed rather than foster any particular ambition for white-collar work (although it did see a demand for qualified immigrant women to work as music teachers). "Russian women in particular make excellent day workers. . . . [M]any well-to-do foreign families coming here to live are usually desirous of obtaining a cook of the same nationality," Sue Barnwell, who ran the employment bureau, observed. "It is not an uncommon thing for the young foreign girls to work in a factory or laundry during the day and do handwork at night. This, they sell through the Institute's exchange to help increase the family's finances." By 1916 the institute employed three full-time case workers: one for girls; one for Italian, French, and Spanish immigrants; and one for the South Slavs (and presumably also the Molokans).[55] With the combined pressures of economic need and organizations like the International Institute at work, it is hardly surprising that the numbers of foreign-born women employed in Los Angeles increased steadily in the first decades of the twentieth century. But the case of the Russian Molokan community illustrates the struggles immigrant women faced in trying to balance work outside the home with cultural expectations about their proper role in society.

White but Not American: The Russian Molokans

Many immigrants did not greet intervention from Anglo-American social agencies with open arms. Los Angeles's Molokan community reveals how some European immigrants, while still participating in Los Angeles's economy, tried to resist assimilation into American society.

The word *Molokan* refers to a particular religious sect originally from Russia. They were evangelicals who refused to follow the Russian Orthodox Church or the czar. The Russian Molokans had been attracted to Southern California as a refuge from religious persecution at the hands of Russian authorities. The Molokans remained a particular concern for the International Institute and other charitable organizations because both their social structures and their values seemed particularly foreign in contrast to those of Progressive Era Americans. Traditional Molokan society had only two formal social organizations, the family and the church. Anglo-Americans did not understand the Molokan church, either—the Molokan church, or *sobranie,* was much more akin to a Quaker meeting than a Protestant, Catholic, or even Greek or Russian Orthodox service. Molokans rejected any form of formal religious practice because they associated them with the Orthodox Church. There were no social classes. Instead, Molokans based their social hierarchy on age, personal merit, and religious activity. In times of crisis they relied on mutual aid from inside the community, not civic agencies.[56]

Even their choice of wardrobe marked the Molokans out as different from other immigrants. They continued to wear traditional dress on the streets of Boyle Heights and the Flats. Molokans initially attempted to graft their farm-based family economies into life in Los Angeles, but found them ill-suited for modern industrial life.[57]

Unable to access indigenous Molokan networks of aid in the community, social workers struggled to find a way to reach them. They observed that these "Slavs," as they called them, suffered from one of the highest rates of illiteracy in English of all the city's immigrant populations. These same workers noted that the much maligned Mexican immigrant community, which most Anglos assumed to be completely illiterate, had more success in learning to read and write English than the Molokans. Since the Molokans could not vote, the City of Los Angeles found it easy to neglect them. The Molokans suffered from health problems, poor housing conditions, and a lack of police.[58]

Most Molokan women worked out of economic necessity because the community suffered from high rates of unemployment among Molokan men. But these women encountered problems trying to balance their families' demands with the need to work outside the home for wages. YWCA case worker Frances Jouromsky fretted about the impact of women's work on the Molokan family. "Children who should be in school have to remain home to care for the little ones while the mother is working. And the mothers come home tired and worn out, only to find that they have all the housework to do," she told the *Los Angeles Tribune*. Alice J. Cushing, principal of the Utah Street School, remembered that so many Molokan children had to bring their infant brothers and sisters to school while their mothers went to work that "the third-grade teacher had as many as six and eight infants crawling all over the classroom while she carried on instruction." Cushing eventually came up with a practical solution to this problem. "Three years later we opened a day nursery, and at a later date were able to secure the service of a Molokan young woman, a reliable and conscientious worker," she reported. "She was married and had a baby of her own attending the nursery." Cushing believed that Molokan mothers trusted the school to care for their infants only because one of their own worked there.[59]

The low-paying jobs held by most Molokan women exacerbated the conflicts between family and work. Molokan women who had learned English at school entered unskilled industrial work. They worked in biscuit factories close to the heart of Molokan Los Angeles or in the candy factory on Utah Street. Other Russian-speaking Molokan women found jobs in laundries. Most of these women earned just four to ten dollars a week. Even if it had been possible for Molokan women to pursue white-collar or office work, which would have paid better, powerful cultural mores prevented them from doing so. Parents and elders feared the Americanizing effects of retail and office work on their young women.[60]

These fears were not unfounded. The story of Cora Jackson that opened this chapter illustrates how one Molokan woman's exposure to American society affected her relationship with her family. Jackson married a Molokan man but eventually left him and her children for life in American Los Angeles. There may have been other stories like Jackson's, because in order to prevent such a breakdown in family relations most Molokans resisted Americanization programs and refused to utilize the International Institute. When Pauline Young studied the community in the 1920s she found that only younger Molokan girls attended classes at the International Institute. Their mothers and older sisters shunned such participation. Young suggested that Molokans may have been more comfortable using institute services than those of settle-ment houses because they did not smack of charity in quite the same way but that most women still saw little value in either. Young found that of the five hundred immigrants enrolled in the institute, very few were adult Molokans, and there were no Molokan women enrolled in parenthood, baby-welfare, cooking, sewing, fancy-work, or swimming classes.[61]

Attitudes held by Anglo-American social workers exacerbated the situa-tion. Many of the Americanization teachers had little patience for the "odd" cultural behavior of this self-segregating group. "Most teachers know little about Molokan culture, and what they do know about it does not appeal to them as worth fostering and promoting. They laugh up their sleeves about the 'Jumpers,'" one retired Americanization teacher remembered. "They [the teachers] have so little to offer that is of immediate practical value to these people that few of them see any use in bothering about school." Social agencies often failed to coordinate their efforts, and heavy caseloads and a high turnover of social workers plagued relief agencies working in Molo-kan neighborhoods.[62]

The problems encountered by both Molokan immigrants and the American women who worked among them, however, were dwarfed by the problems found in the city's Mexican community. Settlement workers and proponents of Americanization wanted Mexicans to become "Americans." But many within the community recognized that such programs did noth-ing to address the persistent racism and discrimination that confined most Mexican men and women to unskilled and semiskilled jobs. Understandably, then, the Mexican and Mexican American community preferred to distrib-ute aid from within the community or to work with volunteer aid workers from the Catholic church.

Mexican Angelenos and Americanization

Increased concerns among Anglo-Americans about how and when Mexicans might become "Americans" resulted from changes in Mexican immigration patterns in the early twentieth century. Los Angeles's Anglo-American popu-lation outnumbered the native-born Mexican American population by the late nineteenth century. Some white observers had gone so far as to predict their eventual disappearance from the area. However, economic and political upheaval in Mexico, particularly the land reforms of the Díaz regime, com-pelled thousands of Mexican immigrants to search for a better future in the United States. The economic and political turmoil of the Díaz regime in Mexico and a subsequent war fueled the trend. So many Mexicans migrated

to Los Angeles in the early years of the twentieth century that they quickly
swamped the smaller population of native-born Mexican Americans. By the
mid-1910s Los Angeles had probably the largest urban colony of immigrant
Mexicans in the United States. Immigrant Mexicans now supplanted what
many Anglos considered the "declining" and "decadent race" of native-born
Mexican Americans.[63]

Many of these new immigrants chose land on the east side of the river in
Belvedere and Maravilla Park, unincorporated neighborhoods where the lack
of municipal taxes and building regulations made housing and land cheap.
But Mexicans could be found living in almost any part of the city. Settling in
Los Angeles often became the end of a series of chain migrations from Mexico: first the male head of household found work, and later he would send for
his wife, children, and other kin. This form of migration played an integral
role in both the survival of the family unit in a new country and in the preservation of Mexican culture.[64]

As ever-increasing numbers of Mexican immigrants arrived in Los
Angeles, both reformers and politicians worried about how best to assimilate them into American culture. Unlike the Swedes, Italians, or even a clannish group like the Molokans, to contemporary viewers Mexicans seemed to
be inherently flawed. Anglo-Americans viewed them as lazy, shiftless, and
thriftless. "The Mexican laborer is unambitious, listless, physically weak,
irregular, and indolent," Victor S. Clark noted in a 1908 report he drafted
for the U.S. Department of Commerce and Labor. Decades of economic
and social discrimination had reduced Los Angeles's Mexican and Mexican
American population to the status of second-class citizens. One survey of
more than one thousand Mexican families living near the Plaza found that,
while 60 percent had lived in the city for more than three years, 55 percent of
men and 74 percent of women could not speak English. Literacy rates were
even lower. A baby born to Mexican parents in Los Angeles had just one-
third the chance of survival as a baby born to Anglo-American or European
immigrant parents.[65]

With many immigrant families dependent on the economic contributions of their children for family survival, few Mexican children entered Los
Angeles's public school system. Unsympathetic school administrators noted
that Mexican children rarely progressed as quickly as their Anglo classmates,
a fact that they blamed on limited English-language skills. Unlike Dana Barlett, Clark had no qualms about calling the downtown housing arrangements
of most Mexican immigrants "tenements."[66] The poor housing and health
conditions in Mexican neighborhoods resulted in large part from the eco-

nomic restrictions placed on Mexican wage earners. Few women or men could enter the kind of skilled or white-collar work that would have substantially increased wages and thus materially improved their daily lives.

In Los Angeles Mexican men found work on the railroads, in construction, on public works, and in service industries. In interviews with potential employers Clark found that there remained less hostility to the Mexican worker than to other minorities for two reasons. First, Mexican workers could not and did not attempt to compete directly with Anglo or even European workers in most skilled and semiskilled labor markets. They were far more likely to be competing with Asians or African Americans for low-paid service or unskilled jobs. Second, employers embraced the stereotype of the Mexican employee as more docile and tractable than any other ethnicity, yet less "foreign" than the Chinese or Japanese worker. "In some occupations [in Los Angeles], Mexicans are rapidly displacing Japanese, Greeks, and even Italians. Lack of education and initiative confines most of these immigrants to the simpler forms of unskilled labor. They compete little, if at all, with what is called 'white labor' in the Southwest." Yet Mexican men did not prove to be the tractable labor force California employers had anticipated. Continued attempts to organize and connections to the radical Partido Liberal Mexicano and the local Socialist Party attest to the active role Mexican American and Mexican immigrant men played on the local labor scene.[67]

The same does not appear to have been true of Mexican women workers in the first decade of the twentieth century. Far fewer Mexican women than men worked outside the home for wages. Investigators noted that even when Mexican men could not find steady work, they often preferred to keep their wives at home if at all possible. The Department of Commerce and Labor report suggested this resulted from a combination of a "peasant prejudice" held by Mexican men and a lack of industrial training among Mexican women. Wives often contributed to the family economy in other ways, such as taking in boarders or doing laundry. "For the same reason," Clark wrote, "Mexicans do not become domestic servants. Women of the better laboring classes will not leave home, and the immigrant women have so little conception of domestic arrangements in the United States that the task of training them would be too heavy for American housewives." However, as George J. Sanchez notes, immigration often required gender roles to adapt to changing family needs. Mexican-born women, in fact, worked outside the home more frequently than Mexican American women precisely because family need often compelled them to do so. But they faced the same difficulties as their husbands and brothers. Racial discrimination prohibited them from finding skilled or white-collar work. Instead, the wives and daughters who did work did so in downtown textile factories or in bakeries or canneries.[68]

On average, Mexican women workers earned less and stood less chance of advancement than workers of other ethnicities. Taylor attributes this to the perceived temporary nature of such jobs, as well as a lack of experience. He does note, however, that some Mexican women in Los Angeles's clothing trades occupied positions as skilled seamstresses. Such women often came from less impoverished families and had more education than their counterparts in other industries. Unlike their American and European counterparts, far fewer young Mexican women entered the workforce with any expectation that work would be a path to economic and familial independence. Those women who did work for these reasons told researchers they wanted to escape tradition-bound families or poverty (or both) at home. The population growth in the barrio did have one benefit for Mexican women, however. It allowed for the growth of a small merchant class that owned and operated shops in these areas. Some women found work as clerks or salespeople in these shops, or in Anglo businesses catering to the growing Mexican population.[69]

While settlement houses and the International Institute had seemed fine for work with European immigrants, many proponents suggested more radical measures would be needed to "Americanize" Mexican immigrants. Los Angeles developed a variety of programs determined to reshape Mexican family life, work, and even culture, many of them staffed and managed by women. Concerned about how best to Americanize the children of these new immigrants, the Los Angeles Board of Education added a system of "model bungalows" to the public schools. The board placed the bungalows under the supervision of Ella Flagg, supervisor of domestic science for the district. Flagg argued that many of the immigrant children had "absolutely no idea of housekeeping according to American standards." Elementary schools on Utah Street, Amelia Street, and several other locations built small three-room bungalows to teach students cooking and cleaning skills. Reformers hoped these model schools would train pupils for future jobs. But by teaching girls cooking and sewing and boys gardening and carpentry work, reformers made it clear that they expected immigrant children to fill only the city's need for manual and domestic labor. Trade unions had generally been hostile to immigrants. But some union supporters now tried to argue that unions actually served Americanization by ensuring what Frances Nacke Noel called "an American standard of living, and without an American standard of living you cannot have an American standard of freedom and culture."[70]

The California State Commission on Immigration and Housing, created in 1913, performed similar work under the leadership of former schoolteacher Mary Gibson. With her background in teaching, suffrage, and the Friday Morning Club, Gibson brought to her work an elite Anglo-American Protestant orientation. She focused on the power of education and moral leadership to reshape Mexican American domestic life. Under her guidance, Gibson's hometown, Los Angeles, became an enthusiastic proponent of Americanization programs. The cornerstone of Gibson's system, home teachers, often entered Mexican homes on the pretext of making sure the children attended school regularly. Once there, however, the teacher attempted to persuade the foreign-born women of the household to attend classes in English, civics, and domestic science. Proponents of these Americanization programs, like those in the school district, hoped that domestic science would provide Mexican women with skills they could then apply to finding work as domestic servants. Home teachers neither expected nor wanted such training to instill any more ambition in a Mexican woman or child than needed for her to become unskilled or semiskilled labor in the local economy. By 1918 the State of California employed twelve full-time "home teachers," but by and large Mexican women rejected such programs.[71]

This may have occurred because in some sense such programs attempted to reinvent the wheel. Had proponents of Americanization studied Los Angeles with a more critical eye, they would have found that Mexican women in need already had other options to turn to, options that did not denigrate their culture or their customs. Even the Clark report found that, in times of trouble, Mexican immigrants instinctively turned to their countrymen, not to the state, for help, and that few Mexicans ever became dependent on public charity. Clark may have been referring to local *mutualistas*, self-support groups originally developed in Mexico and then adapted in the United States by Mexican Americans. These organizations recognized that, due to racism on the part of Anglo-American officials, Mexican men and women often could not rely on local social services for help in times of crisis. Each *mutualista* offered different benefits to its members. These could range from low-cost insurance and funeral benefits to low-interest loans and social services. Although some Mexican clubs and organizations remained segregated by gender, Mexican American and Mexican immigrant women often played active roles in female auxiliaries. The earliest such organization appeared in Southern California in the 1850s, and by the turn of the century several new ones, most notably La Sociedad Hispano-Americana de Beneficia Mutua, provided aid for members in distress. This organization appears to have also used the name Sociedad Española de Beneficencia Mútua. Nelson A. Pichardo found an additional twenty-four other Mexican and Mexican American community organizations active in Los Angeles County between 1910 and 1923. Los Angeles also had a chapter of the largest national *mutualista,* the Alianza Hispano-Americana, which after 1913 admitted women on the same basis as men. Prior to 1913 women belonged to Alianza ladies' auxiliaries. The Alianza evolved from a local mutual society into a fraternal insurance society, and lasted until the 1960s.[72]

California's *movimiento de mutualistas* (*mutualista* movement) became increasingly active after 1917. This occurred largely because such organizations also helped ease the strain that new immigrants placed on Los Angeles's Mexican communities. Mexican immigrants thus arrived not in a social vacuum but rather a well-developed Mexican American community with a long tradition of mutual aid. Had the leaders of Americanization programs recognized the significant role of mutual-aid organizations in Mexican American life and adapted their efforts accordingly, perhaps they would have met with more success. Mexican women often performed charitable works within their own community.[73]

The Mexican immigrant community could also turn to several local religious institutions in time of need. Several Protestant churches near the Plaza offered classes in industrial work as well as social services. One even operated an employment bureau. During World War I the YWCA's International Institute finally began working with the city's Japanese and Mexican immigrants. To help speed assimilation, it added classes on food regulations, draft registrations, and loyalty to the U.S. government to its curriculum. The institute hired two Spanish-speaking secretaries who served an estimated six hundred Mexican families. These secretaries served as translators when needed and also as liaisons between the immigrant and city social services.[74]

An even more popular option may have been Greater Los Angeles's six Catholic social service agencies. The Catholic Church in Los Angeles recognized the need to respond effectively to Mexican immigrants' practical as well as spiritual needs. Church leaders focused on four key goals: educating immigrants in Catholic doctrine, giving the church's blessing for civil marriages that had been performed in Mexico, providing charitable relief, and protecting Catholics from Protestant missionaries and other "false philosophies."[75]

Catholic settlement houses played a key role in both relief and Americanization efforts. It should be noted that Catholic immigrants to the United States had long had to "prove" their national loyalty to skeptical Anglo-American Protestants. The church thus had considerable experience with and interest in Americanization programs. The largest Catholic aid organization remained the Brownson House Settlement at 711 Jackson Street, less than a mile from the heart of the Plaza District.[76] Mary Workman, who had gained experience as a volunteer at the College Settlement House and teacher at the Utah Street public school, managed the settlement. She echoed Dana Barlett's views on the proper role of the settlement house. Rather that trying to force an immigrant to assimilate, Workman believed that "a more permanent good is accomplished by helping people to help themselves through friendly cooperation with them, and by setting in motion the proper agencies to this end." Sixty women and a handful of men served as the Brownson House's volunteer staff. The staff offered a range of services, from a sewing club to an employment bureau; they also permitted the local *mutualistas* to use Brownson House space for meetings.[77] Unlike the Protestant settlements or the Americanization centers, Mexican visitors to Brownson and the other Catholic agencies could also attend religious services held by priests. In 1917 Los Angeles's Bishop John J. Cantwell took the church's relief efforts one step further. He unified the church's disparate efforts under one umbrella, the Associated Catholic Charities. The new bureau included an Immigrant Welfare Division.[78]

The bureaucratization of Catholic charities did not meet with everyone's approval. Mary Workman believed that the new style of management would eliminate the personal contact between settlement worker and immigrant. In 1919 she refused a job in the new charities office, and in 1920 she resigned from the board of directors of the Brownson House Association. The regime change clearly reshaped how Brownson operated. In 1920, instead of a staff of sixty-plus volunteers, the settlement had three full-time employees, only two of whom (a trained nurse and a "field visitor" who worked outside of the settlement) lived at Brownson.[79]

In spite of the efforts of women like Gibson and Workman, Americanization programs had only limited success in Los Angeles. Many Mexican immigrants who had arrived in Los Angeles before World War II never became American citizens.[80] Recognizing this, and faced with a rising tide of anti-Mexican sentiment, the city abandoned most of these programs in the 1920s.[81] While the secular Americanization programs shut down, the Catholic Church and the *mutualistas* continued to provide community support and social services to Los Angeles's Mexican community. But without citizenship, Mexicans in Los Angeles could not vote, and thus few lasting economic or political advances would be made in the next two decades. Many Mexican and Mexican American women who worked outside the home would, like their counterparts in other minority groups, remain in the lowest-paid and least-desirable jobs.

Conclusion

The movement to assimilate immigrant women into the life of the city clearly indicates how rapid change had begun to reshape Los Angeles. But while the well-being of working and immigrant women remained a primary concern of city reformers, economics, not social welfare, remained in the forefront of most Angeleno minds. The long-awaited opening of the Panama Canal on August 15, 1914, had cut eight thousand miles off the journey from New York to Los Angeles, reducing the trip to a mere twenty days. The development of a manufacturing sector along the lines of San Francisco or Chicago finally seemed within reach. Garment, canning, and other industrial businesses continued to spring up across the city. The opening of the Panama Canal also heralded another change for the city, this one more troubling: the first ship to make the journey to Los Angeles via the canal, the *Missourian,* had departed New York City on the very day, August 4, 1914, that England declared war on Germany. In the years between the start of the European war and the U.S. entry into it, Los Angeles's manufacturing industries thrived under increased wartime demand. World War I also required manufacturers to increase production. Statewide production doubled between 1914 and 1919. Much of the increase occurred in existing industries, such as canneries, meatpacking, and printing, but Los Angeles also became a busy center of shipbuilding and airplane manufacturing. With the war in Europe under way, immigration to Los Angeles slackened, helping to ease the city's unemployment problem. An influx of rural Americans to the city also created a surplus of skilled labor.[82]

These trends accelerated with the entry of the United States into World War I in 1917. The war not only helped the local economy, but it also allowed some women to enter jobs that had previously been occupied only by men. A few war workers even obtained equal pay for equal work under guidelines produced by the State of California and the federal government. By and large, however, employers considered these women to be only temporary workers, and had no qualms about pushing them out of the labor force when the war ended.

But Los Angeles's female workers had not given up on organization. After 1915, buoyed by both the business recovery and wartime demand, union organizers returned to Los Angeles with a vengeance. The California State Federation of Labor appealed to the AFL for help, and the union recommended every international union send an organizer to Los Angeles.[83] In spite of the city's ever-increasing fear and distrust of trade unions and Socialists, known as the Red Scare, this new push for organization resulted in a new wave of unionization and strikes that culminated in strikes in 1919.

As the city moved into the 1920s, racial privilege continued to play an important role in what kinds of work a woman might find in Los Angeles. The association of "whiteness" with "ladyhood" became a trope that allowed only certain women entry to new jobs. The respectability of some kinds of work also became a key issue, particularly in the burgeoning film industry. By the 1920s thousands of young and not-so-young women worked in motion pictures or related industries. Possible connections between low pay and a lack of morality in Hollywood ultimately stimulated both investigations of and unionization in the film business. Working women once again actively sought to define for themselves what it meant to be both a "lady" and a "worker" in the City of Angels.

Cover of *Sunset* magazine, January 1905. Collection of *Sunset* Magazine.

Portrait of Mrs. Robert Burdette, date unknown.
Special Collections, Libraries, University of
Southern California, Doheny Memorial Library.

Maria de Lopez. Los Angeles High School yearbook,
Blue and White, Summer 1913. Los Angeles
Unified School District Archives.

Bessie Bruington Burke, *back row far left.* Burke was the first African American teacher in the Los Angeles City Schools. She is shown with the graduating class of Holmes Avenue School, June 1924. Collection of the Los Angeles Public Library, Shades of L.A.

Meeting of female employees, Bullocks Department Store, Los Angeles, ca. 1920. Bullocks Department Store Collection, The Huntington Library, San Marino, California.

The Los Angeles YWCA Clark Memorial Home. Author's collection.

Women working at sewing machines in a garment factory in Los Angeles, ca. 1928.
Special Collections, Libraries, University of Southern California,
Doheny Memorial Library.

Mexican American woman workers at the Side Way Baby Carriage Company, 1922.
Collection of the Los Angeles Public Library, Shades of L.A.

English class for Korean women at YWCA International Institute, 1922.
Collection of the Los Angeles Public Library, Shades of L.A.

7

Wartime, Protest, and New Industries

"I AM READY TO WORK"

In the midst of 1919's citywide labor unrest, Los Angeles's Friday Morning Club invited representatives from several female trade unions to address its members. The meeting's results exemplified the lack of understanding that remained between elite club women and working-class women. Frances Nacke Noel served as presiding chairperson of the evening. Lettie Howard of the Waitress' Union, Hilda Weinburg of the Laundry Workers' Union, Mrs. E. H. Wright of the Journeyman Tailors' Union, Miss Borg from the Telephone Operators' Union, and Daisy Houck all took turns speaking to club members about the challenges facing women workers and the opportunities presented by unionization. Borg told the audience how young college girls on vacation worked as scab operators, thus unknowingly undermining women striking for improved conditions in telephone exchanges. Borg urged mothers to take more interest in the cause of female strikers. The most heated moment of the evening came when Dora Hale of the newly organized Domestic Workers' Union spoke to the audience. Hale complained that employers called their stenographers by their surnames, but domestic workers continued to be known by their first name. Then, the *Los Angeles Citizen* reported, "a woman in the rear of the house challenged the right of an 'uneducated' maid to be called by her surname. Quick as a flash the chairman [Noel] challenged back: 'Is education necessary before respect is due a worker?'" Clearly, the two groups of women still had a long way to go to appreciate each other's point of view.[1]

Los Angeles had suffered through a business slump in 1914–1915 that had hit women particularly hard. The U.S. entry into World War I in 1917 encouraged more women than ever to enter the workforce. However, many Angelenos' growing fear and distrust of radical politics made it again difficult for female workers to unionize in the city. After the war, however, Los Angeles's long-standing feud between capital and labor flared once more, and female union members took to their pickets to hold on to prewar gains. In Los Angeles women workers played an active role in both the strikes and settlements that followed, often in the face of resistance from both employers and male trade unionists.[2]

Women also entered new jobs, most notably in the communications and entertainment industries, where their identity as respectable white women—what Nan Enstad has called "the cultural practices of ladyhood"—played a critical role. The trope of "lady," however, was not interchangeable with that of "woman." Prostitutes and, as we shall see, some working women did not get to claim the status of "lady." But as white skin increasingly became associated with "ladyhood," even respectable women of color were excluded from these professions on the grounds they were not, and never could be, "ladies." Ideals of proper behavior for women had their roots in transformations of gender systems in the early nineteenth century. A "lady" was expected to be the moral guardian of her husband, children, and society at large, as well as pious, obedient, and virtuous. The public visibility of striking women and women in the film industry raised questions about these women's social and sexual respectability. Unions, reformers, and social critics all focused on the need to protect such women rather than on the economic systems that exploited them. But the women themselves, worried about the day-to-day reality of making a living, did not mindlessly internalize this image of "the lady" as passive and docile.[3]

This chapter considers how World War I sparked a new wave of labor unrest. While many American cities had similar experiences immediately after the war, I argue that Los Angeles's unrest was largely the result of old problems left too long unresolved.[4] In this chapter special attention is also given to the newest sector of the regional economy, the film industry, and how it gendered work. Its female employees tried to exert at least some control over their social and economic lives by articulating their rights both as women and as workers.

Bending the Rules: Women and World War I

World War I offered some women a socially acceptable reason to step out of established divisions of labor and into new professions. Likewise, government agencies also found in the war a patriotic reason to grant female war workers equal pay for equal work. But the war did not stimulate any real change in the gender and ethnic division of work in Greater Los Angeles. Once the war ended, advances quickly evaporated.

The war forced regional employers to accept women into positions vacated by men. With the entry of the United States into the war in 1917, the *Los Angeles Times* boasted that "ten thousand girls and women in Los Angeles are preparing to take the place of an equal number of men who have joined the colors." The numbers of women enrolled in local law and professional schools also jumped. So did enrollment in telegraph-operator training courses, considered a vital war service, and in automotive-repair classes. As part of the war effort, the Young Women's Christian Association adapted its commercial school to offer courses in dietetics and Parisian-style French for those women wishing to serve with the Red Cross in France as nurses' aides. Maria de Lopez temporarily gave up her teaching job and moved to New York City. There she trained as an ambulance driver and even learned to fly a plane. She served in the ambulance corps in France and was later cited for bravery by the French government.[5]

More than patriotism drew women into the workforce. Maud McAllister of the YWCA Employment Bureau observed that many of the women coming to her were the wives of servicemen, "proud that they can work while their husbands fight, and in that way they do not become a burden on the men who are drawing small pay." Most of these women had been stenographers or office workers before marriage, she explained to the *Times,* and thus had no trouble returning to similar work now. For the first time factories in the city complained of a shortage of female labor. "We must destroy the present prejudice against the factories, and women and girls must be made to realize that the power-machine operator has a much better time than the girl in the department store," one factory owner commented. "Factory workers can earn more money than the department store workers and the factory girl does not have to spend all of her earnings for clothes." Canneries also experienced labor shortages, particularly when Southern California's farmers produced a bumper crop of peaches and tomatoes. One cannery near Los Angeles estimated that it canned more than two hundred tons of fruit a day in 1917. Recognizing that most of the crop had already been sold to the government to feed troops overseas, the Los Angeles Chamber of Commerce issued a plea for more women to work the canning lines as part of the war effort. Such pleas for women to enter industrial work had mixed success. They seem to have appealed most to some women in underpaid white-collar jobs such as teaching. Across the nation so many teachers abandoned the classroom for the factory floor that by 1918 many states faced a shortage of qualified teachers.[6]

While some women gave up more traditional white-collar work for industrial employment, others took on jobs that had previously belonged only to men. With the car now in common use in the city, women found work in the automobile and automobile-related industries. Three women, for example, found work at the Just-Crackel Rubber Company, a tire distributor: two worked as vulcanizers, and the third tended the stockroom. A local newspaper expressed awe that a woman would be strong enough to move around the heavy tires in a stockroom, but the firm's managers told reporters they were completely satisfied with their new female workers. Some jobs, however, remained closed to women even in wartime. A municipal law prevented women from working as bartenders in Los Angeles. Pacific Electric, which ran the streetcar lines, argued that the work of being a trolley conductor would be too strenuous for a woman to perform. Instead, the company hired women to clean the cars at terminals.[7]

A smaller group of women also entered the labor force to counter the use of immigrant Mexican labor. The war had triggered a widespread shortage of farm labor. In 1914 California's farmers had begun to import Mexican braceros to work on seasonal harvests. Although the growers encouraged these workers to return home during the off-season, many decided to stay. They settled in Los Angeles, forming new communities in emerging barrios. To stem the use of Mexican labor California organized a branch of the Women's Land Army. Patriotic students from Occidental College, the California State Normal School's Los Angeles branch, and the Westlake School all gave up their studies and joined. The number of Los Angeles's women volunteering for the Land Army surpassed the need for their labor. "The feminine sex have been vindicated in the eyes of the scoffer," one man observed. "They have proven the practicability of their claim that they could do a man's work better than a man when the occasion demanded it."[8]

But not all women's wartime work met with such societal approval. The war sparked a revival in the city's prostitution trade, particularly in areas near railroad stations. Centers of the sex industry included Aliso Street near Chinatown, where it operated largely free of police interference, and around the Southern Pacific Depot on Fifth Street. Prostitutes and their clients used nearby small cottages, dark alleyways, and even vacant lots. One enterprising house on Merchant Street that employed both black and white prostitutes allegedly developed a variety of signals in their windows to alert potential customers without attracting either crusading reformers or the police.[9]

Prostitutes were not the only women wandering wartime Los Angeles's streets. The Los Angeles branch of the YWCA continued to find women who worked in hotels, bakeries, cafeterias, sweet shops, telephone and telegraph exchanges, and motion picture companies spending their evenings downtown. Many of these women told investigators that they had only an hour or two off between shifts and preferred wandering the street to returning to their "dark, dingy, cold room[s]." Others explained that they got off work between eight and eleven at night and wanted to enjoy the "light and brightness on the street" before going home to sleep. "The danger is not far off for the girl who is released at 10 o'clock at night," YWCA general secretary M. Belle Jeffrey fretted. Of particular concern were women employed in the theaters, who "seemed inclined to drift. They go from one thing to another until they do not care what sort of work they do." In Los Angeles's theaters, Miss Jeffrey observed, "the older girls were generally concerned for the health and safety of the younger ones." Worse, strangers might mistake unaccompanied women for prostitutes and proposition them. To try to ameliorate these problems, in 1916 the Los Angeles YWCA opened a special club in the main YWCA building. It was open until midnight every night to serve women who either worked nights or needed somewhere to go in the evening. The YWCA also tried to publicize the dangers facing unemployed and underemployed young women in the city. "Every family that advertising brings to this city presents a possible problem for the YWCA," a YWCA secretary announced in a local paper, "especially if there is a girl in the family. . . . [I]ndustries employing women and girls have not kept pace with the incoming population and it makes a larger and more serious problem for those who must support themselves and others who may be dependant on them." The YWCA continued to warn city leadership that women who arrived without a job and a place to stay could all too easily become prey for those who would exploit them.[10]

For the duration of the war those female workers not already organized had little recourse to unions. Union membership had been on the upswing before the war. In Los Angeles overall union membership jumped from an estimated 15,000 to 17,000 members in 1915 to an estimated 19,500 to 21,500 members in 1917. But in 1917 local sentiment turned more sharply than ever against anything smacking of left-wing politics. For many Angelenos union activity during wartime seemed unpatriotic. Instead, Los Angeles's local branch of the "Four Minute Men," an organization devoted to promoting the U.S. war effort, gave speeches at public meetings and sometimes on the street. Some were translated into Armenian, Greek, Chinese, Japanese, Italian, Spanish, and Russian for the benefit of listeners. Founded in 1917, the Better America Federation, a group of businessmen, devoted itself to verbally attacking union members and other "leftists." It also organized its own speaker's bureau advocating conservative, antiunion principles. Sentiments against the Los Angeles's branch of the Industrial Workers of the World grew particularly hard.[11]

Both the U.S. government and the State of California recognized the need to keep women safe and content on the job, at least for the duration of the war. Both took an interest in the welfare of these "temporary" workers and developed programs to address women's industrial conditions and pay scales. In early 1917 the Council of National Defense established a Committee on Women in Industry to advise the council on how to safeguard the health of women war workers. Nationally known public health crusader Florence Kelley directed the new organization. Katherine Phillips Edson chaired its California branch, headquartered on South Hill Street in Los Angeles. Frances Noel, now working at Los Angeles's Municipal Employment Bureau, contributed to the war effort by serving on the Committee on Industry and Employment of the California Women's Committee of Councils on National and States Defense.[12]

To prevent a reduction in wage scales the Committee on Women in Industry mandated that women performing work customarily done by men be paid the same rates as men. Equal pay for equal work had far less to do with female workers' rights than it did with a desire to protect jobs for returning men. In June 1918 President Wilson announced an eight-point program for new service sections of the War Labor Administration. One point called for a "Woman-in-Industry Service" to help streamline the transition of women into war work. By August the service had formulated guidelines for women in war industries, including equal pay for equal work, a forty-hour week, and appropriate safety precautions. Although after the war interest in equal pay for equal work waned, the federal government did continue to pay closer attention to issues surrounding women's work in the United States.[13]

Katherine Phillips Edson agreed with other public officials that women in industry should be prepared to give up their jobs when men returned home from the war. But she drew the line at white-collar female workers. Edson argued that white-collar workers were engaged in creative work that rewarded self-expression and made them happy. She contrasted this kind of work to what she perceived to be the dreary hours spent in a factory. "Women should be in a home," she said, "men should be paid a living wage, that they may maintain their homes, and it is my belief that women would go back willingly and gladly into a home and take care of their house and babies, if they have any, if their men were able to provide for them."[14]

Edson's concerns about women taking men's jobs proved unfounded. Nationally, the United States did not suffer as severe a labor shortage as it had anticipated, and the demand for women workers remained about the same as in the prewar era. Only a few of the nation's largest manufacturers, particularly those with war contracts, employed large numbers of women.[15] World War I ultimately produced little long-term change in women's employment patterns in Los Angeles. Indeed, women increasingly feared they might lose the jobs they'd always held in the city. As antiunion sentiment solidified and the cost of living rose, women in several different segments of the local economy launched a new round of labor protest in an attempt to hold on to prewar gains.

Los Angeles After the War: Women and Labor Protest

Although newer unions, such as the Industrial Workers of the World, all but disappeared from the local labor landscape after the war, older unions in Los Angeles refused to be cowed by postwar antiradical hysteria. Indeed, even before the end of the war California labor leaders had been looking ahead to the future. At its 1918 annual convention held in San Diego, the California State Federation of Labor recognized that California's wartime industrial expansion left it in a unique position. "California and the other Pacific Coast states now lead the world in the production of tonnage. Our resources of labor and utilized resources have been increased while those of other countries have been diminished," the organization wrote in its official statement on the convention. "We have practically everything that the world needs, and we alone among all the industrial nations seems to be in a position to export in vast quantities the materials needed for reconstruction." The State Federation of Labor renewed its call for a universal eight-hour day and the organization of workers statewide.[16]

Unionization both in Los Angeles and across the country accelerated immediately after the war. Postwar prosperity was tempered by soaring prices. The rising cost of living financially strained workers across the region. Some workers became convinced that the time had come to demand better pay and improved working conditions. Indeed, the decline in union participation during the war proved temporary. Overall union membership almost doubled between 1915 and 1920 and included an influx of workers— clothing and textile workers, longshoremen, steelworkers, and so forth—

who had previously been excluded from many unions. Although the cost of living did not rise as sharply in Los Angeles as it did in the rest of the country, it did rise more than in closed-shop San Francisco. Union members seized on this fact to argue that Los Angeles's open-shop status had not saved the city from inflation, and that workers needed wage increases to pay their bills. Such demands renewed tensions between Los Angeles's employers and employees.[17]

The telephone industry experienced more labor unrest in 1919 than perhaps any other industry with a predominantly female labor force. Los Angeles's telephone workers struck initially without the international's approval, but throughout the strike these women proved themselves active and vocal members of the local labor scene. But, like many early-twentieth-century workers, these women also found themselves hemmed in by expectations about the proper behavior of Anglo-American working-class women. Telephone work emerged as one of the most sex-segregated industries in early-twentieth-century America. Ruth Milkman was among the first historians to demonstrate how sex segregation in the workforce emerges out of a complicated mix of historically specific economic, political, and social factors. This was certainly true in the telephone industry. The switch from male to female telephone operators had begun as early as the 1870s due to several factors. Employers considered men and boys temperamentally unsuited for telephone work; they dominated telegraphy instead. Men and women had initially received the same wages in the industry. But as the job became feminized, female operators' pay remained low compared to men's because women did not have access to upward mobility in their profession.[18] The highest position most women could hope for would be that of chief operator. Only a few women in the United States ever obtained the rank of supervisor. However, telephone work attracted women because society regarded it as respectable white-collar work, more akin to teaching or clerking than to factory work. Venus Green suggests that the image of womanhood crafted by the telephone industry both excluded minority women and inhibited the development of a feminist working-class consciousness among Anglo-American women. She argues that this allowed the Bell system, for example, to control their workers for generations.[19]

Telephone work's exclusivity reinforced its desirability. Like retail work and teaching, not just any woman could obtain work in the Southern California telephone exchange. She had to be single and young (usually between eighteen and twenty-five years old) and demonstrate "proper," or "ladylike,"

Wartime, Protest, and New Industries

behavior. An applicant needed to have a grammar school education (and ideally some high school as well), and, above all, she had to be white. Women also had to pass a strict physical examination that declared them fit for the nervous strain of telephone work, and the height of the switchboard generally ruled out any woman under five feet tall. In addition to the virtual exclusion of minority women from telephone exchanges, large numbers of native English speakers and the fashionable dress of operators also helped to reinforce the job's relatively high status in women's minds.[20]

Los Angeles's telephone companies believed they practiced benevolent paternalism, with the company providing the kind of guidance and supervision a parent gave a child, or a teacher gave a student. Employers expected "ladylike" behavior and demeanor from all potential employees, and reinforced these expectations whenever and wherever possible. The Pacific Telephone Company, the West Coast subsidiary of AT&T, went so far as to compare the "dainty rest room" in its Los Angeles branch to "the reading or sewing room of Miss ——'s private school for girls." The Southern California Telephone Company offered a Traffic School to train operators. The woman who supervised this school, Miss Dickey, reported that "especial attention is directed to the culture and preservation of the voice." Clearly, not only did an operator need to *be* a white lady, but she needed to *sound* like a white lady as well. The Southern California Telephone Company also offered a Good Welfare Department, a sickroom, and a cafeteria, and invited the telephone operators' mothers to visit on Mother's Day. The company wanted their employees' mothers to see and approve of their daughters' workplace.[21]

Telephone companies' paternalism also applied to how they disciplined their female workforce. Rather than firing a girl outright for poor performance, as other businesses would do, the Southern California Telephone Company used a variety of tactics to "punish" her. The company occasionally forced an operator to work from 1:00 PM to 10:00 PM instead of the regular hours of 6:00 AM to 7:30 PM. Southern California also made operators work an evening shift at the daily rate (fifteen cents less an hour) as a form of punishment. By the 1910s the entire AT&T system employed a complex system of codified rewards and punishments to control their workforce.[22]

Women who worked the switchboards in Los Angeles's telephone exchanges lacked the protection of a union. At the Sunset Telephone Company, for example, switchboard operators made only twenty-five dollars a month. Although the company claimed to pay overtime, it never did, and it also charged its operators for lost keys and broken telephone horns. The Sunset even held back seven dollars of each woman's first month's wages to prevent her from quitting. Each operator worked under strict supervision: she had to make up the time spent on each visit to the restroom before she could go home. As Elizabeth Banks had noticed in the retail trades, company owners preferred to hire girls who lived at home with their families so wages could remain low. In 1909 the *Los Angeles Citizen* observed that while operators in San Francisco had already unionized and obtained a "living wage," operators in Los Angeles remained at the mercy of employers and benevolent organizations. In fact, the *Citizen* pointed out that one telephone company, the Home, was right across the street from the Young Women's Christian Association's downtown headquarters. "A mint of money was subscribed for this structure by the rich and charitable people of Los Angeles—and scores of these very same subscribers are drawing dividends from the stock of the Home Telephone Company which is paying starvation wages to its girl employees," the paper complained. Job Harriman, as part of his mayoral campaign in 1911, had made the same point in a speech, arguing that it was a blatant injustice for the Home Telephone Company, worth more than ten million dollars in stocks and bonds, to pay its workers so poorly. Unfortunately, the International Brotherhood of Electrical Workers (IBEW), the American Federation of Labor international under whose auspices telephone work fell, initially took little interest in organizing female telephone operators.[23]

World War I provided a boon to the unionization of telephone workers. The vital role played by the telephone on the home front created a new sense of power in the industry. The rapid rise in the cost of living created by the outbreak of war in Europe, however, created strife between employees demanding wage increases and employers determined to maintain prewar salaries. Worse, labor relations in the telephone industry suffered during the government's brief takeover of the telephone and telegraph system between August 1918 and July 1919. During this period Postmaster General Albert Burleson, who had been placed in charge of this temporary wartime measure, practiced militant antiunionism and steadfastly refused to consider any wage increases. Even the conservative *Los Angeles Times* argued that Burleson's takeover had been a disaster for everyone concerned. Burleson's administration had raised rates for the public, hired inefficient and inexperienced operators, and antagonized a workforce that hitherto had seemed relatively content. "A playful kitten never tangled a skein of wool more effectually than our government controllers have raveled up this network of wires," it editorialized. The *Times* noted that the mess Burleson had made of the wire system held special importance in Los Angeles. Many Angelenos were already flirting with the idea of municipal ownership of utilities, a move the

Times vigorously opposed. Burleson's intransigence with labor, in particular, precipitated a wave of telephone strikes across the United States in 1919.[24]

That year the IBEW threatened a general strike if Burleson refused to meet its demand for an end to discrimination against union members in the telephone industry. Burleson hastily issued an order guaranteeing telephone workers the right to organize, but relations between the two groups did not improve. In several cities across the nation the telephone and telegraph operators voted to strike as soon as the IBEW gave the order. On June 10, the day before the strike was to take effect, Congress hastily repealed the law authorizing federal control over telephone, telegraph, cable, and radio lines, with private ownership to resume in June 1920.[25]

Somewhat mollified, the IBEW canceled the general strike order. But many locals still wanted to strike. On the Pacific Coast the strike began in San Diego when male telephone linemen rebelled against the IBEW and struck anyway. Female operators joined them by walking out of the exchanges. Union leaders urged the strikers to postpone action until the operators could be better organized, but as the strike continued to spread, the union had no choice but to give it their grudging support. Venus Green suggests that operators frequently yielded leadership to their male allies, who often changed operators' demands to conform to male craft-union ideology. This does not appear to have been the case in Los Angeles. Telephone Operators' Union no. 52A, part of the IBEW, struck when the Southern California Telephone Company refused members' demands for union recognition and a wage increase. Los Angeles experienced its first "real, genuine, A1, 18-karat, honest-to-goodness strike" as several hundred telephone girls employed across the city and county walked off the job. Estimates of the numbers of strikers in Los Angeles vary. Union representatives argued that 95 percent of operators left their jobs to strike, while the Southern California Telephone Company argued that most workers remained loyal and stayed on the job. The IBEW gave the official number of strikers in Los Angeles as twelve hundred, including both linemen and operators. With the strike under way, the Southern California Telephone Company quickly converted its downtown offices into an improvised hotel to keep those women still at work from having to cross picket lines. It advertised for new workers with or without experience to staff vacant switchboards and hired former employees who had left the workforce upon marriage. The *Times* called such workers "the Sisterhood of the Golden Circle," a pithy reference to these women's wedding bands. However, the company evidently recognized the importance of maintaining the connection between racial exclusion and the ladyhood of its operators. It vehemently denied charges that it had hired African American women as strikebreakers. The strike hit some cities harder than others. It had little reported impact on service in Santa Monica or Pasadena, for example, but in Long Beach only two operators remained on the job, leaving the city without local telephone service. Customers could not get any connection at all to Glendale, San Bernardino, or Calexico. As the strike spread up and down the Pacific Coast, union leaders estimated that five thousand men and seven thousand women in cities such as San Francisco, Portland, Seattle, and Los Angeles had left their jobs for the picket lines.[26]

Los Angeles's operators employed a variety of tactics to publicize their plight and win the strike, all of which increased their public visibility. These women evidently saw no contradiction between their identity as "white ladies" and their identity as workers with legitimate grievances. The operators started by picketing local telephone exchanges. Picketing served two functions: it made it difficult for scabs to take the strikers' jobs, and it drew public attention to the women's demands. Picketing women often faced accusations or insinuations that they were prostitutes. Some women repeatedly called telephone exchanges to convince strikebreakers to join the union; others used public phones to place fake long-distance calls and thus tie up the city's telephone service. This practice became such a nuisance that the company unplugged all the city's pay phones during the strike. Holed up in the Southern California Telephone Company offices, women still on the job expressed hopes the strike would last another six months because the company now gave them not only free room and board but as much candy and ice cream as they could eat. It may well have been the free room and board, and not loyalty to the company, that kept some women at work. This possibility, however, never seems to have occurred to either company officials or strike opponents. On June 18 the Los Angeles City Council adopted a resolution asking for the striking workers to meet with telephone company representatives. The Southern California Telephone Company refused, arguing that the strike was a national issue, directed at Burleson, and therefore could not be addressed at the local level. A June 20 meeting held in San Francisco between representatives of all the striking Pacific Coast unions and their employers failed to reach a settlement. In Southern California the Union Home Telephone and Telegraph, hearing that Burleson remained in negotiations with the IBEW, issued a statement that strikers had twenty-four hours to return to work or they would lose their jobs entirely. Fifty-eight women refused and remained on strike. Union Home claimed that they had issued the ultimatum based on a direct order from Burleson himself, but they were the only telephone company in Southern California to make this claim.[27]

While the city's telephone operators attempted to assert their rights as workers to strike, the popular press more often focused on the appropriateness of these women's public behavior. Nan Enstad demonstrates that nineteenth- and early-twentieth-century newspaper editors often seized on negative stories about women strikers because they helped sell papers. The *Los Angeles Times* took particular interest in reporting how the strikers acted, pointing out how the strike appeared to encourage women to abandon "lady-like" behavior. Once again the *Times* accused unions of manipulating naive women into striking. Criticizing a "jazz time" union meeting that drew three to four hundred telephone operators to Symphony Hall, the newspaper wrote that "a lot of girls who stood at the door complaining that they didn't get enough money to dress themselves decently went in and signed applications, not realizing that, once in the union, considerable of their weekly pay will go hereafter to support loud-mouthed and high salaried organizers." Playing on the idea of the operators' being too young and naive to understand the implications of what they were doing, the *Times* noted that "they were a good-looking bunch of girls, apparently without a leader. . . . [F]rom time to time they hopped up upon the stage, hit the old grand piano a knockout wallop, and chorused, 'Come on, Puppah,' and 'Honey, Honey, Hold Me Tight.'" The paper also argued that the striking women would spend the proposed pay increase only on silk hosiery and facial massages.[28] Such articles clearly hoped to stem public support for the strikers by suggesting that they did not have legitimate grievances against their employers.

To Los Angeles's political leadership the female strikers presented a public nuisance, and the city council determined to keep the women under control. This was not the case elsewhere: in closed-shop Oakland and Berkeley society ladies even brought the picketers lunches and entertained them with automobile rides. Lacking such open community support, the women striking against Southern California Telephone wanted to hold a parade in downtown Los Angeles to show their unity to the cause. But the police chief, under pressure from the city council, denied the women a parade permit. The Southern California Telephone Company then went to court and obtained a restraining order against both Local 52A and Local 370 to prevent striking workers from contacting those still on the job. The striking operators drafted an open letter addressed to "the citizenship especially the women of Los Angeles," arguing:

If [the] modern conception of democracy is worth anything it is worthy of every day practice. We have hoped until now that the telephone company would make the first step and meet all parties in public conference. . . . [W]e seek nothing but fair play. We are willing at all times that you should scrutinize our every move. . . . We further direct your attention to the ultra autocratic procedure against working girls. A procedure protecting solely the interest of employers and utterly ignoring the rights of employees. Following a European war which called forth the utmost strength of this nation to establish world democracy, it ill becomes any judge to assume the role of autocrat.[29]

But while forbidden from marching in a parade, the strikers did receive help from other quarters. The California State Federation of Churches publicly offered the strikers its support. Unions of theater and stage employees as well as those of street-railway workers donated money. Local merchants supplied food for a cafeteria established at the Labor Temple to feed striking workers. The Motion Picture Players Union gave a dance to benefit the telephone girls. The lineman's Local 370 even offered to lower their wage demand from $6.40 to $6.00 a day and return to work if the telephone companies met the women's demands. Employers refused this compromise.[30]

On June 25 representatives of the strikers in California and Nevada broke off negotiations and left the future of the strike in the hands of a general strike committee. Over the next six weeks the strike spread to some 90 percent of the operators on the Pacific Coast and in Nevada before the strike committee reached a settlement. The settlement provided for a retroactive wage increase for both male and female telephone employees. The IBEW urged the women to accept the compromise, and by July 23 all the Southern California strikers were back at work.[31]

Riding the wave of the 1919 successes the Telephone Operator's Department of the IBEW emerged with a peak membership of some 18,000 operators across the United States. Leah Dobkin served as the key organizer in Los Angeles's new Telephone Operators' Union. Dobkin had been born in Russia and was fluent in both Yiddish and English. After working in a department store Dobkin had become a telephone operator. One of the few women to work her way up on the telephone exchange, Dobkin became a supervisor and then joined the Plant Department. Of an estimated 1,650 telephone girls in Los Angeles, the Young Women's Christian Association chose to send her to its 1919 conference on industrial relations because she was a "splendid 'soap-box' orator . . . known to hold her own against a crowd of men and come out with flying colors." In 1921 Katherine Phillips Edson, who personally considered the strike a failure, nonetheless helped raised funds so Dobkin could attend the Bryn Mawr summer school on industrial relations. In a fund-raising letter to fellow Progressive John Randolph Haynes, Edson stressed that the school was "not a radical movement and does not mean leadership for trade unionism only, but general leadership among working girls. You know how seriously we need it in Los Angeles."[32]

Operators and employers did not reach any long-term settlement about union status following the strike. This left union-member operators vulnerable to discrimination once the strike ended. Nor did the strikers make any demands that would have fundamentally changed the organization of telephone work or its pace. Green again blames male trade unionists for pushing issues of pay over those of control over the pace of work. There is no evidence in the primary sources from the Los Angeles strike to suggest that local telephone operators ever demanded or even recognized the need for such control. Their protests, instead, revolved around wages and the right to organize. One prominent organizer reckoned that the strike had served only to antagonize the telephone companies. In the early 1920s Los Angeles's telephone companies launched a counteroffensive (similar to that used by department stores twenty years before): they organized company unions. These unions, restricted to the employees of a particular company or exchange, promised to represent them in dealings with employers. These management-controlled company unions refused to affiliate with larger outside trade unions. In effect, employees chose job security and seniority rights over unionization. International unions, like Local 52A, shrank in the face of such opposition. In 1920 Pacific Bell ordered that all of its employees join its company union. When male members of IBEW locals struck up and down the Pacific Coast (including Los Angeles) later that year, the strike drew far less support than anticipated. The strike ended in failure after two weeks. Several more strikes followed, centered in New England, but the shift to company unions signaled the end of IBEW power in the telephone industry.[33]

Workers in Los Angeles's garment industry had long been keen on organization, and they continued to pursue unionization during the war. Local 52 of the International Ladies' Garment Workers struck for two weeks in 1915, with mixed results, and again in 1917. Clearly, Local 52 did not let the war interfere with its union's activities. In 1917 employees at thirteen shops walked out. After three days the union compromised on a 7.5 percent wage increase but nothing else. ILGWU organizers then negotiated a new wage agreement between employees and employers. When this agreement expired in June

1919 and employers refused to meet union demands, workers struck again. In fact, the strike came so quickly that Local 52 failed to secure the approval of the ILGWU's General Executive Board in New York, which sharply rebuked the Los Angeles local for acting so hastily. ILGWU president Benjamin Schlesinger even urged the strikers to go back to work and accept any terms the employers would offer. Local 52 refused to do so. The strike lasted for five weeks and produced a minimum weekly wage for women of eighteen to forty-two dollars, depending on skill, and a forty-four-hour week.[34]

Local 81 of the Journeyman Tailors' Union tried to renegotiate its agreement with employers in 1919 to include pay increases, limitations on hours, and paid holidays. However, the proposed pay increases still favored skilled men over women in the trade. The union demanded forty-four dollars a week for tailors, pressers, and machine operators and thirty-nine dollars a week for helpers and trimmers, but just twenty-nine dollars a week for women "assistants." Recognizing that Los Angeles had a shortage of skilled tailors, when employers refused to give in by September the tailors walked out. The *Los Angeles Citizen* printed a special edition of its newspaper for striking workers to sell. But one employer, the venerable Harris and Frank on South Spring Street, objected to the sales and called the police. The police arrested two men and one woman for picketing. The *Citizen* then suggested that Harris and Frank had appealed directed to the Merchants and Manufacturers Association, and that the M&M had forced the police to act. Employers retaliated against the unions by forming the Los Angeles Merchant Tailor's Exchange and locking out the strikers, throwing several hundred tailors out of work. The strike soon spread up and down the Pacific Coast, but businesses dependent on custom tailoring reopened in November with scab labor. Given the choice between returning to work in open shops or losing their jobs completely, the tailors returned to work without achieving their goals.[35]

With signed agreements with most employers ensuring regular wage increases already in place, United Garment Workers Local 125 fared better than the city's other two garment unions. The local participated in a few small strikes directed at specific employers between 1915 and 1919. But Local 125 focused most of its attention on the needs of members. Recognizing that many foreign-born women belonged to the local, it arranged to offer citizenship classes at the Labor Temple. Under pressure from Local 125, the Los Angeles Board of Education established a regular public night school at the Labor Temple to prepare union members for citizenship examinations.[36]

Hoping to end the strikes plaguing the city, in June 1919 Cap. Charles T. Connell, a "federal conciliator," held meetings with striking members of the

United Garment Workers' Union, the Tailors' Union, and the Retail Shoe Men's Association. Although he may have facilitated better communication between employer and employee, none of these meetings produced an immediate settlement. In fact, Connell's visit did not slow strike activity in the city at all. Los Angeles's bakers struck that same month, this time in pursuit of a wage increase. In September the city's cigar makers won a one-day strike against their employers. In 1919 male and female orange pickers, on strike against unsanitary conditions and low pay, met at the Labor Temple to discuss the creation of a new union chartered by the AFL. The union was never created.[37]

Los Angeles's teachers also showed a revived interest in organization. Teachers belonged to one of three independent organizations—the High School Teachers' Association, the City Teachers' Club, or the Principal's Association. But in 1918 a county tax-rate cut threatened to lower salaries of teachers across the board, and the Los Angeles Central Labor Council assembled a committee to help. Under the combined pressure of this committee and the superintendent of schools, the Los Angeles Board of Education granted teachers a flat increase of three hundred dollars a year. "This increase is fifteen percent below the average increase in the cost of living during the last four years, and is not as great as the wage increases given to skilled workers," a coalition of Los Angeles teachers' organizations wrote in the *Citizen*. "However, the teachers feel that their salary raise is based on a just understanding of their needs and they deeply appreciate the support given them by the citizens of this community." Flushed with victory, the Central Labor Council then determined to help create a local of the American Federation of Teachers. But with pay raise in hand, many teachers and principals now went on record as firmly opposed to the new union, Local 77 of the AFT. Angry at the sudden defection, city labor leaders threatened to reject the next school bond issue. In December 1919 the Board of Education announced that it banned all teachers from joining outside unions, and that any who had joined Local 77 had to give up membership. Los Angeles's teachers had no choice but to accept the board's decision. The city's High School Teachers' Association wrote a poignant open letter to the school board that circulated in the city's labor community: "We accept these contracts, not because we think the compensation adequate, but rather with a deep feeling of injustice. Unwilling to forsake the children whose interests we have championed, or to break with the public, whom we know to be with us, we acknowledge that for the moment you hold the key to the situation, and that neither we nor the public can control your immediate action. We are nevertheless confidant that having faithfully held to the obligations of our profession, we shall eventually secure a belated injustice."[38]

Domestic workers, who had been excluded from the protection of the eight-hour law and most Industrial Welfare Commission orders, also pursued better conditions in 1919. That year a bill to establish a ten-hour day for domestic workers passed in both houses of the California legislature, only to be vetoed by Governor Stephens. In response, domestics in Los Angeles established the Domestic Workers' Union with Frances Nacke Noel as president. "If domestic workers are worthy of hiring because their labor is needed," one flyer argued, "then they are also worthy of the legal protection accorded to other workers." Noel herself told one meeting that "the comforts of many homes, especially the households of business women who cannot look after their home and family affairs, depends on the hired ingenuity of domestic service." The union took the formal name of the Association for the Improvement of Domestic Service and resolved to continue to work for the ten-hour day and the extension of California's workmen's compensation laws to cover domestic workers injured on the job. In 1920 a union of domestic workers in Los Angeles affiliated with the American Federation of Labor, one of only ten unions of domestic workers nationally to do so.[39]

As the case of domestic workers illustrates, California's protective legislation still did not benefit all employed women in the state. In 1919 the Industrial Welfare Commission estimated that the minimum-wage law covered only some 191,429 of the 286,647 working women in California because many worked in supervisory or professional positions that the law did not cover. The IWC also said that it would be impossible to enforce minimum-wage laws among agricultural and domestic workers. Applying the law, the IWC argued, would be "practicable" for only 54.9 percent of female workers, those "most commonly thought of when women wage earners are discussed—the women in stores, offices, factories, and hotels and restaurants." They also noted that the federal census of 1920 had undercounted the number of women employed in California because it had been taken in January during the slack season for the canning industry. The IWC estimated the cannery workers should have added another 25,000 female workers to the state totals.[40]

But of all the new professions a woman might choose, none stirred more controversy in the years before and after World War I than working in motion pictures. Women in Hollywood, whether behind or in front of the camera, stimulated debate not only about their rights as workers but also about the very respectability of the industry itself.

Hollywood: New Opportunities in the Film Industry

Greater Los Angeles held distinct advantages for filmmaking. The climate allowed for year-round production, and the dazzling array of scenery available within one hundred miles of Los Angeles made location shoots much easier, particularly for popular westerns. Los Angeles's open-shop orientation also seemed to promise a steady supply of cheap labor. Col. William Selig, a Chicago movie producer, was the first to move his production facilities to Hollywood; in short order D. W. Griffith's company, Biograph, and the Nestor Film Company followed.[41]

With studios now settling permanently in the city, the budding film industry became a major employer. By the beginning of World War I some two hundred actors and actresses worked in the area, making films that cost anywhere from five hundred to three thousand dollars, sometimes took a whole week to shoot, and could be seen in fourteen minutes. The motion picture industry proved relatively immune to business fluctuations, and thus an excellent source of income for the area. David Horsely, founder of the Universal Picture Company, touted the new industry in a local paper. Horsely estimated that the film industry brought more than five million dollars into California each year and, unlike oil or mining, took nothing out of it. The tremendous success of *The Birth of a Nation,* which premiered at Clune's Auditorium in Los Angeles in February 1915, convinced many that there might be a financially promising future for the film industry in Los Angeles.[42]

But not everyone in Los Angeles welcomed this new business. Many Angelenos feared the potentially disruptive impact of the film industry on the community. To help limit such an impact residents in 1919 forced the City of Los Angeles to enact zoning ordinances restricting studios to seven prescribed areas. Hollywood's residents also complained repeatedly about the "circus" atmosphere of the film shoot disrupting daily life. Others tried to be philosophical about the film industry. "Locally, the motion picture people may be something of a pest, but their value to the community as national and international advertisers is inestimable," the *Los Angeles Times* reasoned.[43]

Working women formed an integral part of this new industry from its very beginning. As early as 1910 women from all over the country descended on Hollywood in the hopes of finding fame and fortune. Known as "movie-struck girls," such women had attended films at their hometown cinemas, read the movie magazines, and now hoped to break into the industry themselves. There seems to have been no equivalent "movie-struck boy," but as Wendy Holliday points out, male migration for opportunity had long been considered perfectly normal. The fact that some actresses, among them Mary Pickford, the Gish sisters, and Marion Cooper, had successfully made the transition from extra to star gave these new arrivals hope.[44] The fluidity of early Hollywood also created new opportunities for women behind the camera. The film industry itself had not yet established any definition of "male" versus "female" work. Moreover, occupations such as screenwriting, editing, and directing seemed to many Americans simply new forms of white-collar work that had long been socially acceptable work for women. The one exception was financing pictures: this has been an almost exclusively male job for most of industry history. During World War I, in particular, women in the entertainment industry took up jobs behind the camera as directors, shifters, and carpenters. "We can't all go to the front as Red Cross nurses any more than all the men can go, but the girls at home should relieve the men of whatever work they can," actress Olga Grey of Triangle Studios reported. "I am ready to work a camera any time I am called, and, while I hate to brag, I know that I can do as well as some of the cameramen on the lot." The same egalitarian spirit did not apply to race. Opportunities both in front of and behind the camera in major studies were open only to whites.[45]

By 1919 twenty-nine studios in and around Los Angeles made 95 percent of the films shown in the United States. With no way to count the numbers of people employed by the industry, the YWCA estimated the number at some six thousand people, with somewhere between two and three thousand of those being girls and women. Seasonality remained the greatest problem in the industry. The "rainy" season between December and March every year led to periods of slack employment. The film industry generally adhered to the eight-hour law for women, but often worked them overtime in order to meet rigid shooting schedules.[46]

Investigation and Reform in the Film Industry

By 1919 the film industry was increasingly segregated by gender, with women occupying many of the lowest-paid positions with the least chances for upward mobility. The number of women working in positions of power behind the scenes (as directors, writers, and so on) waned in the 1920s. As these jobs became more respectable and better paid, men wanted them. "Some of the early pioneers, particularly writers such as Frances Marion, Anita Loos, and Jeanie Macpherson and the editors Margaret Booth, Blanche Sewall, and Anna Bauchens continued to be in demand," scholar of early Hollywood Cari Beauchamp explains, "but by 1930, they were the exception and no longer the rule."[47] With so many women in poorly paid, low-status jobs, social reformers worried about possible connections between low pay and a lack of morality in Hollywood. This stimulated both investigations of and unionization in the film business.

Women in Hollywood who worked behind the scenes did so now in jobs usually considered secondary to those held by men. Men worked as directors and screenwriters, for example, while women often read "scenarios," rejecting stories too outlandish to be filmed. These women often started out as typists and worked their way up. Pay in the scenario department averaged from twelve to twenty dollars a week. Among the most skilled jobs occupied by women in the film industry were continuity writers, expert film cutters, and some film editors. Although steady work, these jobs paid only thirty to forty dollars a week, low considering the responsibility and skill they entailed. Unskilled girls worked in film laboratories splicing and polishing film for ten dollars a week. Like their counterparts elsewhere in the United States, large numbers of women also worked in studio dressmaking and sewing jobs. In Hollywood they worked for wardrobe departments rather than factories, but the pay remained equally low: about twelve to fifteen dollars a week for an experienced seamstress. Women in these jobs remained vulnerable to sudden layoffs, as studios often sacked them during slack periods to save money. Studios also employed women in a variety of newer jobs. The YWCA found a handful of women working as casting agents for studios, interior decorators, and research experts for wardrobe departments and art directors. Women in these enviable positions could usually name their own salaries.[48]

Most men and women employed in Hollywood worked as actors and actresses, and it was here social agencies focused most of their attention. The top tier of actors and actresses, the stars, consisted of perhaps only two hundred people. An actress in the next tier, playing supporting roles, could make anywhere from a hundred and fifty to two hundred dollars a week per picture. Following in both prestige and pay, the "character" actresses generally played the same part in different pictures. Inexperienced "characters" could earn thirty to forty dollars a week, with experienced actors making perhaps ten dollars more a week. At the very bottom of the acting hierarchy was an enormous pool of floating "extras." Pay ranged from three dollars a day for appearing in a crowd scene to seven and a half dollars for a "bit" role in a film, but there was never any guarantee of a day's work. Stars and minor leads could be hired directly by a director or through a high-class employment agency, but either the studio or an employment bureau hired the extras. Casting directors were well known for often-inexplicable discrimination, and for promising work that never came.[49]

In 1918 motion picture producers established the Motion Picture Producers' Service Bureau. The bureau deducted a percentage from the salaries of players and from individual studio returns based on the number of people employed. Most in the community viewed this as merely an attempt by producers to reduce salaries, and steered clear of it. The bureau paid extras with vouchers instead of cash. The vouchers could be cashed only in-house, and the bureau took seven cents from every paycheck an extra received as a "fee." Its location downtown, instead of near the studios, made many extras complain about the travel time required to collect their pay. Nor was it particularly good at finding registrants work. A *Times* investigation found that ten thousand hopeful extras had registered with the bureau but that there was usually only work for six hundred.[50]

The "limousine" extra, the married woman who dabbled in extra work, hoping to be discovered, compounded this problem. Full-time extras bitterly resented such women as a hindrance to their ability to make a living. Expected by the studios to provide their own wardrobe and makeup, female extras often found themselves using their earnings for gowns and shoes rather than food and rent. Studios did not provide any form of health care or workers' compensation for those injured on the job. These injuries ran the gamut from broken bones to pneumonia contracted while sitting in a drafty studio all day in an evening gown to "kleigitis," a painful inflammation of the eyes caused by working in front of the powerful kleig lights used in close-up shots. Even the usually proemployer *Los Angeles Times* conceded that many of the extras' complaints were valid. The female extra "is the product of the industry. Sometimes she rises to stardom after a long struggle. But more often not," one article concluded. "Usually the word is passed about that 'so and so is out.' The renaissance of an 'out' extra girl is not a matter of record. When she's 'out' she's 'out' and the studios know her no more." Nonetheless, the motion picture industry was proud to point out that it was one of the few industries of the era truly practicing "equal pay for equal work," because male and female extras were paid the same.[51]

Extra work also suffered from a poor reputation outside of the entertainment industry. For many Angelenos it seemed to be merely another name for prostitution. Such beliefs were not entirely unfounded: the seasonal nature of film work required extras and low-paid actresses to scramble to make ends meet, working as waitresses, secretaries, and unskilled nurses. A few extras undoubtedly succumbed to the temptation of allowing a man to support them in return for sexual favors. But what investigators perceived as the overall lax morals of picture girls concerned them more than the fall of a few individuals. They pointed out that these girls tended to be either extremely young and of limited education (making them vulnerable to exploitation) or older women already hardened by life in the theater (whose morals were presumably lax to begin with and who exerted a bad influence on the younger girls). Immorality came not from acting per se, reformers argued, but from the men who hung around studios and film crews.

In reality, what reformers perceived as immoral behavior was more likely simply a recognition by aspiring actresses of what it took to get ahead in the business. In the tightly knit Hollywood community gossip spread quickly, and a girl with the reputation of being too conservative or unapproachable could materially hurt her chances to succeed. In its 1919 investigation even the YWCA softened its conclusions somewhat, reporting that "the industry is so young and changes have been so frequent that probably all its weaknesses are not due to an attempt to exploit so much as thoughtlessness."[52]

If finding work in the film business could be difficult for white women, it proved well nigh impossible for minority women. Studios generally preferred to use Anglos made up as African Americans, Asians, or Native Americans to using minority actors and actresses themselves. There were, however, a few notable exceptions in the teen and twenties. African American actress Madame Sul-te-Wan had cut her teeth on the black vaudeville circuit in the eastern United States before moving to Hollywood. She had difficulty finding work, finally accepting a role in *The Clansman*. When Los Angeles's black population protested the finished film, the studio temporarily fired Madame Sul-te-Wan, blaming her for provoking the protests. She eventually got her job back and made films for the next two decades, but never in a leading role. Mexican actresses Dolores Del Rio and Lupe Velez, who began their careers in 1925 and 1927, respectively, had more success. Alicia Rodríquez-Estrada notes that old stereotypes of "'good' Spanish and 'bad' Mexican" women were simply transferred onto the screen. Del Rio, who was from an upper-class Mexican family and had very light skin, was cast in a variety of roles, but Velez was often typecast as a hypersexual "hot tamale." Like Del Rio and Velez, Japanese-born Tsuru Aoki also found some success in films, but only by carefully controlling her public image. Aoki was a curious blend of modernity and tradition. In publicity stills she often dressed in kimonos. But newspaper and magazine articles emphasized the equality within her marriage to actor Sessue Hayakawa. The two raced about Hollywood in roadsters and even taught jujitsu to members of the Los Angeles Police Department.[53]

At a time when Anglos were regularly cast in Asian roles, Aoki's success in finding work suggests that audiences responded positively to her carefully crafted image.

While they paid little attention to racial discrimination, organizations like the YWCA worried about the gender and relative youth of Hollywood's new workforce. In addition to low pay, reformers fretted about how the residential patterns and leisure time of young women in Hollywood might promote immoral behavior. The women, however, seem to have had very clear ideas of where they wanted to live and how they liked to spend their time. What motion-picture girls considered to be a good time often did not meet with middle-class Angelenos' approval, but they do not seem to have cared. One example of this was the Dug-Out Club. One of the most popular locations for entertainment in post–World War I Hollywood, the club had started as a recreational club for soldiers and sailors during the war. The Dug-Out allowed men who could not afford other accommodations to sleep on the floor. Young women enjoyed the dances held there every week; a different actress greeted guests at the door each time. While the YWCA report recognized that the Dug-Out seemed to fill a need, it worried about the club's being used as a place for prostitutes to find clients. The YWCA was not able to have the club closed, and actresses continued to happily patronize it for several more years.[54]

Outside of clubs where they could mix freely with men and with each other, many of these young women suffered from social isolation. The segregated nature of Hollywood society, where "picture people are not able to and do not like to mix with Hollywood residents," contributed to this problem. Neither Hollywood nor Los Angeles provided many recreational outlets for picture girls. Like the women employed in other parts of the city, during their off hours the picture girls tended to wander the streets of Hollywood or go downtown in search of amusement. By 1919 downtown Los Angeles featured several large dance halls (evidently unsupervised), two live theaters featuring regular vaudeville performances, and six "first-class" motion picture palaces where people waited in line for up to an hour to catch the latest flick.[55]

Finding safe, affordable housing also posed a challenge for an aspiring actress. Most of the women working for studios lived in Hollywood, while men favored the cheap hotels downtown. An apartment in Hollywood cost from eighteen to twenty-five dollars a month, but the YWCA calculated that if two girls shared an apartment and cooked their own breakfast and dinner it would be possible to make ends meet. However, a housing shortage brought on by the large numbers of people arriving in Hollywood forced some women to find accommodations downtown. Like their male counter-parts, these women found temporary housing in hotels. Interestingly, they avoided the YWCA boardinghouses, recognizing that "the usual restrictions will interfere with their late working hours and [they] are sceptical [sic] as to the reception they might have."[56]

Responding to the particular needs of women employed in this grow-ing industry, in 1916 the YWCA helped organize the Studio Club on San Car-los Street as a residence for women. The Studio Club had begun as a social club for young women in the Hollywood branch of the city library. The head librarian, Miss Jones, organized some twenty-eight women for gymnasium classes, which she held in the library's basement. The club, one newspaper lauded, "means a personal interest and a good guiding influence in the lives of the hundreds of girls who are engaged in the motion picture industry." When membership grew to 150, the club rented a hall and later that year opened its own boardinghouse.[57] The colonial house set on an acre of land provided residents with the services of a full-time cook and housekeeper. The club moved into what had been the Twist home at 6129 Carlos Avenue in the heart of Hollywood.[58] Here it housed single girls, provided a meeting place for dramatic classes, and held dances and Sunday-night teas. Some 200 actresses from nearby studios belonged to the club, including the number-one female box-office draw of the era, Mary Pickford. The Community Chest's Assistance League also got creative when providing aid to extras. To assist those extras who had children, it funded and operated a day nursery directly across the street from Fox Studios.[59]

The Extra and Actor's Equity

While some women took advantage of organizations like the Studio Club, they also appear to have recognized that private charities could not address the underlying issue of low pay and exploitation in the industry. In 1918 film employees organized the Motion Picture Players Union no. 16377. The union affiliated with the American Federation of Labor and met twice a month to pursue four stated goals: reducing the oversupply of workers, enforcing pay-ment, encouraging the reporting of violations of the eight-hour law, and standardizing the daily minimum rates for extras. The Motion Picture Play-ers welcomed women into the union, but it remained at best unreceptive to the persistent discrimination against and needs of minorities in Hollywood. Like other unions in Los Angeles, representatives of the Motion Picture Play-ers carefully explained to employers and the public that they had no inten-tion of calling a strike. However, if necessary they threatened to advertise the names of unfair producers across the country, appealing to other union members and to movie audiences for sympathy. Hollywood's elite, however, belonged not to the Motion Picture Players Union but to the Actor's Equity League. Stage actors had formed Actor's Equity in New York City in 1913, and the Los Angeles branch appeared sometime around 1915.[60] In 1919, the same year it affiliated with the American Federation of Labor, Equity struck against the powerful Producing Managers' Association, which had determined to crush the fledgling union. Before the creation of Actor's Equity the Producing Managers' Association had had total control of wage scales as well as the often arbitrary hiring and firing of actors.[61]

The strike centered on the live theaters of New York, but many Hollywood film managers also reluctantly supported their East Coast counterparts and refused to recognize Actor's Equity. By August, however, representatives of the National Association of the Motion Picture Industry (NAMPI), embarrassed by the negative publicity surrounding the strike, quietly notified the union that it intended to remain neutral and would not bar any striking actor from employment. The union then agreed to direct future activity against individual theaters but not NAMPI. Actor's Equity apparently feared live-theater owners might switch to showing films rather than hire striking actors: these were the theaters Equity targeted with their pickets. Actor's Equity and the Producing Managers' Association reached a formal agreement in September 1919. Equity then turned its attention to the motion picture industry. In 1923 union president John Emerson argued that one of Equity's first tasks would be making it easier for extras to collect their pay. The following year, spurred by a threatened pay cut in the industry, Equity began to require the exclusive use of its contract for both stage and film productions. Unlike unions in other industries, Equity did not seek any particular wage or hour requirements but rather individual contracts for performers and union recognition. It eventually got both, ensuring at least a minimum set of working conditions for its members.[62]

Perhaps it was Hollywood's uniqueness that made it relatively easy to organize both female and male workers even in an open-shop city like Los Angeles. After all, there would be little danger of a union like Actor's Equity spreading to other American workers. But for the rest of the city's working women, the successes of 1919 marked only a brief victory in the ongoing war against organized labor. As the city moved into the 1920s and 1930s, commitment to the open shop among local employers hardened, and both male and female workers lost many of their hard-won gains.

Conclusion

On paper, Los Angeles's working women appeared to be in excellent shape by the end of the 1920s, but the reality was more complicated. Many union contracts from 1919 remained in place. California still had laws limiting working hours for some women, which was more than could be said of many other states. Hollywood and the motion picture industry had created new jobs for women, and the war had temporarily opened up new possibilities as well. By 1920 Los Angeles's businesses, now openly competing for their share of global business, employed almost as many women of all ages and ethnicities as the city's longtime rival, San Francisco. Just over 36 percent of Los Angeles's working women worked in a handful of clerical and sales occupations. Domestic service remained the second-largest source of jobs, employing 13 percent of female workers. Ten percent of working women had entered professional and white-collar occupations, but more than half of those worked as teachers. Women remained underrepresented in the city's skilled trades.[63]

More ominously, protections for female workers were being dismantled. As the political climate of the 1920s shifted to the right, many of the reforms heralded by Progressives seemed suspect. Nor did national woman suffrage, beginning in 1920, turn out to be the new force for female-led reform its proponents had expected. Instead, just as Los Angeles's women had learned in the municipal election of 1911, American women often voted along the same class and ethnic lines as their fathers, husbands, and brothers.

In 1920 California's Industrial Welfare Commission had raised the statewide minimum wage for women to $16 a week, making this the highest such wage in the United States at the time. IWC legislation protected an estimated 150,000 working women statewide. Katherine Phillips Edson's political influence had helped sustain the IWC and provided valuable continuity in the state's labor policies. But after 1923 that was no longer possible as a conservative Supreme Court dealt Progressive reform a major blow. That year the U.S. Supreme Court decision in the case of *Adkins v. Children's Hospital* set a legal precedent by throwing out minimum wages for women in the District of Columbia on the grounds that such laws violated the Fifth Amendment by denying employers due process of law.[64] Only in 1937 did the Supreme Court overturn *Adkins*, in *West Coast Hotel Co. v. Parrish*, setting the stage for a raft of new legislation setting limits on hours for both women and men.[65]

In California the first blow to the minimum wage had actually come with the recession of 1921–1922. Employers pleaded with the IWC to reconsider the wage scale, and the commissioners, Katherine Phillips Edson included, decided to reduce the state minimum wage from $16 to $15 a week. The San Francisco Labor Council then launched a campaign against Edson that lasted until the economy improved enough to restore the minimum wage to $16 a week in 1923. But that year the *Adkins* decision sharply undercut the IWC's authority to legislate a women's minimum wage. The commission soldiered on, however, focusing not on minimum-wage legislation but on the employment rights of the state's women and children. Edson finally resigned from the IWC in 1931. Across the country women's earning power continued to lag far behind that of men. By the end of 1920, while all workers nationwide earned an average weekly wage of $28.71, women workers earned an average of just $17.09 per week.[66]

Minority women had made some inroads into low-status, feminized white-collar jobs like sales and secretarial work in the 1920s. Most economists and scholars of women's work now refer to such jobs as "pink collar."[67] Some Molokans, for example, had moved out of Los Angeles, hoping to escape the divisiveness of American urban life. Those who remained in Los Angeles increasingly moved into fuller participation in American society. In the late 1920s Pauline V. Young found young Molokan women working in offices, in department stores, and even as extras in the film industry. However, the handful of women working in Hollywood understandably kept such work secret from their parents.[68]

But protections for female workers were inconsistent at best. Minority women workers in particular still did not enjoy the same attention from politicians as white women. Following the failure of Americanization programs, most reformers and politicians went back to at best ignoring and at worst trying to limit the rights of minority women. Jobs like domestic service remained outside the purview of protective legislation for decades. Private charitable organizations did little more. Only in 1919 did the Los Angeles YWCA rent a room at 1108 East Twelfth Street and start the city's first YWCA Center for Colored Girls. By 1921 the Center for Colored Girls occupied its own building. In 1922 the YWCA finally responded to the city's changing demographics by opening the Magnolia Residence, a boardinghouse for Japanese and Japanese American girls. Women also remained vulnerable to change within industries. As sound became a regular part of motion pictures, job opportunities for extras, for example, began to decline. By 1929, although more and more people registered with extra agencies and pay had improved somewhat, it was becoming harder and harder to place all of them in films.[69]

The most serious development of the 1920s was the backlash against organized labor. Stung by the 1919 strikes and fearing the spread of radical politics, Los Angeles's employer organizations redoubled their efforts to prevent the spread of unions in the city. With the help of the *Los Angeles Times,* employers refused to renew union contracts and fired workers who tried to organize other employees. Workers in several unions, including members of the International Ladies' Garment Workers' Union and the Fruit and Vegetable Workers Union, struck in 1920, but none of these walkouts was successful. By the late 1920s Los Angeles seemed to be back to the open-shop bastion it had been in the first few years of the twentieth century. Making matters worse, the proponents of the open shop in Los Angeles once again went on the offensive. When the postwar boom turned to recession between the middle of 1920 and the end of 1922, it added fuel to the open-shop fire.

The Merchants and Manufacturers Association and the Chamber of Commerce remained at the head of Los Angeles business interests. Members of these two organizations continued to insist that they, not the unions, had the city's best interests at heart. Businesses that relocated to the city seemed to confirm this: a representative for Goodyear Tires even told a meeting of the Chamber of Commerce that one of the things that had attracted his company to Los Angeles was its open-shop orientation. In reality Los Angeles's open-shop philosophy in and of itself probably did little to attract industry. Rather, businesses like Goodyear wanted unskilled laborers, and post–World War I immigration to Los Angeles provided this in abundance.[70]

But such developments did not stem the tide of women working in Los Angeles. Working women's grievances would lay dormant for most of the 1920s while the open shop held sway across Southern California. In the 1930s, however, women would again become active players in labor protest in Los Angeles. While issues of class, gender, and ethnicity continued to complicate such efforts, working women would again forcefully assert their rights as women, as workers, and as a critical part of Los Angeles's economic future.

Epilogue

Standing in downtown Los Angeles in 1929, a young working woman could find much about the city to celebrate, but also much to condemn. In just fifty years Los Angeles had grown from a small cow town with little infrastructure into a city that offered residents and business owners abundant and inexpensive water, gas, electricity, and oil. National companies now recognized that the West Coast's rapid population growth had created promising new markets for goods and services. Los Angeles seemed to many to be the ideal location for tapping these new markets. Between World War I and World War II the city became the center of the oil-equipment and -service industry; the second-largest tire-manufacturing center in the United States; the headquarters of the western furniture, glass, and steel industries; and a regional center for aircraft, automotive, chemical, and trucking industries. By 1924 Los Angeles had become the fourth-largest garment center in the United States. Alongside traditionally "female" work such as teaching and garment work were new opportunities, such as the motion picture industry, that seemed to promise a bright future for at least some women. But for others, who because of race, class, or ethnicity could not get hired for such positions, the future must have looked increasingly dim. A nationwide political tilt to the right was eroding away even the limited protections created by Progressive reformers, club women, and unions.[1] Once the Great Depression took hold, women might have been marginalized even further. But instead the working women of Greater Los Angeles used the challenges of the Depression as a catalyst to reinvigorate not only their links to former allies, such as club women, but to unions as well. They once again forcefully asserted their rights as economic, social, and political contributors to the region.

Business slumped in Southern California during the Depression, just as it did across the United States. The federal census estimated that 3.3 out of every 100 people in Los Angeles had been thrown out of work. Of the other major Southern California cities, Long Beach had the highest unemployment, at 3.8 out of 100. Angelenos recognized that their unemployment situation was not nearly as bad as in some eastern and midwestern cities. But many women were now either out of work or once again working in poorly paid jobs with long hours.[2]

Upper- and middle-class club women did their best to help. They urged other women to buy as many locally made products as possible to keep workers on the job. One club raised funds to keep unemployed women supplied with cosmetics, arguing that if a woman did not keep herself presentable, it would materially hurt her chances of being hired. In 1932 Los Angeles's Midnight Mission opened a Woman's Talent Shop where women could make crafts and sew items to sell and earn forty cents an hour in return. Observers were troubled by how quickly the Depression had driven some women out of good jobs and into the mission. One woman working there had been a seamstress at a major studio, two had been opera singers, another had once run her own business raising chickens. *Los Angeles Times* columnist Alma Whitaker, besieged by pleas for help and advice, angrily noted that most social agencies handed women "'round from agency to agency. They become more hopeless, more undernourished, more nervous and unemployable every day. Their clothes get shabby, their faces gaunt," she argued, "so that employers fear to hire them." Eva Hance of the Los Angeles Council of Social Agencies agreed, admitting that most Depression-era solutions to unemployment, such as breadlines and dormitories, did not fit the needs of women. Sadly, she admitted, female unemployment was "a new development consequent upon women's advent into the business world."[3]

Happily, working women found allies in the state and national political arenas of the 1930s. In 1937 the Supreme Court, in *West Coast Hotel Co. v. Parrish,* overturned the *Adkins* decision, setting the stage for a raft of new legislation setting limits on hours for both women and men.[4] On the local level Los Angeles had the Associated Women's Committee for Women's Unemployment, which operated a clearinghouse in the Chamber of Commerce Building. It linked needy women with appropriate social service agencies. By 1935 the committee had served more than 9,000 women. California's State Emergency Relief Administration (SERA) launched fifteen new work projects in and around Los Angeles, creating jobs for 1,121 men and 1,008 women on projects ranging from office work to sewing. Only women with dependents were eligible for this program, but they could earn anywhere from nine to twelve dollars a week, depending on the number of children they supported. However, only one family member could be employed on a SERA job at a time, and the state expressed a clear preference that it be the husband if at all possible. The Los Angeles County Relief Administration used federal Works Progress Administration funds to create jobs for another 5,000 women. Most of those jobs consisted of sewing clothing and other items for relief efforts, but a woman could still earn up to thirty-five dollars a month. Workers so depended on those funds that in 1936, when the WPA threatened to lay off more than 2,000 women, they appealed directly to local and state government. California in turn pleaded with the federal government to restore funding for the program, but to no avail. By 1938 the handful of women still employed by the program had joined the Workers' Alliance, a coalition of those employed with government funds. The women had the public support of such notables as Robert Noble of Long Beach, a pioneer of the old-age pension plan, and Los Angeles County supervisor Legg, from the city of Downey. For more than a year women aggressively lobbied city supervisors to keep the sewing projects operating. The WPA shut down the last of the projects in 1939, arguing that it was no longer necessary. Instead, it urged women to apply for direct aid from the State of California.[5]

In spite of (or in many cases because of) the economic upheaval of the Depression, working women also expressed new interest in the labor movement. This was part of a national trend. The numbers of women in the labor movement increased across the United States in the 1930s due to dramatic shifts in both government attitudes toward unions and how the unions themselves dealt with female workers. The National Industrial Recovery Act (NIRA), passed in 1933 as part of the New Deal, guaranteed workers the right to organize. Unions affiliated with the Congress of Industrial Organizations welcomed workers of all genders and ethnicities into the movement. The American Federation of Labor expanded into new industries such as hospitality and retail that employed large numbers of women.[6] As had happened after the turn of the century, women in Los Angeles's garment industry took the lead in a new wave of labor agitation in the 1930s.

Garment workers had many grievances against employers. Since the 1920s, when many of the old contracts had expired, the rates of pay for Los Angeles's garment workers had lagged far behind those elsewhere in the country. In 1920 an experienced dressmaker in Southern California earned as little as twenty dollars a week, and unskilled workers made even less. While the minimum hourly wage in New York garment factories was sixty-five cents, in Los Angeles it was closer to thirty. Anita Castro, whose story opened this book, had been born in what was then the Austro-Hungarian Empire but was raised in Argentina before moving to the United States. She married a Mexican man, spoke Spanish as her first language, lived in Los Angeles's Mexican community, and identified as a Latina. She worked as a finisher. She remembered that her factory of more than seventy women still used the piecework system. If a worker was unlucky enough to lose the tickets proving how much work she had done, she might take home only four or five dollars at the end of the week. Those women who objected to the pay or conditions lost their jobs.[7]

At first it appeared ethnic divisions would again doom unionization. The Los Angeles local of the International Ladies' Garment Workers' Union struggled to reconcile the largely unskilled Mexican women who did much of the work in Los Angeles factories with union management geared toward skilled European men. By 1926 the ILGWU had only three thousand members in the city. A 1930 strike by Local 65 of the cloak and suit makers failed miserably. John Laslett and Mary Tyler identified three reasons for this failure. First, the strike took place before NIRA was in place. Second, the M&M, the *Los Angeles Times,* and other employers provided financial support to the threatened businesses. Third, an explosion in one of the factories, caused by a gas leak, reminded too many Angelenos of the 1910 *Times* bombing and turned public opinion against the strike.[8]

But an organizing drive led by the ILGWU's Rose Pesotta in the 1930s helped to increase the local's influence on the Los Angeles garment trade. Pesotta was part of a new generation of female labor organizers active in the 1930s and 1940s. Dorothy Sue Cobble characterizes these women as the first true "labor feminists" because they both "articulated a particular variant of feminism that put the needs of working-class women at its core and because they championed the labor movement as the principle vehicle through which the lives of the majority of women could be bettered." Pesotta, a veteran of union activity in New York's garment trade, estimated that by the early 1930s Los Angeles had 150 dress factories employing two thousand workers. She astutely recognized that organizing minority women would be the key to union success in Los Angeles's garment trade. Employers routinely took advantage of language barriers and the large pool of unskilled labor to prevent organization.[9]

Women in several shops began to organize without direct help from the ILGWU. Anita Castro found out about the union from other garment workers. At her first union meeting she was thrilled to hear that women in unionized shops worked limited hours and had enough free time to go to the library if they liked. "I used to read an awful lot in those days because I was trying to learn English," she recalled. "So that sounded very good to me, you know." When her employer found out she had attended the meeting, he refused to give her enough work, and then fired her. She appealed to the shop's union leader, Sally. As Castro later recalled, Sally immediately rose, took off her apron, shook it, and said, "'Let's go, sisters.'" Castro's shop went out on strike a few days before the ILGWU called a general strike. That began in October 1933, following an industry lockout of union workers. Two thousand dressmakers from several factories across Los Angeles struck. An estimated 75 percent of the strikers were Mexican or Mexican American. Even by Los Angeles standards the strike was bitter and often violent. Strikers harassed strikebreakers; police harassed strikers. The National Recovery Act State Recovery Board assembled an arbitration committee that included Frances Nacke Noel. On November 6 an arbitrated settlement ended the lockout. The settlement produced mixed results. Although it was supposed to limit hours and raise pay, in reality the terms of the settlement were not always enforced. The most important result of the strike was not the settlement but the experience it provided for workers. As John Laslett notes, dressmakers' "strength, solidarity, and militancy contradicted the widespread belief that Latina dressmakers could not be organized." By 1940 more than half the garment businesses in Los Angeles worked with union labor and union contracts.[10]

The film industry weathered the Depression better than most other businesses. In 1933 it broke a seven-year record by employing more than thirty-nine thousand extras in the month of September alone. These high rates of employment might not have catapulted many extras to stardom, but it helped keep bread on their tables. Actor's Equity continued to press its demands as well. In 1926 it helped hammer out the first basic film studio agreements. When the New Deal created a friendlier climate for organized labor in the 1930s, the writers, actors, publicists, story analysts, directors, and other skilled workers in the industry unionized in often bitter but ultimately successful struggles with studio tycoons. Clearly, the M&M and the Los Angeles Chamber of Commerce found that they could no longer maintain leadership in a city now dominated by aircraft firms, the film industry, and local branches of national corporations that had little interest in maintaining the open shop unless it was in their own best interests.[11]

It is not surprising that Mexican and Mexican American women took such active roles in the 1933 strike. With immigration from Mexico continuing unabated, almost 40 percent of Mexican and Mexican American wives worked outside the home. In the barrios of Brooklyn Heights and Lincoln Heights, where residents were most likely to be first-generation immigrants, the percentages increased to 73 and 57, respectively. Interestingly, Mexican women in these neighborhoods appear to have had more success than Mexican men in entering semiskilled white-collar work such as retail in the 1920s. Many of these women had attended night school while working in industrial jobs in order to move into white-collar work. But George J. Sánchez still found 62 percent of Mexican women and 70 percent of Mexican men working in blue-collar jobs.[12]

Considering such jobs paid little more than factory work and had considerably less flexibility, this raises the interesting possibility that first- and second-generation Mexican American women expressed the same preference for "ladylike" white-collar work as their Anglo-American counterparts. Scholars recognize the 1920s and 1930s as a time when the Mexican American community increasingly absorbed and adapted American popular culture. American cultural expectations about "women's work" thus may have also had an impact on the job choices of some young Mexican American women.[13]

But for other minority women Los Angeles remained a city of dead-end, unskilled jobs. The 1920s had seen in boom in the city's African American population, as thousands of rural blacks immigrated to the city. Most settled around Central Avenue, soon one of the most famous African American districts in the country. However, in 1918 the California Supreme Court had ruled that restrictions against African American property ownership were not unconstitutional, opening the way for a flurry of such covenants to be passed. Restrictive housing covenants and increasing segregation of and discrimination against African Americans in the city meant that their plight increasingly looked similar to that found elsewhere in the United States. Forty percent of the city's African Americans lived in the district surrounding thirty blocks of Central Avenue. Few African American women found work beyond domestic service and unskilled factory work. Nonetheless, another wave of African American migration would follow during World War II.[14]

Asian American women, too, remained segregated from Anglos both inside and outside of the labor force. Asian women remained confined to the very bottom of the occupational hierarchy in Los Angeles. They could work as stock girls but not sales ladies; they could work as cigarette girls in a restaurant but not as waitresses. Even college-educated Asian women found work only in service and semi- and unskilled jobs. Some Chinese American newspapers even encouraged second-generation Chinese to return to China to escape the pervasive employment discrimination in the United States.[15]

Some Anglo-American working women also found their occupational opportunities shrinking, but in their case economic and technological changes, not discrimination, were to blame. Servants in Los Angeles had long been fighting for the ten-hour day for domestics, and some belonged to a union affiliated with the American Federation of Labor. But attempts at reforming domestic work in the United States became largely redundant in the 1930s, as the live-out cleaning woman took the place of the domestic servant. As more and more jobs opened up to women, and public programs eased the more pressing needs of the poor, the numbers of women working as servants in the United States continued to plummet. Like domestic service, the numbers of women working in commercial laundries also dropped significantly in the thirties, done in by the invention of an electrically powered automatic washing machine small enough for household use. Similar changes reshaped the telephone industry, drastically reducing the numbers of women employed as operators across the United States. The advent of the Depression combined with the conversion to dial service doomed any chance for a renewal of organization among telephone operators, although poor working conditions during World War II did produce a brief flurry of unionization. After a 1947 strike was defeated, operators decided a national organization was again needed. They created the Communications Workers of America in June of that year. It affiliated with the Congress of Industrial Organizations in 1949, but due to the diminishing importance of telephone operating, this organization never reached the power of its early-twentieth-century counterparts.[16]

Greater Los Angeles would change again in the 1940s as World War II ushered in a whole new era. More than 1 million people moved to California between 1941 and 1945, and at least 660,000 of them flooded into Southern California. The war created some 250,000 new jobs in the region, attracting workers from all over the United States. World War II completed the transformation of the City of Angels into California's premier economic power. Women continued to pursue full economic citizenship. More than ever before the war placed women to the front and center of this issue, as they struggled to combine work, family, and patriotic duty.[17] But the phenomenal growth of post-1941 Los Angeles should not be allowed to obscure the vital role women played in helping to build Los Angeles in the nineteenth and early twentieth centuries.

Southern California's women did not passively accept their place in the social or economic life of the city. Representing as they did such a wide variety of backgrounds, it is not surprising working women proved extremely adaptable in this developing region. When club women and social reformers offered their help, such as intervening in labor disputes or providing affordable housing, working women accepted. In periods of labor militancy, when they could expect more support from male workers, Los Angeles's women workers organized unions and pursued formal agreements with employers to achieve their goals. Unfortunately, after women in both the labor and the reform movements cooperated in the successful suffrage campaign of 1911, they never again forged a successful alliance with one another. Likewise, many of the city's Anglo-American working women did not hesitate to claim racial privilege when doing so gave them access to "respectable" employment.[18]

Women from the city's racial and ethnic minorities remained at a disadvantage in the labor market. But even when fragmented into smaller groups by ethnicity, job, or interest, these women continued to push for change. Whether employed as teachers, maids, or bookkeepers, Los Angeles's working women used a variety of tactics to pursue better pay, better working conditions, and the respect of both male workers and a society that had historically undervalued women's work. The paid labor of women from a variety of ethnic and sociocultural backgrounds, many of them in underpaid, undervalued jobs, laid the foundation for the economic, social, and political development of Southern California in the twentieth century.

NOTES

Introduction

1. Anita Castro, interviewed by Sherna Berger Gluck, January 16, 1976, "Labor History: Garment Workers," Virtual Oral/Aural History Archive, California State University, Long Beach, Interview 2a, Segment 1 (0:00–1:31), Segkey: xxg1025, September 26, 2007, available at http://www.csulb.edu/voaha.

2. Robert M. Fogelson, *The Fragmented Metropolis: Los Angeles, 1850–1930*, 78.

3. Barbara Mayer Wertheimer, *We Were There: The Story of Working Women in America*, 255n. See also T. A. Larson, "Women's Role in the American West," 4, cited in Joan M. Jensen and Darlis A. Miller, "The Gentle Tamers Revisited," 190. The western states in 1870 were California, Oregon, Nevada, and Texas; the western territories were Washington, Utah, Idaho, Wyoming, the two Dakotas, New Mexico, Colorado, Montana, and Arizona.

4. In descending order, the percentage of women engaged in wage work in the mountain and Pacific states from 1880 to 1900 are as follows: California, 1880: 13.0; 1890: 17.5; 1900: 18.7; Nevada, 1880: 12.1; 1890: 17.1; 1900: 17.6; Colorado, 1880: 11.6; 1890: 17.4; 1900: 17.2; Wyoming, 1880: 11.4; 1890: 13.6; 1900: 17.3; Montana, 1880: 7.8; 1890: 16.4; 1900: 16.9; Utah, 1880: 7.1; 1890: 12.3; 1900: 13.6; Oregon, 1880: 6.9; 1890: 13.1; 1900: 15.3; Washington, 1880: 6.5; 1890; 13.5; 1900: 15.3; Arizona, 1880: 6.3; 1890: 11.7; 1900: 20.3; New Mexico, 1880: 6.3; 1890: 8.7; 1900: 11.1; Idaho, 1880: 5.0; 1890: 10.1; 1900: 11.5 (Joseph A. Hill, *Women in Gainful Occupations, 1870–1920: A Study of the Trend of Recent Changes in the Numbers, Occupational Distribution, and Family Relationship of Women Reported in the Census as Following a Gainful Occupation*, 30).

5. Glenn S. Dumke, *The Boom of the Eighties in Southern California*, 10; Fogelson, *Fragmented Metropolis*, 84.

6. U.S. Bureau of the Census, *Thirteenth Census of the United States Taken in the Year 1910*, 207–13; Walton Bean and James J. Rawls, *California: An Interpretive History*, 193.

7. John C. Putnam, *Class and Gender Politics in Progressive-Era Seattle*, ix.

8. For help in assembling this definition I drew on Dana Frank, "White Working-Class Women and the Race Question," 80–102; and Mary Lou Locke, "'Like a Machine or an Animal': Working Women of the Late-Nineteenth-Century Urban Far West, in San Francisco, Portland, and Los Angeles," 7, 21.

9. Claudia Goldin, *Understanding the Gender Gap: An Economic History of American Women*, 11; Lynn Y. Weiner, *From Working Girl to Working Mother: The Female Labor Force in the United States, 1820–1980*, 18–25.

10. Karen Oppenheim Mason and Barbara Laslett, "Women's Work in the American West: Los Angeles, 1880–1890, and Its Contrast With Essex County, Massachusetts, in 1890," 23–24.

11. Ibid., 19–20; U.S. Department of Labor, *Fourth Annual Report: Working Women in Large Cities*, 625, quoted in Weiner, *Working Girl*, 25.

12. Weiner, *Working Girl*, 14; Locke, "'Like a Machine or an Animal,'" 7, 21; Putnam, *Class and Gender Politics*, ix.

13. On the importance of the urban West to western women's history, see, for example, Susan Armitage, "Women and Men in Western History: A Stereoptical Vision"; and Susan Lee Johnson, "'A Memory Sweet to Soldiers': The Significance of Gender in the History of the American West."

14. Barbara J. Fields, "Ideology and Race in American History," 150. For an excellent critique of this approach, see Eileen Boris and Angelique Janssens, "Complicating Categories: An Introduction."

15. Rosaura Sánchez, *Telling Identities: The "Californio Testimonios,"* 188; Putnam, *Class and Gender Politics*, 2, 172; Sara Alpern et al., eds., introduction to *The Challenge of Feminist Biography: Writing the Lives of Modern American Women*, 7.

16. David R. Roediger, *The Wages of Whiteness: Race and the Making of the American Working Class*, 178–80.

17. See Cheryl I. Harris, "Whiteness as Property," 284; and Frank, "White Working-Class Women," 82–83.

1 | Women in White-Collar Work

1. "1898–1923," *Sunset* 50, no. 6 (June 1923): 14–15; Kevin Starr, "*Sunset* Magazine and the Phenomenon of the Far West," in *"Sunset" Magazine: A Century of Western Living, 1898–1998*, 32.

2. Bertha H. Smith, "What Women Are Doing in the West," pt. 1, *Sunset* 26, no. 3 (March 1911): 316–24. See also, for example, Clara M. Greening, "Western Personalities: Policewoman Number One," *Sunset* 27 (September 1911): 305–6.

3. Wertheimer, *We Were There*, 255; Gayle Gullett, *Becoming Citizens: The Emergence and Development of the California Women's Movement, 1880–1911*, 25.

4. Locke, "'Like a Machine or an Animal,'" 349–58.

5. Dumke, *Boom of the Eighties*, 10, 18–19, 272, 276; Fogelson, *Fragmented Metropolis*, 84.

6. Albert Camarillo, *Chicano in a Changing Society: From Mexican Pueblos to American Barrios in Santa Barbara and Southern California, 1848–1930*, 120; Lisbeth Haas, *Conquest and Historical Identities in California, 1769–1936*, 86; Deena J. Gonzalez, "The Widowed Women of Santa Fe: Assessments of the Lives of an Unmarried

Population, 1850–1880"; Deena J. Gonzalez, *Refusing the Favor: The Spanish-Mexican Women of Santa Fe, 1820–1880,* 5; Richard Griswold del Castillo, *"La Familia": Chicano Families in the Urban Southwest, 1848 to the Present,* 32–35. I have chosen to use *"Californiana"* to denote women of Mexican descent living in California. After 1848 I use this term interchangeably with *Mexican American* in order to distinguish these women from later Mexican immigrants. I use *Anglo-American* or *Anglo* to describe white, non-Hispanic Californians. While there certainly were white European immigrants in Los Angeles at this time, their numbers were dwarfed by native-born Anglo-American immigrants from the East Coast and the Midwest.

7. Dumke, *Boom of the Eighties,* 9, 21–24, 27.

8. Charles O. Slosser, "Social Mobility in Nineteenth Century Los Angeles, 1880–1890," quoted in Mason and Laslett, "Women's Work in the American West," 5. See also Carey McWilliams, *Southern California Country: An Island on the Land,* 127; and Dumke, *Boom of the Eighties,* 223.

9. Dumke, *Boom of the Eighties,* 9, 43–48, 55, 200, 221.

10. Ibid.

11. *Los Angeles Times,* June 15, 1887; Tom Zimmerman, "Paradise Promoted: Boosterism and the Los Angeles Chamber of Commerce," 24.

12. Dumke, *Boom of the Eighties,* 50, 226, 272, 276.

13. Ibid., 51, 265–70.

14. Fogelson, *Fragmented Metropolis,* 120–21.

15. Locke, "'Like a Machine or an Animal,'" 157.

16. The most famous boom of all is, of course, the California Gold Rush. As Susan Lee Johnson notes, that boom was structured in such as way that many women found economic opportunity only in fandangos, saloons, and brothels (*Roaring Camp: The Social World of the California Gold Rush,* 293–97).

17. Amy G. Richter, *Home on the Rails: Women, the Railroad, and the Rise of Public Domesticity,* 137–40, 147.

18. Southern Pacific advertisement, *Sunset* 14, no. 1 (November 1904); cover illustration, *Sunset* 14, no. 3 (January 1905). For more on the Southern Pacific Railroad and its publicity machine, see Richard J. Orsi, *Sunset Limited: The Southern Pacific Railroad and the Development of the American West, 1850–1930.*

19. Lee Simpson, *Selling the City: Gender, Class, and the California Growth Machine, 1880–1940.*

20. Oscar Osburn Winther, "The Use of Climate as a Means of Promoting Migration to Southern California," 414, 422; John E. Baur, *The Health Seekers of Southern California, 1870–1900,* 41, 50; Dumke, *Boom of the Eighties,* 32.

21. *Los Angeles Herald,* November 25, 1874, quoted in Baur, *Health Seekers,* 50.

22. Clara Burdette, "The College Woman and Citizenship," *Syracusan* 9, no. 14 (June 15, 1917), Folder 1, Box 125, Clara (Bradley) Burdette Collection, Huntington Library, San Marino, California; Clara Burdette biography manuscript, Folder 5, ibid.

23. "Mrs. Jessie Benton Fremont," *Los Angeles Times*, August 15, 1897; "Relief for Mrs. Benton," *Los Angeles Times*, January 19, 1901; "The Widows of Presidents," *Los Angeles Times*, July 26, 1908; "Mrs. Garfield Answers Call," *Los Angeles Times*, March 14, 1918. The *Los Angeles Times* even briefly ran a "relief" collection for the Frémonts before Mrs. Frémont finally received a pension from the federal government.

24. Dumke, *Boom of the Eighties*, 45–46.

25. Weiner, *Working Girl*, 25. For information on men and white-collar work, see Clark Davis, *Company Men: White-Collar Life and Corporate Cultures in Los Angeles, 1892–1941*.

26. Larson counted actresses as "professionals" ("Women's Role in the American West," 5); I do not.

27. Wertheimer, *We Were There*, 233; Locke, "'Like a Machine or an Animal,'" 27. See also Mary Lou Locke, "Out of the Shadows and Into the Western Sun: Working Women of the Late-Nineteenth-Century Urban Far West," 172–74; and Mason and Laslett, "Women's Work in the American West," 39–40.

28. "Old School Methods," *Los Angeles Times*, May 22, 1896. On the opening of the first city high school and the first kindergarten, see "Los Angeles Schools Got Off to Slow Start," *Los Angeles Times*, September 18, 1949.

29. Dumke, *Boom of the Eighties*, 245–52.

30. David B. Tyack, *The One Best System: A History of American Urban Education*, 61–65; Gloria Ricci Lothrop, "Westering Women and the Ladies of Los Angeles: Some Similarities and Differences," 52; "County School Statistics," *Los Angeles Times*, July 31, 1898.

31. John Aubrey Douglas, *The California Idea and American Higher Education: 1850 to the 1960 Master Plan*, 79.

32. This is speculation on my part, but 1873–1874 did also see the passage of legislation making women eligible for election to school offices (*Index to the Laws of California, 1850–1893: Index to Statutes, the State Edition of the Codes, 1872, and Subsequent Amendments, and the Constitution of 1879; Prepared Under the Supervision of A. J. Johnson*, 611). For more on this time period, see Roy W. Cloud, *Education in California: Leaders, Organizations, and Accomplishments of the First Hundred Years*, 60.

33. "Dr. Susan Dorsey Typifies Pioneer Spirit," *Los Angeles Times*, February 13, 1938; "Dorsey, Susan Almira Miller"; Joan M. Jensen and Gloria Ricci Lothrop, *California Women: A History*, 33; Faye E. Dudden, *Serving Women: Household Service in Nineteenth-Century America*, 45.

34. "Rites Set for Ex-Principal Ethel Andrus," *Los Angeles Times*, July 15, 1967; Walt Secor, "Organization Offers Solutions to Boring Days of Retirement," *Los Angeles Times*, April 12, 1970.

35. Locke, "'Like a Machine or an Animal,'" 184.

36. *Los Angeles Citizen*, March 29, 1907. See also the *Los Angeles Union Labor News*, February 15, 1907.

37. Tyack, *One Best System*, 88–104.

38. The Los Angeles Teachers' Association appears to have been mainly a social club, although it was often at odds with the NEA over the latter's policies. It appears to have later taken the name the Los Angeles Teachers' City Club. See "Teachers' Sociability," *Los Angeles Times*, October 25, 1902; "The Phalanx of Teachers," *Los Angeles Times*, November 30, 1909; and "Looking for Fray," *Los Angeles Times*, July 1, 1911.

39. Grace Heilman Stimson points out how far ahead of its time the Council of Labor's suggestion really was, coming four years before the first-known teachers' union in the country and nine years before the first alliance between a teachers' union and the labor movement (*Rise of the Labor Movement in Los Angeles*, 127). Tyack notes that teachers all over the United States also steered clear of unions in this era. Militant teachers' unions would not appear until the 1960s and 1970s (*One Best System*, 268, 289–90).

40. "The Phalanx of Teachers"; "Merit System Not Enough?" *Los Angeles Times*, June 28, 1912.

41. Debra Gold Hansen, Karen F. Gracy, and Sheri D. Irvin, "At the Pleasure of the Board: Women Librarians and the Los Angeles Public Library, 1880–1905," 315, 317.

42. Elizabeth L. Banks, "Studying the Women Who Toil," *Los Angeles Express*, February 5, 1904.

43. Apostol, "Mary Emily Foy," 109–18; Hansen, Gracy, and Irvin, "At the Pleasure of the Board," 318.

44. Dolores Hayden, "Biddy Mason's Los Angeles, 1856–1891," 89–99; Harris Newmark, *Sixty Years in Southern California, 1853–1913*, 138.

45. Douglas Flamming, *Bound for Freedom: Black Los Angeles in Jim Crow America*, 71. See also Lawrence B. de Graaf, "Race, Sex, and Region: Black Women in the American West, 1850–1920," 294–96.

46. Kate Bradley Stovall, "The Negro Woman in Los Angeles and Vicinity—Some Notable Characters," *Los Angeles Times*, February 12, 1909; "Called by Washington," *Los Angeles Times*, March 15, 1903; de Graaf, "Race, Sex, and Region," 294–96; "A History of Mexican Americans in California: Historic Sites—Casa Blanca School, Riverside, Riverside County," in *Five Views: An Ethnic History Site Survey for California* (Sacramento: California Department of Parks and Recreation, Office of Historic Preservation, December 1988), available at http://www.nps.gov/history/history/online_books/5views/5views5h10.htm. In 1909 the *Los Angeles Times* reported that Rowan had been the first African American to graduate from the school back in 1888 (Stovall, "Negro Woman in Los Angeles and Vicinity"). When Harrison graduated in 1903, however, it reported that she had been the first ("Called by Washington").

47. "The African American Registry" (Minneapolis: African American Registry, 2005), available at http://www.aaregistry.com/african_american_history/1571/Bessie_Burke_a_Los_Angeles_educational_icon.

48. De Graaf, "Race, Sex, and Region," 302; Flamming, *Bound for Freedom*, 72.

49. For more on school segregation, see "A History of Mexican Americans in California: Historic Sites—Casa Blanca School, Riverside, Riverside County," in *Five Views*.

50. Antonia I. Castaneda, "The Political Economy of Nineteenth-Century Stereotypes of *Californianas*."

51. The de Lopez family were descendants of Claudio Lopez, a prominent figure in the history of Mission San Gabriel. Belen de Lopez never married and died in 1892. See "Casa Adobe Notes," Casa de Adobe—Reports about the Casa, 1929, Braun Research Library, Southwest Museum, Autry National Center, Los Angeles; U.S. Census ms., 1880, San Gabriel, Los Angeles, ED 34, p. 417.1000; and "Obituary," *Los Angeles Times*, March 19, 1892.

52. U.S. Census ms., 1880, San Gabriel, Los Angeles, ED 34, p. 417.1000; ibid., 1910, San Gabriel, Los Angeles, ED 34, p. 23A; Margaret Jimenez Page, "The Adobes of San Gabriel, California," 73; "Obituary," *Los Angeles Times*, January 23, 1904.

53. "The City in Brief," *Los Angeles Times*, July 27, 1902. On her work in the suffrage campaign, see chapter 4. On her career at UCLA, see "Extension Classes to Open Next Week," *Los Angeles Times*, November 8, 1926; and "Lowther, Mrs. Maria Lopez De," Biographical File, University of California at Los Angeles, University Archives.

54. For an excellent account of the impact of McGroarty's work, see "The Drama of Los Angeles History," chap. 6 in William Deverell, *Whitewashed Adobe: The Rise of Los Angeles and the Remaking of Its Mexican Past*, 207–50.

55. John S. McGroarty, "The Need of Knowing Spanish," *Los Angeles Times*, July 26, 1914.

56. Ernestina de Lopez worked with Irving Richman on his *California Under Spain and Mexico, 1535–1847: A Contribution Toward the History of the Pacific Coast of the United States, Based on Original Source (Chiefly Manuscript) in the Spanish and Mexican Archives and Other Repositories* (Boston: Houghton Mifflin, 1911). Among the translations Maria de Lopez worked on were McGroarty's *Mission Play* (see "Society," *Los Angeles Times*, February 27, 1916); Rueben Dario's *Poetic and Prose Selections* (New York: D. C. Heath, 1931); *Botica general de los remedios esperimentados, Sonoma, 1838* (Los Angeles: privately printed, 1954); and *Los pastores* (Hollywood: Homer H. Boelter Lithography, [n.d.]).

57. U.S. Census ms., Los Angeles, ED 115, p. 20B; "Pioneers to Be Honored by Pomona," *Los Angeles Times*, October 12, 1934; "The Lee Side o' L.A.," *Los Angeles Times*, November 6, 1935; Fiesta program, May 5, 1940, Casa Adobe—Events, Fiesta, 1931–1948, Braun Research Library, Southwest Museum, Autry National Center, Los Angeles.

58. This is speculation on my part, based on my own research and the persistent discrimination that African American teachers faced. Mexican American teachers in the nineteenth and early twentieth centuries deserve a great deal more study. On discrimination in the teaching profession, see Tyack, *One Best System*, 225–29.

59. Richard Griswold del Castillo, *The Los Angeles Barrio, 1850–1890: A Social*

History, 92; Camarillo, *Chicanos in a Changing Society*, 137; Locke, "Out of the Shadows," 173.

60. Susan B. Anthony and Ida Husted Harper, eds., *History of Woman Suffrage*, 507; Joan Jacobs Brumberg and Nancy Tomes, "Women in the Professions: A Research Agenda for American Historians," 277–78.

61. Jennifer Lisa Koslow, "Eden's Underbelly: Female Reformers and Public Health in Los Angeles, 1889–1932," 91–122.

62. "Rose Talbott Bullard," 252; "Jordon, M. Evangeline"; "Kenney, Elizabeth L." Very little is known about the Women's Pacific Coast Oil Company; it appears to have been in operation for less than a year. See display ad, *Los Angeles Times*, May 20, 1900.

63. Bertha H. Smith, "What Women Are Doing in the West," pt. 4, *Sunset* 27, no. 1 (July 1911): 44–52; "Mrs. Summers, 'Oil Queen,' Dies," *Los Angeles Times*, November 28, 1941; Gerald T. White, *Formative Years in the Far West: A History of Standard Oil Company of California and Predecessors Through 1919*, 313; Kenny A. Franks and Paul F. Lambert, *Early California Oil: A Photographic History, 1865–1940*, 74.

64. "Interesting Westerners," *Sunset* 41, no. 1 (July 1918): 45; "Romances of Industry Shade Aladdin's Lamp," *Los Angeles Times*, January 1, 1927; "June Rand Forms New Firm Here," *Los Angeles Times*, March 4, 1923. The Sassy Jane firm went under in 1923. Rand then launched a new garment business, the June Rand Company.

65. Flamming, *Bound for Freedom*, 17. For more on how racism functioned in local hiring, see 26–28.

66. Maxine Leeds Craig, *Ain't I a Beauty Queen: Black Women, Beauty, and the Politics of Race*, 34; Stovall, "Negro Woman in Los Angeles and Vicinity"; Kathy Peiss, *Hope in a Jar: The Making of American Beauty Culture*, chap. 3; Tiffany Melissa Gill, "'I Had My Own Business . . . So I Didn't Have to Worry': Beauty Salons, Beauty Culturists, and the Politics of African American Female Entrepreneurship."

67. Flamming, *Bound for Freedom*, 17, 26–28.

68. "Women Owners Have Third of Property," *Los Angeles Times*, March 5, 1905; Simpson, *Selling the City*, 15–20.

69. Flamming, *Bound for Freedom*, 78–79; "Women Owners Have Third of Property."

70. "Miss Adelia Edwards Hickman," in *California of the South: A History*, by John Steven McGroarty, 723–25; "Little Mary's Big Idea," *Sunset* 51, no. 1 (July 1923); "Senora Consuelo Castillo de Bonzo," in *California of the South*, by McGroarty, 777–78; Celeste Durant, "'Queen of Olvera Street' Dies at 87," *Los Angeles Times*, October 24, 1977. Hickman was also a self-published poet.

71. "Local Women's Success Hailed," *Los Angeles Times*, November 21, 1924; "Five Hundred Business Women Appeal for Economic and Political Equality," *Los Angeles Times*, March 12, 1935; "Women's Bank Department Is Proved Success," *Los Angeles Times*, March 22, 1925; "Woman's Bank Ready to Open," *Los Angeles Times*, December 10, 1922; "All-Feminine Bank Wins Instant Popular Favor," *Los Angeles Times*, May 20, 1923.

72. The local NAACP's greatest victory came in 1919 when it forced the county hospital's nursing school to admit African American applicants (Flamming, *Bound for Freedom*, 139, 141, 148).

73. Mark Wild, *Street Meeting: Multiethnic Neighborhoods in Early-Twentieth-Century Los Angeles*, 16; John D. Weaver, *Los Angeles: The Enormous Village, 1781–1981*, 37; Douglas Monroy, *Rebirth: Mexican Los Angeles From the Great Migration to the Great Depression*, 114.

74. Newmark, *Sixty Years in Southern California*, 123. For more on the difficulties of recovering Chinese women's history in Los Angeles, see Lucie Cheng and Suellen Cheng, "Chinese Women of Los Angeles: A Social Historical Survey," 1–2, 6–7.

2 | *Servants and Retail Workers in Los Angeles*

1. Dumke, *Boom of the Eighties*, 46.

2. Janet Hooks, *Women's Occupations Through Seven Decades*, 139; Locke, "Out of the Shadows," 176.

3. Ruth Milkman, preface to *Women Work and Protest: A Century of U.S. Women's Labor History*, edited by Milkman, 2–3. See also Christine Stansell, *City of Women: Sex and Class in New York, 1789–1860*, 105–54; and Alice Kessler-Harris, *Out to Work: A History of Wage-Earning Women in the United States*, 68–69, 139–42, 157–58, 203–97.

4. McWilliams, *Southern California Country*, 158.

5. Dudden, *Serving Women*, 1, 18–27.

6. Ibid., 46–48, 65, 107–8, 132.

7. De Graaf, "Race, Sex, and Region," 287, 296–300; Gerald Nash, *The American West in the Twentieth Century: A Short History of an Urban Oasis*, 79; Wild, *Street Meeting*, 20. As late as 1900 there were only two thousand African Americans living in Los Angeles. There remains a need for a comprehensive study of this early community in the historiography.

8. Locke, "'Like a Machine or an Animal,'" 167–75.

9. Banks, "Through an Expatriate's Eyes: Domestic 'Help' Problem," *Los Angeles Express*, November 30, 1903; Evelyn Nakano Glenn, "The Dialectics of Wage Work: Japanese-American Women and Domestic Service, 1905-1940," 445. See also unidentified newspaper clipping, February 12, 1907, Scrapbook 3, Los Angeles Young Women's Christian Association Collection, Urban Archives Center, California State University, Northridge; and *Los Angeles Times*, September 6, 1913.

10. "Burdette, Clara," U.S. Census ms., 1900, Pasadena Precinct 5, Los Angeles, Enumeration District: 117, p. 8A; Burdette biography manuscript, Folder 5, Box 125, Burdette Collection, Huntington Library, San Marino, California.

11. "Severance, Caroline," U.S. Census ms., 1910, Los Angeles Assembly District 71, Enumeration District: 202, p. 4B; Emily K. Abel, *Suffering in the Land of Sunshine: A Los Angeles Illness Narrative*, 64, 125–27.

12. Elizabeth L. Banks, "Studying the Eternal Question: Anything but an American Girl," *Los Angeles Express*, December 16, 1903.

13. Sarah Deutsch, *Women and the City: Gender, Space, and Power in Boston, 1870–1940*, 64–68, 74–75.

14. Dudden, *Serving Women*, 84, 107–8, 132.

15. Elizabeth L. Banks, "Through an Expatriate's Eyes: Enterprise of Los Angeles Women—How They Have Solved the 'Servant Problem' by Doing the Work Themselves, Keeping Young Meanwhile," *Los Angeles Express*, November 23, 1903.

16. Banks, "Studying the Eternal Question: Viz: The Domestic Problem," *Los Angeles Express*, December 11, 1903.

17. Banks, "Through an Expatriate's Eyes: Los Angeles 'Help' and London Servants," *Los Angeles Express*, November 27, 1903.

18. Ibid.; Banks, "Through an Expatriate's Eyes: Engaging and Discharging of Domestic Help"; Banks, "Through an Expatriate's Eyes: Domestic 'Help' Problem," *Los Angeles Express*, November 30, 1903; *Los Angeles Express*, December 2, 1903; *Los Angeles Times*, December 31, 1905; Dudden, *Serving Women*, 120.

19. Burdette biography manuscript, Folder 5, Box 125, Burdette Collection, Huntington Library, San Marino, California.

20. Lucy M. Salmon, *Domestic Service*, 109, quoted in Elizabeth Ross Haynes, "Negroes in Domestic Service in the United States: Introduction," 393; Banks, "Studying the Eternal Question," *Los Angeles Express*, December 16, 1903; Zimmerman, "Paradise Promoted"; David M. Katzman, *Seven Days a Week: Women and Domestic Service in Industrializing America*, 14; Banks, "Through an Expatriate's Eyes: Question of the 'Evening Out' for Domestic Workers," *Los Angeles Express*, December 4, 1903; Dudden, *Serving Women*, 120, 169, 179, 182, 198; Banks, "Through an Expatriate's Eyes," *Los Angeles Express*, December 4, 1903.

21. Banks, "Studying the Eternal Question: More of Domestic Problem," *Los Angeles Express*, December 14, 1903; Banks, "Studying the Eternal Question: Letters From Domestic Employees in Which Charges Are Made Against Employers," *Los Angeles Express*, January 25, 1904; Salmon, *Domestic Service*, 90, cited in Haynes, "Negroes in Domestic Service," 416.

22. Banks, "Studying the Eternal Question: Letters From Domestic Employees"; Salmon, *Domestic Service*, 90, quoted in Haynes, "Negroes in Domestic Service," 416. For more on African American women's clubs, see, for example, Elizabeth Lindsay Davis, *Lifting as They Climb*.

23. Salmon, *Domestic Service*, 90, cited in Haynes, "Negroes in Domestic Service," 416.

24. Banks, "Studying the Eternal Question: One Worker Gives Her Reasons Why She Will Not Engage as a Domestic," *Los Angeles Express*, February 1, 1904; "Points About Servant Question," *Los Angeles Citizen*, June 18, 1909.

25. Robert Gottlieb and Irene Wolt, *Thinking Big: The Story of the "Los Angeles Times," Its Publishers, and Their Influence on Southern California*, 17–23.

26. Katzman, *Seven Days a Week*, 234.

27. "First Week in the New YWCA Building Notable for Los Angeles Organiza-

tion," *Los Angeles Express,* June 27, 1908; "A Short Historical Sketch of the Los Angeles Y.W.C.A.," Series I, Administrative Records, 1894–1972, Los Angeles Young Women's Christian Association Collection, Urban Archives Center, California State University, Northridge.

28. "First Week in the New YWCA Building Notable for Los Angeles Organization," *Los Angeles Express,* June 27, 1908. An alternative account of the founding of the Hermosa Club spells Sanger's name differently ("Saenger") and gives the year of her arrival as 1901, but the basic facts remain the same ("Short Historical Sketch of the Los Angeles Y.W.C.A.").

29. "Short Historical Sketch of the Los Angeles Y.W.C.A."

30. "First Week in the New YWCA Building Notable"; "Short Historical Sketch of the Los Angeles Y.W.C.A."

31. Unidentified newspaper clipping, February 12, 1907, Scrapbook 3, Los Angeles Young Women's Christian Association Collection, Urban Archives Center, California State University, Northridge; *Los Angeles Times,* September 6, 1913; "First Week in the New YWCA Building Notable."

32. *Los Angeles Times,* September 6, 1913. There are nine "Hannah Andersons" listed in the 1910 U.S. Census for Los Angeles County; four of those were servants, and three of those servants were Swedish. It is thus impossible to determine which one is the Hannah Anderson associated with the Progressive Household Club. However, other club officers who could be located in the census confirm that many were Scandinavian born or the American-born offspring of Scandinavian parents. See "Anderson, Hannah," U.S. Census ms., 1910, Los Angeles County.

33. *Los Angeles Times,* September 6, 1913; "First Reception," *Los Angeles Times,* September 19, 1913; "Women's Work, Women's Clubs," *Los Angeles Times,* April 7, 1914; "Women's Work, Women's Clubs," *Los Angeles Times,* April 21, 1914; "Women's Work, Women's Clubs," *Los Angeles Times,* March 31, 1916. Elizabeth Ross Haynes notes that a "Progressive Household Club" existed in Los Angeles, but says it was formed in 1919–1920 ("Negroes in Domestic Service," 435). This may actually be the Progressive Housemaid Club under a new name.

34. Susan Porter Benson, *Counter Cultures: Saleswomen, Managers, and Customers in American Department Stores, 1890–1940,* 14; Industrial Welfare Commission of the State of California, *First Biennial Report of the Industrial Welfare Commission of the State of California, 1913–1914,* 23–25; Wertheimer, *We Were There,* 156–58; *Los Angeles City Directory, 1901,* 95.

35. Industrial Welfare Commission of the State of California, *First Biennial Report,* 23–25, 31–32. The California Retail Dry Goods Association Study of women working in retail produced a much lower figure for single women employed in Los Angeles's retail dry-goods stores (30 percent). However, this study did not include all the city's retail workers, as the IWC investigation did. See the *First Biennial Report* for the California Retail Dry Goods Association Study.

36. Elizabeth L. Banks, "Studying the Women Who Toil: Young Women and Girls in the Los Angeles Stores," *Los Angeles Express,* December 31, 1903; "Beauty Behind the Counter in Los Angeles One of the Charms of the Great Stores," *Los Angeles Times,* July 21, 1912; Industrial Welfare Commission of the State of California, *First Biennial Report,* 23–25, 31–32.

37. Benson, *Counter Cultures,* 193, 209, 211, 221; Locke, "Out of the Shadows," 173.

38. Industrial Welfare Commission of the State of California, *First Biennial Report,* 31–32; Benson, *Counter Cultures,* 193, 209.

39. Industrial Welfare Commission of the State of California, *First Biennial Report,* 23–25; Wertheimer, *We Were There,* 238; Benson, *Counter Cultures,* 92; Elizabeth L. Banks, "Studying the Women Who Toil: Among the Holiday Saleswomen," *Los Angeles Express,* December 29, 1903; Banks, "Studying the Women Who Toil," *Los Angeles Express,* December 31, 1904.

40. "Beauty Behind the Counter in Los Angeles"; Wertheimer, *We Were There,* 238–40; Benson, *Counter Cultures,* 37, 193, 209.

41. Benson, *Counter Cultures,* 211; "Beauty Behind the Counter in Los Angeles"; Banks, "Studying the Eternal Question: One Worker Gives Her Reasons Why She Will Not Engage as a Domestic," *Los Angeles Express,* February 1, 1904; Elizabeth L. Banks, "Studying the Women Who Toil: Among the Holiday Saleswomen," *Los Angeles Express,* December 29, 1903.

42. Kessler-Harris, *Out to Work,* 160–61.

43. Stimson, *Rise of the Labor Movement,* 43, 126, 187, 260–61.

44. "Clerks' Holidays Are in Danger," *Los Angeles Record,* June 19, 1907; "Clerks to Hold Mass Meeting," *Los Angeles Record,* June 22, 1907; "Clerks to Meet to Oppose Saturday Night Opening," *Los Angeles Record,* June 19, 1907.

45. *Los Angeles Citizen,* July 22, 1910, April 5, 1912, March 13, April 24, 1914.

46. Stimson, *Rise of the Labor Movement,* 260–61; Kessler-Harris, *Out to Work,* 161.

47. Mary E. Odem, *Delinquent Daughters: Protecting and Policing Adolescent Female Sexuality in the United States, 1885–1920,* 104; *Los Angeles Citizen,* September 1, 1911.

48. See, for example, Sarah Heath's account of the YWCA's problems conducting welfare work in Cincinnati stores ("Negotiating White Womanhood: The Cincinnati YWCA and White Wage-Earning Women, 1918–1929," 91).

49. Benson, *Counter Cultures,* 141–45; "Greater Broadway Department Stores," *Los Angeles Citizen,* January 8, 1915.

50. *Los Angeles Times,* January 1, 1906; unidentified newspaper clipping, February 12, 1907, Scrapbook 3, Los Angeles Young Women's Christian Association Collection, Urban Archives Center, California State University, Northridge; "Busy Girls Make Frolic of Work," *Los Angeles Express,* May 18, 1905; "Gifts to Add to Extension Fund," *Los Angeles Herald,* February 17, 1907; "First Week in the New YWCA Building Notable"; "For Workers in the Stores," *Los Angeles Times,* September 13, 1905;

unidentified newspaper clipping, February 12, 1907, Scrapbook 3, Los Angeles Young Women's Christian Association Collection, Urban Archives Center, California State University, Northridge; *Los Angeles Times,* January 1, 1906.

3 | *Working Women and the Limits of Welfare Capitalism*

1. Elizabeth L. Banks, "Studying the Eternal Question Among Los Angeles Working Girls—Do Many of Them Go Hungry? An Arithmetical Problem Which May Be Solved by a Visit to the YWCA 'Noon Rest,'" *Los Angeles Express,* December 18, 1903.

2. Ibid. Banks died in London in 1938. See Maude Andrews, "A London Success," *Los Angeles Times,* November 29, 1896; and "Authoress Succumbs," *Los Angeles Times,* July 19, 1938.

3. Haarsager, *Organized Womanhood: Cultural Politics in the Pacific Northwest, 1840–1920,* 230. Sandra Haarsager's work focuses on the Pacific Northwest, but her statement holds true for club women across the United States.

4. Gullett, *Becoming Citizens,* 2–3, 33.

5. For a discussion of the problems inherent in finding a single term to describe women's activities in this period, see Nancy F. Cott, "What's in a Name? The Limits of 'Social Feminism'; or, Expanding the Vocabulary of Women's History."

6. Mrs. William A. Spalding, "Madame Severance and the First Woman's Club of Los Angeles—1878," October 1935, unpublished paper bound in "How Firm a Foundation" Collection, Friday Morning Club Archives, Friday Morning Club, Los Angeles, cited in Gullett, *Becoming Citizens,* 23–24.

7. Gullett, *Becoming Citizens,* 3, 11–12; Wertheimer, *We Were There,* 195; Dudden, *Serving Women,* 7, 91–92; Gwendolyn Mink, "The Lady and the Tramp: Gender, Race, and the Origins of the American Welfare State," 94; Gayle Gullett, "Constructing the Woman Citizen and Struggling for the Vote in California, 1896–1911," 575. See also Estelle Freedman, "Separatism as Strategy: Female Institution Building and American Feminism, 1870–1930"; and Paula Baker, "The Domestication of Politics: Women and American Political Society, 1780–1920."

8. Sherry Jeanne Katz, "Dual Commitments: Feminism, Socialism, and Women's Political Activism in California, 1890–1920," 58, 69.

9. Ibid., 66, 68, 38; Gullett, *Becoming Citizens,* 11–12, 18.

10. Katz, "Dual Commitments," 25; Gullett, *Becoming Citizens,* 12; Wertheimer, *We Were There,* 195.

11. Gullett, *Becoming Citizens,* 27–28, 214n44; Apostol, "They Said It With Flowers," 70–71.

12. Gullett, *Becoming Citizens,* 29–31.

13. Highland Park Ebell Program, Los Angeles, 1907–1908, n.p., Braun Research Library, Southwest Museum, Autry National Center, Los Angeles.

14. "Club Life for Young Women," *Los Angeles Times,* November 13, 1910.

15. "For Settlement Work," *Los Angeles Times,* February 8, 1902.

16. On the Ruskin Art Club, see, for example, "What Women Are Doing," *Los*

Angeles Times, May 5, 1927. On the Los Angeles Travel Club, see "Clubdom Today," *Los Angeles Times,* October 23, 1934. Suffrage clubs appeared as early as the 1890s but really took off in 1911 during California's suffrage campaign of that year. See "Officers Are All Women," *Los Angeles Times,* May 3, 1911.

17. Katz, "Dual Commitments," 68–69.

18. De Lopez's official entry in the 1914 *Woman's Who's Who* listed membership in five organizations; she would also later join the Ebell Club ("Lopez, Maria De G. E.").

19. Gullett, *Becoming Citizens,* 32, 33.

20. Eileen V. Wallis, "Mexican-American Women, Clubs, and the 'Spanish' Auxiliary in Southern California, 1880–1930"; Gullett, *Becoming Citizens,* 114.

21. Gullett, *Becoming Citizens,* 123–24.

22. "In the Vale of Shadows: Notable Woman Lingers at Brink of Divide," *Los Angeles Times,* September 4, 1912; "The Color Line Invades Fiesta," *Los Angeles Times,* April 21, 1902; Gullett, *Becoming Citizens,* 126.

23. For an excellent discussion of the Fiesta, see Deverell, *Whitewashed Abode,* 84–90.

24. "The Color Line Invades Fiesta," *Los Angeles Times,* April 21, 1902.

25. "The Color Line," *Los Angeles Times,* April 20, 1902; Gullett, *Becoming Citizens,* 123–24.

26. There are several accounts paraphrasing what Severance said, but the differences between them are minor. See "The Color Line Invades Fiesta"; Gullett, *Becoming Citizens,* 120, 125; and "The Color Line."

27. John M. Nieto-Phillips, *The Language of Blood: The Making of Spanish-American Identity in New Mexico, 1880–1930s,* 16.

28. "The Color Line Invades Fiesta"; "An Absurd Blunder," *Los Angeles Times,* April 22, 1902.

29. Helen Densmore, "A Defense That Does Not Defend," letter to the *Los Angeles Times,* April 25, 1902.

30. Castaneda, "Political Economy," 225; Wallis, "Mexican-American Women, Clubs, and the 'Spanish' Auxiliary"; Gullett, *Becoming Citizens,* 114. While this incident is justly famous and has been cited by several historians, most neglect to see the combination of class and race dynamics at work. On this subject, see Flamming, *Bound for Freedom,* 136; and Deverell, *Whitewashed Abode,* 88. For a deeper exploration of the GFWC debate, see Gullett, *Becoming Citizens,* 125–26.

31. Unidentified newspaper clipping, Saturday, March 5, 1904, Publicity Files, Los Angeles Young Women's Christian Association Collection, Urban Archives Center, California State University, Northridge; unidentified flyer, Scrapbook 8, ibid.; "Short Historical Sketch of the Los Angeles Y.W.C.A." (see chap. 2, n. 27).

32. Heath, "Negotiating White Womanhood," 87; unidentified newspaper clipping, January 20, 1906; "Volunteer Rally for Campaign to Aid Girls," unidentified newspaper clipping, ca. 1910, Publicity Files, Los Angeles Young Women's Christian Association Collection, Urban Archives Center, California State University, Northridge.

33. YWCA of Los Angeles General Information, 1910–1911, Los Angeles Young Women's Christian Association Collection, Urban Archives Center, California State University, Northridge; "Employment at Board Meeting, July 2, 1914," ibid.; Series II: Records of the Board, 1903–1966, ibid.; "Need a School to Train Girls for House Work," *Los Angeles Record,* June 3, 1907.

34. YWCA of Los Angeles General Information, 1910–1911, Los Angeles Young Women's Christian Association Collection, Urban Archives Center, California State University, Northridge; brochure, n.d., Scrapbook 40, ibid.; card of introduction, n.d., Scrapbook 40, ibid.

35. *Los Angeles Herald,* November 20, 1911; YWCA of Los Angeles General Information, 1910–1911, Series IV: Records of YWCA branches, 1909–1976, Los Angeles Young Women's Christian Association Collection, Urban Archives Center, California State University, Northridge.

36. "Short Historical Sketch of the Los Angeles Y.W.C.A."; "How Do You Plan to Spend Your Evening This Winter?" ca. 1914 and "Vocational Schools at the YWCA Hill Street," ca. 1914, Series IV: Records of YWCA Branches, 1909–1976, Los Angeles Young Women's Christian Association Collection, Urban Archives Center, California State University, Northridge; "YWCA Teaches Girls to Make Living in Pleasant Line of Work," *Los Angeles Record,* November 19, 1912.

37. "Hungry Little Tots Who Slave in Stores Fed for Penny at YWCA," *Los Angeles Record,* February 15, 1913; "Short Historical Sketch of the Los Angeles Y.W.C.A."; *Los Angeles Times,* January 1, 1906; YWCA of Los Angeles General Information, 1910–1911, Series IV: Records of YWCA branches, 1909–1976, Los Angeles Young Women's Christian Association Collection, Urban Archives Center, California State University, Northridge; Mary Andrews Clark Memorial Home brochure, ca. 1913, YWCA I 12-36 [11-32], 1913–1915, ibid.

38. Mary Andrews Clark Memorial Home brochure, ca. 1913, YWCA I 12-36 [11-32], 1913–1915, Los Angeles Young Women's Christian Association Collection, Urban Archives Center, California State University, Northridge; *Some Points of Information Concerning the Mary Andrews Clark Home,* YWCA I 12-35 [11-31], 1916–1965, ibid.; "Low Living Cost Solved for Women: Comforts of Home at $8.50 a Week," *Los Angeles Herald,* March 21, 1913.

39. Data drawn from 128 Clark Memorial Home cards used to check residents in and out (Los Angeles Young Women's Christian Association Collection, Urban Archives Center, California State University, Northridge).

40. Kessler-Harris, *Out to Work,* 128.

41. *Los Angeles Eagle,* April 8, 1911; de Graaf, "Race, Sex, and Region," 307; Adrienne Lash Jones, "Struggle Among Saints: African-American Women and the YWCA, 1870–1920," 161; Gullett, *Becoming Citizens,* 123–24.

42. De Graaf, "Race, Sex, and Region," 307.

43. Heath, "Negotiating White Womanhood," 97; David Montgomery, *The Fall of the House of Labor: The Workplace, the State, and American Labor Activism, 1865–1925;*

Los Angeles Times, April 23, 1911, December 31, 1905; "YWCA to Train Saleswomen: Pioneer in This Work for Girls," *Los Angeles Express,* November 3, 1913; "Employment at Board Meeting, July 2, 1914," Los Angeles Young Women's Christian Association Collection, Urban Archives Center, California State University, Northridge; "Dead Center Loan for Needy Girls Aiding Many," *Los Angeles Express,* November 20, 1913.

44. "Employment at Board Meeting, July 2, 1914," Los Angeles Young Women's Christian Association Collection, Urban Archives Center, California State University, Northridge.

4 | *Race, Class, and Gender in Los Angeles's Unions*

1. "Deluded Women Coming Here: They Leave Good Jobs, Expecting to Find Work at Once," *Los Angeles Tribune,* November 2, 1913.

2. Ibid.

3. Vicki Ruiz, *Cannery Women, Cannery Lives: Mexican Women, Unionization, and the California Food Processing Industry, 1930–1950,* xviii.

4. Frederic Cople Jaher, *The Urban Establishment: Upper Strata in Boston, New York, Charleston, Chicago, and Los Angeles,* 636; Harry Ellington Brook, *Los Angeles, California: The City and County,* 78; Charles Frances Saunders, *Under the Sky in California,* 249–50, quoted in Baur, *Health Seekers,* 51.

5. Nash, *American West,* 34–37.

6. Louis B. Perry and Richard S. Perry, *A History of the Los Angeles Labor Movement, 1911–1941,* 34.

7. *Los Angeles, 1900–1961,* 2.

8. Gottlieb and Wolt, *Thinking Big,* 44–46; Fogelson, *Fragmented Metropolis,* 125; Stimson, *Rise of the Labor Movement,* 189.

9. Jaher, *Urban Establishment,* 628; Mink, "Lady and the Tramp," 99.

10. Stimson, *Rise of the Labor Movement,* 104, 123, 128–29, 133; Gottlieb and Wolt, *Thinking Big,* 30.

11. Stimson, *Rise of the Labor Movement,* 172, 190–91.

12. "Ideals of Organized Labor and Our Duty as Members," *Los Angeles Citizen,* September 3, 1915.

13. Stimson, *Rise of the Labor Movement,* 197–99, 204, 208–9, 215.

14. Ibid., 197–99, 204, 208–9, 215; Becky M. Nicolaides, "'Where the Working Man Is Welcomed': Working-Class Suburbs in Los Angeles, 1900–1940," 540–41.

15. Frances Noel, Los Angeles, to Mrs. Frances A. Williamson, Oakland, July 12, 1911, Frances Noel Papers, University of California at Los Angeles, University Research Library, Department of Special Collections.

16. Dorothy Sue Cobble, *Dishing It Out: Waitresses and Their Unions in the Twentieth Century,* 35, 37; Perry and Perry, *Los Angeles Labor Movement,* 38.

17. Roediger, *Wages of Whiteness,* 178–80; *Los Angeles Citizen,* March 13, 1914, January 12, 1912; Cobble, *Dishing It Out,* 214.

18. Stimson, *Rise of the Labor Movement,* 66.

19. Ibid., 66, 76, 126; Cobble, *Dishing It Out,* 61.

20. Cobble, *Dishing It Out,* 62–65.

21. *Los Angeles Citizen,* November 19, 1909, August 5, 1910, December 29, 1911; Wertheimer, *We Were There,* 222.

22. *Los Angeles Citizen,* March 13, 1914.

23. *Los Angeles Citizen,* January 12, 1912; Cobble, *Dishing It Out,* 214.

24. Arwen P. Mohun, *Steam Laundries: Gender, Technology, and Work in the United States and Great Britain, 1880–1940,* 1, 39–42, 49, 67–71.

25. Ibid., 101–2.

26. H. E. Du Pue, "Laundry Workers: A Fighting Organization," *Los Angeles Citizen,* September 1, 1911; Perry and Perry, *Los Angeles Labor Movement,* 46.

27. Mohun, *Steam Laundries,* 74–95, 106, 114.

28. Nancy Woloch, *"Muller v. Oregon": A Brief History with Documents,* 3–12.

29. Mohun, *Steam Laundries,* 128.

30. Industrial Welfare Commission of the State of California, *First Biennial Report,* 35–40; Industrial Welfare Commission of the State of California, *Second Biennial Report of the Industrial Welfare Commission of the State of California, 1915–1916,* 31–32; Mohun, *Steam Laundries,* 97.

31. Stimson, *Rise of the Labor Movement,* 244–46; Mohun, *Steam Laundries,* 129–30; *Los Angeles Citizen,* November 11, 1911; Du Pue, "Laundry Workers."

32. *Los Angeles Citizen,* November 11, 1911; Du Pue, "Laundry Workers."

33. Du Pue, "Laundry Workers."

34. Stimson, *Rise of the Labor Movement,* 260, 297; Du Pue, "Laundry Workers."

35. Mohun, *Steam Laundries,* 134–36.

36. "Union and Non-union Laundries," *Los Angeles Union Labor News,* February 2, 1906; U.S. Bureau of the Census, "Census of Steam Laundries," 4, cited in Mohun, *Steam Laundries,* 136–37.

37. Industrial Welfare Commission of the State of California, *Second Biennial Report,* 191, 203–17; Kessler-Harris, *Out to Work,* 158; Mohun, *Steam Laundries,* 136–37.

38. Mohun, *Steam Laundries,* 50, 67–71; Industrial Welfare Commission of the State of California, *Second Biennial Report,* 191.

39. *Los Angeles Citizen,* July 1, 1910, Stimson, *Rise of the Labor Movement,* 297; *Los Angeles Citizen,* March 3, 1911; *Los Angeles City Directory, 1901; Los Angeles City Directory, 1911.*

40. *Los Angeles Times,* October 9, 1900; Stimson, *Rise of the Labor Movement,* 246–47, 258–300.

41. Gottlieb and Wolt, *Thinking Big,* 50–51. Such failures characterized organized labor across the country in this era (Montgomery, *Fall of the House of Labor,* 274).

42. Paul Greenstein, *Bread and Hyacinths: The Rise and Fall of Utopian Los Angeles,* 23–27; Gottlieb and Wolt, *Thinking Big,* 82.

43. Stimson, *Rise of the Labor Movement*, 336, 360; Wild, *Street Meeting*, 159; *Los Angeles Citizen*, June 23, 1911.

44. Geoffrey Cowan, *The People vs. Clarence Darrow: The Bribery Trial of America's Greatest Lawyer*, 76–78, 87, 273; Greenstein, *Bread and Hyacinths*, 45–46, 53–54; McWilliams, *Southern California Country*, 283.

45. "Women Unionists and Club Women Hold Heart-to-Heart Conference," *Los Angeles Citizen*, July 11, 1919.

46. Mohun, *Steam Laundries*, 151.

5 | *Suffrage and Politics in Los Angeles*

1. "After Votes Via Stomach," *Los Angeles Times*, July 13, 1911.

2. The motives behind suffrage campaigns in other cities varied. For example, Putnam argues that it was a concern over vice and prostitution that largely drove the suffrage movement in Seattle (*Class and Gender Politics*, 99–100).

3. McWilliams, *Southern California Country*, 281; *Los Angeles, 1900–1961*, 12–13; Gullett, *Becoming Citizens*, 151, 160–61.

4. Gullett, *Becoming Citizens*, 151, 160–61; *Los Angeles, 1900–1961*, 13.

5. Odem, *Delinquent Daughters*, 110; Gullett, *Becoming Citizens*, 161–62.

6. Gullett, *Becoming Citizens*, 180.

7. Stimson, *Rise of the Labor Movement*, 218–25.

8. Wild, *Street Meeting*, 159.

9. Daniel J. Johnson, "'No Make-Believe Class Struggle': The Socialist Municipal Campaign in Los Angeles, 1911," 31; Wild, *Street Meeting*, 159–63.

10. Wild, *Street Meeting*, 154–58; *Los Angeles Citizen*, July 22, 1910; Stimson, *Rise of the Labor Movement*, 346–47.

11. Katz, "Dual Commitments," 100–102, 175; "Report by M.E.G.," *Los Angeles Socialist*, May 10, 1902, cited in ibid., 100–102, 175.

12. Katz, "Dual Commitments," 157–58, 166–77; Stimson, *Rise of the Labor Movement*, 250–51; *Common Sense*, February 9, 1907.

13. Gullett, *Becoming Citizens*, 179; Frances Noel, Los Angeles, to Mrs. Frances A. Williamson, Oakland, July 12, 1911, Noel Papers, University of California at Los Angeles, University Research Library, Department of Special Collections; Katz, "Dual Commitments," 273.

14. Katz, "Dual Commitments," 273–74, 330n71; "The Woman's Conference of Los Angeles County: Its Aim and Object," Box 4, Folder 12, Noel Papers, University of California at Los Angeles, University Research Library, Department of Special Collections; *Los Angeles Citizen*, February 10, 1911.

15. "The Sisters: They Hold a Momentous Meeting with Closed Doors," *Los Angeles Times*, October 31, 1888.

16. Anthony and Harper, *History of Woman Suffrage*, 497–99; Gullett, "Constructing the Woman Citizen," 581; Katz, "Dual Commitments," 499–500.

17. Gullett, *Becoming Citizens,* 95–96; Katz, "Dual Commitments," 581.

18. "After Votes Via Stomach"; Gullett, *Becoming Citizens,* 181–84.

19. "The Wage Earner's Suffrage League," n.d., Box 1, Folder 7, Noel Papers, University of California at Los Angeles, University Research Library, Department of Special Collections.

20. *Los Angeles Citizen,* June 2, 1911.

21. "Suffrage Not Society Fad," *Los Angeles Citizen,* September 9, 1911.

22. Frances N. Noel, "A Word to Socialist Voters," *Los Angeles Citizen,* September 1, 1911.

23. "Activity of the Suffragette," *Los Angeles Citizen,* September 29, 1911. See also, for example, "Whirlwind End, Suffrage Fight," *Los Angeles Times,* October 3, 1911; Gullett, *Becoming Citizens,* 186; *Los Angeles City Directory, 1911,* 876; and "Women Hustle for Big Vote," *Los Angeles Citizen,* October 4, 1911.

24. Jacqueline R. Braitman, "Katherine Phillips Edson: A Progressive-Feminist in California's Era of Reform," 121–22; "The Political Equity League, Los Angeles, California, to Mothers, Fathers, and All Good Citizens," n.d., Katherine Phillips Edson Papers, University of California at Los Angeles, University Research Library, Department of Special Collections; "Wage Earners Suffrage League Ready for Action," *Los Angeles Citizen,* June 30, 1911; "Activity of the Suffragette."

25. Maud Younger, "Why Wage-Earning Women Should Vote," *Los Angeles Citizen,* September 29, 1911.

26. "Yellow Flag Checkmated," *Los Angeles Times,* October 3, 1911. Antisuffrage advocates took particular glee in pointing out the persistence of polygamy in Utah in spite of female suffrage in that state.

27. Mrs. George Stein, "After the Victory," *Los Angeles Citizen,* September 29, 1911.

28. Katz, "Dual Commitments," 356n140.

29. "This Is the New Law," *Los Angeles Citizen,* September 29, 1911; Katz, "Dual Commitments," 297, 358n141; "Women's Work, Women's Clubs," *Los Angeles Times,* November 5, 1911; Gullett, *Becoming Citizens,* 191.

30. *Los Angeles Times,* November 5, 1911; Gullett, *Becoming Citizens,* 194–95; Braitman, "Katherine Phillips Edson," 144.

31. Gullett, *Becoming Citizens,* 194–95.

32. Ibid., 196–97; "Socialists Cannot Raise Wages," *Los Angeles Times,* November 5, 1911; "Vote for the Home and Your Jobs," *Los Angeles Times,* November 11, 1911; "Women Make Converts," *Los Angeles Times,* November 29, 1911.

33. James P. Kraft refers to this organization as the Women's Wage-Earner's League, but I have chosen to use the name as it appeared in newspaper accounts of the time ("The Fall of Job Harriman's Socialist Party: Violence, Gender, and Politics in Los Angeles, 1911," 62; "Laundry Girls for Alexander," *Los Angeles Times,* November 29, 1911). For an opposing view on working women's involvement in these groups, see Kraft, "Harriman's Socialist Party," 61. Not all employers were so tolerant of

political debate. The *Los Angeles Citizen* reported that many department store owners forced their saleswomen to wear Alexander buttons ("Employees Have to Wear Alexander Buttons," *Los Angeles Citizen,* December 1, 1911). After Alexander's victory one woman, employed at the New York Cloak and Suit House on South Broadway, wrote in to the *Citizen* arguing that her employers had not let their employees out to vote at all ("Working Girl Complains," *Los Angeles Citizen,* December 14, 1911). The *Citizen* published several letters alleging voter fraud and discrimination against those registered as Socialists, but no charges were ever filed.

34. D. Johnson, "'No Make-Believe Class Struggle,'" 41; Gullett, *Becoming Citizens,* 194–95; "Women's Work, Women's Clubs," *Los Angeles Times,* November 21, 1911.

35. Stimson, *Rise of the Labor Movement,* 366–419; G. Cowan, *People vs. Clarence Darrow,* 268, 275; D. Johnson, "'No Make-Believe Class Struggle,'" 41–42.

36. Kraft, "Harriman's Socialist Party," 51.

37. D. Johnson, "'No Make-Believe Class Struggle,'" 42, table 2, "Statistics of the General Election"; Kraft, "Harriman's Socialist Party," 59.

38. D. Johnson, "'No Make-Believe Class Struggle,'" 43; Edson, draft of statement to National League of Women Voters, 32, 626, Box 6, Folder 1, Edson Papers, University of California at Los Angeles, University Research Library, Department of Special Collections, quoted in Braitman, "Katherine Phillips Edson," 144–45.

39. "Women Progressives Are Misleading the Voters," *Los Angeles Citizen,* October 18, 1912; "Show Socialist Vote Was Against Suffrage," *Los Angeles Express,* November 30, 1911. For refutation of such claims, see Gullett, *Becoming Citizens,* 191; and Katz, "Dual Commitments," 297, 358n141.

40. Katz, "Dual Commitments," 363.

41. Ibid., 386–92, 445n42.

42. Ibid., 403–5, 418, 573.

43. Gullett, *Becoming Citizens,* 204.

44. "Gaining Suffrage Wasn't All: There's a Bigger Fight Ahead for the Women of California, and It's Time to Be Moving On," *Los Angeles Citizen,* October 10, 1913.

45. Milly Bennet, "San Francisco News," April 1, 1930, Box 7, Envelope 9, Edson Papers, University of California at Los Angeles, University Research Library, Department of Special Collections.

46. Katz, "Dual Commitments," 567–80; *Los Angeles Citizen,* March 29, 1907; "8-Hour Demonstration," *Los Angeles Citizen,* April 14, 1911.

47. Katz, "Dual Commitments," 567–80; *Los Angeles Citizen,* April 14, 1911.

48. "Eight-Hour Law for Women Is Upheld in Test Case," *Los Angeles Citizen,* March 8, 1912; "Court Holds 8-Hours Law Constitutional," *Los Angeles Citizen,* May 31, 1912.

49. Braitman, "Katherine Phillips Edson," 169–74; Earl C. Crockett, "The History of California Labor Legislation, 1910–1930," 298. The California State Bureau of Labor Statistics had been created in 1883.

50. Katz, "Dual Commitments," 581; "Eight Hours for Nurses," *Los Angeles Times,* March 13, 1913; "Eight Hours and Women," *Los Angeles Times,* March 17, 1913; "Nurses Don't Ask for Cut," *Los Angeles Times,* March 25, 1913.

51. Braitman, "Katherine Phillips Edson," 177–78.

52. Katz, "Dual Commitments," 589–90; Edson, "Industrial Problems as I See Them," n.d., Box 7, Folder 5, Edson Papers, University of California at Los Angeles, University Research Library, Department of Special Collections.

53. *Los Angeles Record,* February 11, 1913; "Complete Probe of Local Conditions Is the Promise," unidentified newspaper clipping, Box 6, Folder 14, Noel Papers, University of California at Los Angeles, University Research Library, Department of Special Collections.

54. "Many Fall Below Living Wage Committee Finds," *Los Angeles Citizen,* June 20, 1913; Perry and Perry, *Los Angeles Labor Movement,* 117.

55. Ibid. See, for example, Edson's comments on the potential impact of the Panama Canal on local labor ("Industrial Problems as I See Them").

56. Braitman, "Katherine Phillips Edson," 87, 201.

57. Norris Hundley, "Katherine Phillips Edson and the Fight for California's Minimum Wage Law, 1912–1923," 277; Braitman, "Katherine Phillips Edson," 196–97, 203, 226.

58. Edson, "Industrial Problems as I See Them."

59. Hundley, "Katherine Phillip Edson," 276; Edson, n.d., Box 7, Folder 4, Edson Papers, University of California at Los Angeles, University Research Library, Department of Special Collections.

60. Edson, n.d., Box 7, Folder 4, Edson Papers, University of California at Los Angeles, University Research Library, Department of Special Collections; Industrial Welfare Commission of the State of California, *Third Biennial Report of the Industrial Welfare Commission of the State of California, 1917–1918,* 28–29; Rebecca J. Mead, "'Let the Women Get Their Wages as Men Do': Trade Union Women and the Legislated Minimum Wage in California," 331; bulletin (San Francisco), August 11, 1916, Box 5, Folder 2, Edson Papers, University of California at Los Angeles, University Research Library, Department of Special Collections, quoted in Braitman, "Katherine Phillips Edson," 216–17.

61. IWC minutes, 1920, quoted in Braitman, "Katherine Phillips Edson," 220–21.

62. Braitman, "Katherine Phillips Edson," 221.

63. Ibid., 222–23; Industrial Welfare Commission of the State of California, *Third Biennial Report,* 66, 108, 112. See, for example, criticism of the wage calculations in Agnes H. Downing, "Women's Wages," *Los Angeles Citizen,* March 5, 1915.

64. Katherine Phillips Edson, Los Angeles, to Harry A. Encell, San Francisco, April 1, 1920, Box 1, Folder 8, Edson Papers, University of California at Los Angeles, University Research Library, Department of Special Collections; Industrial Welfare Commission of the State of California, *Third Biennial Report,* 16–17.

65. Katherine Phillips Edson, "The Impact of Limited Hours and Minimum Wage on Women in Industry," *California Outlook*, n.d., Box 6, Folder 13, Noel Papers, University of California at Los Angeles, University Research Library, Department of Special Collections; "Wage Law for Women Effective Thursday," *Los Angeles Express*, May 7, 1918; Industrial Welfare Commission of the State of California, *Third Biennial Report*, 16–17.

66. "Report on the Motion Picture Industry in Los Angeles," n.d. (May 1919?), Los Angeles Young Women's Christian Association Collection, Urban Archives Center, California State University, Northridge.

67. Mead, "'Let the Women Get Their Wages,'" 324–25; Industrial Welfare Commission of the State of California, *Second Biennial Report*, 66–82; "O, That Women Were Self-Reliant!" *Los Angeles Citizen*, July 20, 1917 (emphasis in the original).

68. Frances Nacke Noel, Box 1, Folder 8, Noel Papers, University of California at Los Angeles, University Research Library, Department of Special Collections; Hundley, "Katherine Phillips Edson," 275.

69. Edson, "Impact of Limited Hours."

70. Mead, "'Let the Women Get Their Wages,'" 334–35.

71. Cobble, *Dishing It Out*, 84.

72. "Autocratic Minimum Wage Rule Forced Upon State," *Los Angeles Times*, July 22, 1917; "An Autocratic Commission," *Los Angeles Times*, July 16, 1917.

73. California Industrial Welfare Commission, *Historical Review of Minimum Wage Issues*, December 1983, 9, quoted in Braitman, "Katherine Phillips Edson," 224; Mead, "'Let the Women Get Their Wages,'" 339.

74. "Los Angeles Committee of the NWTLL Los Angeles, October 27, 1914," Noel Papers, University of California at Los Angeles, University Research Library, Department of Special Collections; Frances Noel, Los Angeles, to Minnie Warren, Phoenix, March 23, 1915, Noel Papers, University of California at Los Angeles, University Research Library, Department of Special Collections. See also, for example, Muncy, *Creating a Female Dominion in American Reform, 1890–1935*, 35; and Katz, "Dual Commitments," 593–99.

75. *Los Angeles Citizen*, June 22, 1917; Fogelson, *Fragmented Metropolis*, 130. However, the testimony of witnesses was not published until 1916.

76. "Mrs. Katherine Edson Testifies Before the Industrial Relations Commission," *Los Angeles Citizen*, September 29, 1916. Between 1900 and 1910 the percentage of married women employed in Los Angeles increased from 6.2 percent to 9.8 percent. By 1920 13.7 percent of married women worked. In the same time period the percentage of single women working increased from 40.8 percent in 1900 to 48.7 percent in 1910 and 51.1 percent in 1920 (Hill, *Women in Gainful Occupations*, 270).

77. "Mrs. Edson Continues Testimony Before the Industrial Relations Commission," *Los Angeles Citizen*, October 6, 1916.

78. "Testimony of Mrs. Edson Before She Became a Hughes 'Booster,'" *Los Angeles*

Citizen, October 20, 1916; "Mrs. Edson's Words Compared With Her Deeds," *Los Angeles Citizen,* October 27, 1916; "Mrs. Katherine Edson Testifies Before the Industrial Relations Commission."

79. "Mrs. Noel Cites Underlying Causes of Industrial Ills of Los Angeles," *Los Angeles Citizen,* December 22, 1916; "Mrs. Noel Continues Testimony Before the Federal Industrial Relations Committee," *Los Angeles Citizen,* December 29, 1916; "Mrs. Noel Continues Testimony Before the Federal Industrial Relations Committee," *Los Angeles Citizen,* January 5, 1917; "Mrs. Noel Concludes Testimony Before the Federal Industrial Relations Committee," *Los Angeles Citizen,* January 12, 1917.

80. Perry and Perry, *Los Angeles Labor Movement,* 117.

81. Gullett, *Becoming Citizens,* 205.

82. "What the Friday Morning Club Has to Say About Unemployment," *Los Angeles Citizen,* January 2, 1914; "Mrs. Noel Continues Testimony," January 5, 1917.

83. "California Overcrowded With Women," *Los Angeles Citizen,* January 15, 1915; *Los Angeles Citizen,* November 12, 1915; "Fair Employees Out of a Job," *Los Angeles Citizen,* December 3, 1915. Of the cities studied, unemployment was highest in Portland, Oregon, where 20 percent of wage earners were unemployed, and 17.3 worked only part-time. In Los Angeles the bureau estimated 24.1 percent of workers to be employed only part-time.

84. "Miss Daugherty Addresses Club," *Los Angeles Citizen,* March 5, 1915.

85. *Los Angeles Citizen,* January 2, January 15, February 19, March 26, 1915.

86. Braitman argues that unions failed in the canneries because of a lack of effectiveness and public hostility ("Katherine Phillips Edson," 219–20, 233–34). In contrast, historian Martin Louis Brown argues that the IWC needed the cooperation of cannery owners and thus refused to make any changes (such as encouraging unionization) that might anger them ("A Historical Economic Analysis of the Wage Structure of the California Fruit and Vegetable Canning Industry," 358).

87. Industrial Welfare Commission of the State of California, *Third Biennial Report,* 92.

6 | *Immigrant Women, Work, and Americanization*

1. Pauline V. Young, *The Pilgrims of Russian-Town,* 247–49.

2. Fogelson, *Fragmented Metropolis,* 83; Juan Gómez-Quiñones, *Mexican American Labor, 1790–1900,* 66; Wild, *Street Meeting,* 29; Frank, "White Working-Class Women," 89.

3. Hill, *Women in Gainful Occupations,* 28, 33; John H. M. Laslett and Mary Tyler, *The ILGWU in Los Angeles, 1907–1988,* 4–6.

4. Industrial Welfare Commission of the State of California, *Second Biennial Report,* 66–82, 233–57.

5. Ibid., 66–82, 233–57; John H. M. Laslett, "Gender, Class, or Ethno-cultural Struggle? The Problematic Relationship Between Rose Pesotta and the Los Angeles ILGWU," 24–26.

6. *Los Angeles Citizen,* July 2, 1915; Industrial Welfare Commission of the State of California, *Second Biennial Report,* 85–86.

7. Industrial Welfare Commission of the State of California, *Second Biennial Report,* 90–99, 146.

8. Paul S. Taylor, "Mexican Women in Los Angeles Industry in 1928," 103, 108–10, 112–13, 124–27.

9. Nan Enstad, *Ladies of Labor, Girls of Adventure: Working Women, Popular Culture, and Labor Politics at the Turn of the Twentieth Century,* 91–92; J. Laslett and Tyler, ILGWU *in Los Angeles,* 8–11, 15; J. Laslett, "Gender, Class, or Ethno-cultural Struggle?" 20.

10. Perry and Perry, *Los Angeles Labor Movement,* 36; "Cloak Makers Strike in Local Factory," *Los Angeles Citizen,* July 10, 1914; "Merchants, Manufacturers, and Employers' Ass'n Having Hard Time to Prevent Break in Ranks," *Los Angeles Citizen,* August 15, 1914.

11. Flyer, n.d., Noel Papers, University of California at Los Angeles, University Research Library, Department of Special Collections; "Max Marks' Employees Strike," *Los Angeles Citizen,* July 17, 1914; "Three Important Strikes Won During the Past Two Months," *Los Angeles Citizen,* July 24, 1914.

12. "Max Marks Employees Again Quit Work, Cannot Live on Prices Paid," *Los Angeles Citizen,* June 4, 1915.

13. "Ladies' Garment Workers Battle for Justice," *Los Angeles Citizen,* August 10, 1917; Enstad, *Ladies of Labor,* 160; *Los Angeles Citizen,* August 31, 1917.

14. Perry and Perry, *Los Angeles Labor Movement,* 36; *Los Angeles Citizen,* March 4, 1910.

15. "Haisch, Jeannette," U.S. Census ms., 1910, Los Angeles, AD 70, ED 267, p. 3A; "Houck, Daisy A.," ibid., AD 74, ED 88, p. 22B.

16. Putnam, *Class and Gender Politics,* 87.

17. Perry and Perry, *Los Angeles Labor Movement,* 37; Wertheimer, *We Were There,* 328; "Haisch, Jeannette," U.S. Census ms., 1910, Los Angeles, AD 70, ED 267, p. 3A; "Houck, Daisy A.," ibid., AD 74, ED 88, p. 22B; "Mrs. Houck Addresses Convention Women's Clubs and Shows Right Industrial Conditions Help Homes," *Los Angeles Citizen,* March 24, 1916.

18. *Los Angeles Citizen,* January 7, 1910; J. Laslett and Tyler, ILGWU in Los Angeles, 11; *Los Angeles Citizen,* August 16, 1912.

19. *Los Angeles Citizen,* December 10, 1909; "Mrs. Katherine Edson Testifies Before the Industrial Relations Commission," *Los Angeles Citizen,* September 29, 1916; "Products of White Goods Departments Appeal to Wearers of Label Garments," *Los Angeles Citizen,* April 2, 1915; "Help Wanted," *Los Angeles Citizen,* July 18, 1919; "'Stronghold,' the Overall That Built the Aqueduct," *Los Angeles Citizen,* March 8, 1912; *Los Angeles Citizen,* October 8, 1915.

20. *Los Angeles Citizen,* August 25, 1911; "Garment Workers on Strike," *Los Angeles Citizen,* March 7, 1913; "Police Call Union Bluff," *Los Angeles Times,* March 12, 1913.

21. "Garment Workers on Strike," *Los Angeles Citizen*, March 7, 1913; "Police Call Union Bluff."

22. "Police Call Union Bluff."

23. "Strikers Gain Support of Best Merchants: Settlement Sure to Result From Efforts of Unions," *Los Angeles Citizen*, March 14, 1913; "Striking Garment Workers Gain Support of Outside Unionists," *Los Angeles Citizen*, March 28, 1913; "Striking Garment Workers Gain Recruits From Unfair Factory," *Los Angeles Citizen*, March 21, 1913; "Miss Sutor Says Garment Workers Will Win Strike," *Los Angeles Citizen*, April 18, 1913.

24. "Merchants, Fearing Otis-Zeehandelaar Outfit, Handle Unfair 'Merit' Shirts," *Los Angeles Citizen*, August 8, 1913; "Three Important Strikes Won During the Past Two Months"; "P. A. Newmark and Company Send Labor Day Greetings," *Los Angeles Citizen*, September 4, 1914.

25. "Hail! Trade Unionists! We, the Garment Workers of Los Angeles, Salute You!" *Los Angeles Citizen*, September 3, 1915.

26. *Los Angeles Citizen*, July 20, 1917; "Shoe Workers at Torrance Revolt Against Tyranny," *Los Angeles Citizen*, May 22, 1914; "Torrance Strike Is Won," *Los Angeles Citizen*, June 5, 1914.

27. *Los Angeles Citizen*, January 30, 1914, November 19, 1915, February 18, 1916; "Ideals of Organized Labor and Our Duty as Members," *Los Angeles Citizen*, September 3, 1915.

28. Kessler-Harris, *Out to Work*, 112; Nash, *American West*, 67; Wertheimer, *We Were There*, 217; *Los Angeles Citizen*, July 26, 1914.

29. Frances Noel, letter to the National Women's Trades Union League, n.d., Box 11, Folder 8, Noel Papers, University of California at Los Angeles, University Research Library, Department of Special Collections; *Los Angeles Citizen*, April 16, 1915, March 17, 1911. For more on gender and organization in later decades, see Ruiz, *Cannery Women*, esp. 24–25, 43.

30. Wertheimer, *We Were There*, 221.

31. Perry and Perry, *Los Angeles Labor Movement*, 44; *Los Angeles Citizen*, September 1, March 17, 1911.

32. See, for example, the *Los Angeles Citizen*, April 26, 1912; Perry and Perry, *Los Angeles Labor Movement*, 44; and *Los Angeles Citizen*, March 17, August 4, September 8, 1911.

33. The best study of this development among working men is Roediger, *Wages of Whiteness*. For a consideration of how these issues affected working women, see Deutsch, *Women and the City*, 192.

34. Evelyn Brooks Higginbotham has famously called the intersection of race with class, gender, and sexuality the "metalanguage of race" ("African-American Women's History and the Metalanguage of Race," 252). See also Frank, "White Working-Class Women," 96.

35. Wild, *Street Meeting*, 54–56, 61, 30–31.

36. Ibid., 32–33, 68, 70–71, 124–25.

37. Pauline V. Young, "The Russian Molokan Community in Los Angeles," 393–94.

38. Wild, *Street Meeting*, 28; McWilliams, *Southern California Country*, 323.

39. Wild, *Street Meeting*, 40–44.

40. Ronald Takaki, *Strangers From a Different Shore: A History of Asian Americans*, 10, 14, 40; William A. Edwards, M.D., and Beatrice Harraden, *Two Health-Seekers in Southern California*, 1897), 93; Fogelson, *Fragmented Metropolis*, 122–23; Cheng and Cheng, "Chinese Women of Los Angles," 2–3, 5, 9–10; Mason and Laslett, "Women's Work in the American West," 25.

41. John Modell, "Japanese-Americans: Some Costs of Group Achievement," 105; Wild, *Street Meeting*, 38; Takaki, *Strangers From a Different Shore*, 123; Cheng and Cheng, "Chinese Women of Los Angles," 2–3, 9–10.

42. Takaki, *Strangers From a Different Shore*, 103.

43. Ibid., 46–47, 50, 186; Fogelson, *Fragmented Metropolis*, 77; Patricia Nelson Limerick, *The Legacy of Conquest: The Unbroken Past of the American West*, 269.

44. Glenn, "Dialectics of Wage Work," 432–40; Takaki, *Strangers From a Different Shore*, 50, 193; Modell, "Japanese-Americans," 108; Wild, *Street Meeting*, 24.

45. Koslow, "Eden's Underbelly," 137; Natalia Molina, *Fit to Be Citizens? Public Health and Race in Los Angeles, 1879–1939*, 104.

46. Bean and Rawls, *California: An Interpretive History*, 260; Fogelson, *Fragmented Metropolis*, 77.

47. Nash, *American West*, 79; Lonnie G. Bunch, "A Past Not Necessarily Prologue: The Afro-American in Los Angeles," 101; McWilliams, *Southern California Country*, 325.

48. The percentage of women engaged in gainful occupations in Los Angeles by birth, 1900–1920, is as follows: African American, 1900: 38.4; 1910: 50.0; 1920: 50.5; foreign-born white, 1900: 20.6; 1910: 23.5; 1920: 24.0; foreign or mixed parentage white, 1900: 24.2; 1910: 28.8; 1920: 31.4; native-born white women, 1900: 20.6; 1910: 24.9; 1920: 29.9 (Hill, *Women in Gainful Occupations*, 271–76).

49. Camarillo, *Chicanos in a Changing Society*, 201–3; Dana W. Bartlett, *The Better City: A Sociological Study of a Modern City*, 71, 96 (emphasis added).

50. Muncy, *Creating a Female Dominion*, 9, 13–14; "YWCA Work for Newcomers," *Los Angeles Times*, October 18, 1914; Raymond A. Mohl, "Cultural Pluralism in Immigrant Education: The YWCA's International Institutes, 1910–1940," 114.

51. Peggy Pascoe, *Relations of Rescue: The Search for Female Moral Authority in the American West, 1874–1939*, 10–11, 12; Bartlett, *Better City*, 86–89; Jay P. Nolan and Gilberto M. Hinojosa, eds., *Mexican Americans and the Catholic Church, 1900–1965*, 156; Michael E. Engh, S.J., "Mary Julia Workman, the Catholic Conscience of Los Angeles," 7; Robert A. Woods and Albert J. Kennedy, eds., *Handbook of Settlements*, 9–13; Gayle Gullett, "Women Progressives and the Politics of Americanization in California, 1915–1920," 78.

52. "New Chinese Mission," *Los Angeles Times*, April 1, 1913; Stimson, *Rise of the*

Labor Movement, 294–95; Woods and Kennedy, *Handbook of Settlements,* 9–13; Bartlett, *Better City,* 86–89; Muncy, *Creating a Female Dominion,* 30.

53. Mohl, "Cultural Pluralism," 119.

54. "Confusion of Tongues Reigns at YWCA Meeting Place of Nationalities to Learn English," *Los Angeles Express,* July 18, 1913.

55. "Speak Eight Languages at YWCA Employment Bureau Help Foreigners," *Los Angeles Record,* September 28, 1916; "Short Historical Sketch of the Los Angeles Y.W.C.A." (see chap. 2, n. 27).

56. Young, *Pilgrims of Russian-Town,* 1, 12, 30; Young, "Russian Molokan Community," 396–97.

57. Bartlett, *Better City,* 80–81; Young, *Pilgrims of Russian-Town,* 99.

58. Young, "Russian Molokan Community," 400–401; Victor S. Clark, *Mexican Labor in the United States,* 510.

59. "Woman Angel of Cheer to Slaves: Labor of Love Instructing Poor; Russian Colony Is Scene of Work," *Los Angeles Tribune,* December 3, 1914; Young, *Pilgrims of Russian-Town,* 149, 153.

60. Lillian Sokoloff, "The Russians in Los Angeles," 5–7. See also Young, "Russian Molokan Community," 398–99.

61. Young, "Russian Molokan Community," 398–99.

62. Ibid.

63. Phoebe S. Kropp, *California "Vieja": Culture and Memory in a Modern American Place;* V. Clark, *Mexican Labor in the United States,* 507.

64. Sanchez, *Becoming Mexican American,* 72–78; George J. Sanchez, "'Go After the Women': Americanization and the Mexican Immigrant Woman, 1915–1929," 252.

65. G. Bromley Oxnam, *The Mexican in Los Angeles: Los Angeles City Survey,* 9–12; Gullett, "Women Progressives," 82; V. Clark, *Mexican Labor in the United States,* 496.

66. V. Clark, *Mexican Labor in the United States,* 508, 507.

67. Ibid., 466, 511–12; Gómez-Quiñones, *Mexican American Labor,* 65–89.

68. V. Clark, *Mexican Labor in the United States,* 466, 495–96; Sanchez, *Becoming Mexican American,* 132, 142–43; Monroy, *Rebirth,* 19.

69. P. Taylor, "Mexican Women in Los Angeles," 103, 108–10, 112–13, 124–27. See also Sanchez, "'Go After the Women,'" 260; and Mason and Laslett, "Women's Work in the American West," 16–18.

70. Gullett, "Women Progressives," 82; Sanchez, "'Go After the Women,'" 251–63; "Plans Model Bungalow," *Los Angeles Express,* November 8, 1910; "Macy School Children Make Efficient Workers," *Los Angeles Express,* September 17, 1914; "Trade Union Movement Helps to Americanize," *Los Angeles Citizen,* May 5, 1916.

71. Gullett, "Women Progressives," 79, 81, 85–93.

72. Nelson A. Pichardo, "The Establishment and Development of Chicano Voluntary Associations in California, 1910–1930," 93–95, 110, 117; Kaye Lynn Briegel, "Alianza Hispano-Americana, 1894–1965: A Mexican American Fraternal Insurance Society," 53, 208; Cynthia E. Orozco, "Beyond Machismo, *la Familia,* and Ladies Aux-

iliaries: A Historiography of Mexican-Origin Women's Participation in Voluntary Associations and Politics in the United States, 1870–1990," 13; Jose Amaro Hernandez, *Mutual Aid for Survival: The Case of the Mexican American,* 9.

73. V. Clark, *Mexican Labor in the United States,* 510–11; Hernandez, *Mutual Aid for Survival,* 9; Ricardo Romo, *East Los Angeles: History of a Barrio,* 153; Griswold del Castillo, *Los Angeles Barrio,* 136–37; Pichardo, "Chicano Voluntary Associations," 93–95, 110, 117; Briegel, "Alianza Hispano-Americana," 53, 208; Orozco, "Beyond Machismo," 13.

74. Unidentified newspaper clipping, Box 18, Series V: Publicity Files, Los Angeles Young Women's Christian Association Collection, Urban Archives Center, California State University, Northridge.

75. Nolan and Hinojosa, *Mexican Americans and the Catholic Church,* 137, 155. Before the 1910s Mexican attendance at local Catholic churches had been on the decline.

76. The five other Catholic agencies were El Hogar Feliz/St. Joseph's Settlement at 1441 North Main Street, the Alpine Street Center at 421 Alpine Street, the Guardian Angel Center at 151 North Clarence Street, the Plaza Center at 420 North Main Street, and the Mother Cabrini Preventorium in Burbank (Oxnam, *Mexican in Los Angeles,* 17–20).

77. Engh, "Mary Julia Workman," 5–7, 9; "Brownson House," brochure [1916], Mary Julia Workman Collection, Department of Special Collections, Von der Ahe Library, Loyola Marymount University, Los Angeles, California; Nolan and Hinojosa, *Mexican Americans and the Catholic Church,* 148.

78. Nolan and Hinojosa, *Mexican Americans and the Catholic Church,* 157. This later became the Catholic Welfare Bureau.

79. Oxnam, *Mexican in Los Angeles,* 17–20; Engh, "Mary Julia Workman," 13.

80. Nolan and Hinojosa, *Mexican Americans and the Catholic Church,* 153.

81. Romo, *East Los Angeles,* 90; Gullett, "Women Progressives," 85–93.

82. Weaver, *Los Angeles,* 85; Jaher, *Urban Establishment,* 659; Fogelson, *Fragmented Metropolis,* 131.

83. *Los Angeles Citizen,* June 16, 1916.

7 | Wartime, Protest, and New Industries

1. "Eastern Journal Outlines Progress Unionism Has Made in Los Angeles," *Los Angeles Citizen,* November 22, 1918; "Women Unionists and Club Women Hold Heart-to-Heart Conference," *Los Angeles Citizen,* July 11, 1919.

2. "Appeals in Pews to Get Work for Girls," *Los Angeles Times,* February 1, 1916.

3. Stansell, *City of Women,* xii; Enstad, *Ladies of Labor,* 91, 93, 120; Venus Green, *Race on the Line: Gender, Labor, and Technology in the Bell System, 1880–1980,* 2; Deutsch, *Women and the City,* 217; Higginbotham, "African-American Women's History," 261; Lois Rita Hembold and Ann Schofield, "Women's Labor History, 1790–1945," 503.

4. See, for example, Putnam's exploration of postwar labor unrest in Seattle (*Class and Gender Politics,* 197–216).

5. "New Courses Offered at YWCA," *Los Angeles Examiner,* February 4, 1918; "Ten Thousand Women Prepare to Take Places of Soldiers," *Los Angeles Times,* n.d., Scrapbook 18, Los Angeles Young Women's Christian Association Collection, Urban Archives Center, California State University, Northridge; "Woman Will Do War Work," *Los Angeles Times,* February 23, 1918: "Three Get War Cross," *Los Angeles Times,* March 28. 1919.

6. "Canners Issue Call for Workers to Help Save Banner Fruits and Vegetable Crop," *Los Angeles Express,* September 13, 1917; "Nation's Man Power Found Sufficient for Needs," *Los Angeles Express,* May 13, 1918; "Ten Thousand Women Prepare to Take Places of Soldiers," *Los Angeles Times,* n.d., Scrapbook 18, Los Angeles Young Women's Christian Association Collection, Urban Archives Center, California State University, Northridge.

7. "Women Successful in Doing Tire Work Here," *Los Angeles Express,* September 29, 1918; Norman S. Stanley, *No Little Plans: The Story of the Los Angeles Chamber of Commerce,* 23; "Ten Thousand Women Prepare to Take Places of Soldiers," *Los Angeles Times,* n.d., Scrapbook 18, Los Angeles Young Women's Christian Association Collection, Urban Archives Center, California State University, Northridge.

8. "Women Successful in Doing Tire Work Here"; Stanley, *No Little Plans,* 23; "Farmerettes Leave for Land Army Work," *Los Angeles Express,* July 1, 1918; "Women Prove Their Worth as Workers on Farm," *Los Angeles Express,* May 20, 1918.

9. Wild, *Street Meeting,* 122–31.

10. Lavinia Griffin Graham, "Women's Clubs Urged to Provide Homelike Hotel for Night-Working Girls," *Los Angeles Examiner,* February 18, 1916; "YWCA Opens Club for Girl Night Toilers," *Los Angeles Herald,* October 28, 1916; "YWCA Great Aid to Saleswomen, Adams Says," *Los Angeles Express,* February 11, 1916; "Protection of Girls," *Los Angeles Herald,* March 17, 1915; Wild, *Street Meeting,* 131.

11. "U.S. Officers in L.A. Jail Alleged Alien Enemy, Seize Press," *Los Angeles Express,* September 5, 1917; *Los Angeles Times,* September 20, 1917; Ralph E. Shaffer, "Radicalism in California, 1869–1929," 209, 221, 355–58; *Los Angeles Times,* November 15, 17, 19, 1919; "Labor Temple Closes Its Doors Against the I.W.W.," *Los Angeles Citizen,* March 7, 1919; Perry and Perry, *Los Angeles Labor Movement,* 36; Wild, *Street Meeting,* 170.

12. Braitman, "Katherine Phillips Edson," 243; brochure, "Reconstruction Program Women's Committee of the State Council of Defense of California," 1918, Noel Papers, University of California at Los Angeles, University Research Library, Department of Special Collections; Edson, Los Angeles, to Noel, Los Angeles, September 16, 1917, Noel Papers, ibid.

13. Mary Anderson, Director, Women's Bureau, Washington, D.C., to John P. McLaughlin, Commissioner, Bureau of Labor Statistics, San Francisco, September 19, 1919, Edson Papers, University of California at Los Angeles, University Research

Library, Department of Special Collections; Edson, Los Angeles, to Noel, Los Angeles, September 16, 1917, Noel Papers, ibid.; Wild, *Street Meeting*, 170; "Government for Labor Standards," *Los Angeles Citizen*, December 14, 1917.

14. Jacqueline R. Braitman, "A California Stateswoman: The Public Career of Katherine Phillips Edson," 90.

15. "Nation's Man Power Found Sufficient for Needs."

16. "Plans for Reconstruction," *Los Angeles Citizen*, November 22, 1918.

17. Louis Levine, *The Women's Garment Workers: A History of the International Ladies' Garment Workers Union*, 329; Montgomery, *Fall of the House of Labor*, 332; Perry and Perry, *Los Angeles Labor Movement*, 123; Andrew F. Rolle, *California, a History*, 263–64, 429.

18. Stimson, *Rise of the Labor Movement*, 314–15; Stephen H. Norwood, *Labor's Flaming Youth: Telephone Operators and Worker Militancy, 1878–1923*, 26–27; Ruth Milkman, *Gender at Work: The Dynamics of Job Segregation by Sex During World War II*, 4; Green, *Race on the Line*, 3.

19. However, Green focuses mainly on a black-white binary of female workers (*Race on the Line*, 3). See also Norwood, *Labor's Flaming Youth*, 28–32.

20. Stephen Norwood has written the definitive work on labor unions in the telephone industry. See his *Labor's Flaming Youth*, 40–48; and Frances N. Noel, "Nervous Strain at Switchboard Impairs Health," *Los Angeles Citizen*, June 27, 1919.

21. "The Development of the Telephone in Los Angeles," 6; Norwood, *Labor's Flaming Youth*, 36; "Development of the Telephone in Los Angeles," 6.

22. Jeffrey E. Cohen, *The Politics of Telecommunications Regulation: The States and the Divestiture of AT&T*, 28; Green, *Race on the Line*, 78–79.

23. "The Line Is Busy," *Los Angeles Citizen*, April 5, 1907; "Job Harriman Says Women Must Help Make the Good Laws," *Los Angeles Citizen*, November 17, 1911; Norwood, *Labor's Flaming Youth*, 73–74.

24. "Wire Troubles," *Los Angeles Times*, June 10, 1919; Norwood, *Labor's Flaming Youth*, 158–69.

25. "Want All to Strike," *Los Angeles Times*, June 9, 1919; Norwood, *Labor's Flaming Youth*, 198–99: "Want All to Strike," *Los Angeles Times*, June 9, 1919; "Hasten Return of Wires," *Los Angeles Times*, June 11, 1919.

26. Green, *Race on the Line*, 90; Norwood, *Labor's Flaming Youth*, 202–3; "1,200 Telephone Girls Fighting for Justice," *Los Angeles Citizen*, June 20, 1919; "Phone Strike Starts Today?" *Los Angeles Times*, June 16, 1919; "Strike Fails to Tie Up Telephone Service," *Los Angeles Times*, June 17, 1919; "Telephone Operators Wanted," *Los Angeles Times*, June 19, 1919; "Say Telephone Strike's Practically Broken," *Los Angeles Times*, June 18, 1919; "Strike Conference Fails," *Los Angeles Times*, June 20, 1919; "Phone Strike Starts Today?"

27. "Ultimatum to Strikers," *Los Angeles Times*, June 22, 1919; "Strike Situation Clears," *Los Angeles Times*, June 23, 1919: Green, *Race on the Line*, 91; Enstad, *Ladies of Labor*, 91–92: Perry and Perry, *Los Angeles Labor Movement*, 142; "Phone Com-

pany Cannot Treat With Strikers," *Los Angeles Times,* June 19, 1919; "Strike Conference Fails," *Los Angeles Times,* June 20, 1919.

28. Enstad, *Ladies of Labor,* 86; "Attack in Times Answered by Girl," *Los Angeles Citizen,* July 4, 1919; "Jazz Phone Girls Into Labor Union," *Los Angeles Times,* June 14, 1919.

29. "A letter from telephone girls to the citizenship especially women of Los Angeles," Los Angeles, July 14, 1919, Noel Papers, University of California at Los Angeles, University Research Library, Department of Special Collections; "Attack in Times Answered by Girl"; "1,200 Telephone Girls Fighting for Justice"; "Court Is Asked to Gag Striking Telephone Girls," *Los Angeles Citizen,* June 27, 1919; "Restraining Order Stands Against Telephone Girls," *Los Angeles Citizen,* July 4, 1919.

30. "Court Is Asked to Gag Striking Telephone Girls"; "Restraining Order Stands Against Telephone Girls"; *Los Angeles Citizen,* July 11, 1919; Perry and Perry, *Los Angeles Labor Movement,* 143.

31. "Phone Company Cannot Treat With Strikers"; Norwood, *Labor's Flaming Youth,* 202–3; "Phone Strike Parleys Ended," *Los Angeles Times,* June 26, 1919; Perry and Perry, *Los Angeles Labor Movement,* 144.

32. Perry and Perry, *Los Angeles Labor Movement,* 217; "Soap-Box Girl Goes East to Attend Industrial Conference," *Los Angeles Record,* October 18, 1919; Edson to Shelley Tolhurst, June 3, 1921, Edson Papers, University of California at Los Angeles, University Research Library, Department of Special Collections; Edson to John R. Haynes, June 3, 1921, Edson Papers, ibid.; U.S. Census ms., 1910, Los Angeles, AD 73, ED 135, p. 4B; Dorothy Sue Cobble, *The Other Women's Movement: Workplace Justice and Social Rights in Modern America,* 26.

33. Green, *Race on the Line,* 104; Perry and Perry, *Los Angeles Labor Movement,* 142, 144; Norwood, *Labor's Flaming Youth,* 202–3, 257–60.

34. Perry and Perry, *Los Angeles Labor Movement,* 148–49; J. Laslett and Tyler, *ILGWU in Los Angeles,* 19.

35. "Union Tailors Fighting for Their Existence," *Los Angeles Citizen,* April 18, 1919; Perry and Perry, *Los Angeles Labor Movement,* 150–51.

36. Perry and Perry, *Los Angeles Labor Movement,* 151.

37. "Orange Pickers to Meet at the Temple," *Los Angeles Citizen,* February 14, 1919.

38. Perry and Perry, *Los Angeles Labor Movement,* 159; "A Living Wage for Teachers," *Los Angeles Citizen,* May 23, 1919; "Teachers Beaten in Their Battle for Living Wages," *Los Angeles Citizen,* July 9, 1920; *Los Angeles Citizen,* October 24, 31, 1919.

39. "Domestics in Mass Meet to Urge 8 Hour Day: Women Workers to Discuss Employment Problems in Households," *Los Angeles Herald,* December 3, 1919; flyer, n.d., Noel Papers, University of California at Los Angeles, University Research Library, Department of Special Collections; "Domestic Workers Organize Forever," *Los Angeles Citizen,* June 27, 1919; Haynes, "Negroes in Domestic Service," 435. This union was likely the Association for the Improvement of Domestic Service.

40. U.S. Department of Labor, *The Development of Minimum Wage Laws in the United States, 1912 to 1927,* 15.

41. Weaver, *Los Angeles,* 79; Nash, *American West,* 129; Wendy Holliday, "Hollywood's Modern Women: Screenwriting, Work Culture, and Feminism, 1910–1950," 32; Stanley, *No Little Plans,* 22, reprinted from *Southern California Business,* September 1956.

42. Weaver, *Los Angeles,* 73; Nash, *American West,* 103; "California's Great Movie Industry Brings $5,000,000 Yearly to the State," *Los Angeles Citizen,* April 9, 1915; McWilliams, *Southern California Country,* 332.

43. McWilliams, *Southern California Country,* 332; *Los Angeles Times,* January 17, 1911, quoted in Weaver, *Los Angeles,* 78.

44. Holliday, "Hollywood's Modern Women," 42. On leading actresses and actors who started out as extras, see "How Famous Film Stars Have Been Discovered," *Los Angeles Times,* October 18, 1914.

45. Holliday, "Hollywood's Modern Women," 36, 46, 67; "Ten Thousand Women Prepare to Take Places of Soldiers," *Los Angeles Times,* n.d., Scrapbook 18, Los Angeles Young Women's Christian Association Collection, Urban Archives Center, California State University, Northridge; "Report on the Motion Picture Industry in Los Angeles," n.d. (May 1919?), ibid., 1–2, 6–7.

46. "Report on the Motion Picture Industry in Los Angeles," 1–2, 6–7.

47. Valeria Belletti, *Adventures of a Hollywood Secretary: Her Private Letters From Inside the Studios of the 1920s,* 205–6.

48. "Report on the Motion Picture Industry in Los Angeles," 1–2, 4–5.

49. Ibid., 3, 7–9, 11–13.

50. "Extras Charge Illegal Ways," *Los Angeles Times,* January 26, 1923.

51. Ibid.; "Report on the Motion Picture Industry in Los Angeles," 16–120.

52. "Report on the Motion Picture Industry in Los Angeles," 16–120.

53. De Graaf, "Race, Sex, and Region," 302; Alicia Rodríquez-Estrada, "Dolores Del Rio and Lupe Velez: Images On and Off the Screen, 1925–1944," in *Writing the Range: Race, Class, and Culture in the Women's West,* edited by Elizabeth Jameson and Susan Armitage, 476, 481, 485; Sara Ross, "The Americanization of Tsuru Aoki: Orientalism, Melodrama, Star Image, and the New Woman"; "Jiu-Jitsu for Police Force," *Los Angeles Times,* December 27, 1914.

54. Report on the Motion Picture Industry in Los Angeles," 14; Mary P. Ryan, *Civic Wars: Democracy and Public Life in the American City During the Nineteenth Century,* 68–76; Sharon E. Wood, *The Freedom of the Streets: Work, Citizenship, and Sexuality in a Gilded Age City,* 53.

55. "Report on the Motion Picture Industry in Los Angeles," 14–16.

56. Ibid., 9, 14.

57. Ibid.; "Short Historical Sketch of the Los Angeles Y.W.C.A." (see chap. 2, n. 27); "Unique Girls' Club at Hollywood Founded in Little Life Incident," *Los Angeles Record,* February 27, 1918.

58. Unidentified newspaper clipping, ca. 1916, Box 16, Series IV: Records of the YWCA Branches, 1909–1976, Los Angeles Young Women's Christian Association Collection, Urban Archives Center, California State University, Northridge; "$250,000 Studio Club to Be Dedicated at Ceremonies Tomorrow," *Los Angeles Citizen*, May 6, 1926.

59. "Report on the Motion Picture Industry in Los Angeles," 14; "$250,000 Studio Club to Be Dedicated"; brochure, n.d., unidentified newspaper clipping, Scrapbook 32, Los Angeles Young Women's Christian Association Collection, Urban Archives Center, California State University, Northridge; "Day Nursery Helps Mothers," *Los Angeles Times*, July 7, 1929.

60. "Report on the Motion Picture Industry in Los Angeles," 12–13; *Los Angeles Citizen*, September 12, 1919; Grace Kingsley, "At the Stage Door," *Los Angeles Times*, July 19, 1915. A Chorus Equity Association was also created in 1919. Accounts vary as to whether Actor's Equity absorbed a previous vaudeville union, the White Rats of America, or if it was wiped out by company unions. See Alfred Harding, *The Revolt of the Actors*, 14–15, 66–67.

61. *Los Angeles Citizen*, September 12, 1919; Harding, *Revolt of the Actors*, 8–9.

62. Harding, *Revolt of the Actors*, 88–89, 189–90, 230–36; Paul F. Gemmill, "Equity: The Actor's Trade Union"; "Actor's Equity Seeks Reforms," *Los Angeles Times*, January 4, 1923; "Cinema Salary Cut Postponed," *Los Angeles Times*, July 1, 1927.

63. The total number of employed women in that year was 68,061. The percentages were as follows: professional and other white-collar jobs, 10.7 percent; petty proprietorships, 3.2 percent; semiprofessional occupations, 7.2 percent; clerical and sales occupations, 36.3 percent; skilled occupations, 0.39 percent; domestic service, 13.2 percent; personal service occupations, 11.5 percent; manufacturing in a nonfactory setting, 6.7 percent; manufacturing in a factory setting, 8.1 percent; miscellaneous semiskilled occupations, 1.3 percent; unskilled occupations, 1.5 percent. See Eileen V. Wallis, "Women Employed in Certain Selected Occupations, Los Angeles, 1920," appx. F in "At Work in the Urban West: Gender, Ethnicity, and Employment in Los Angeles, 1883–1920"; and Hill, *Women in Gainful Occupations*, 212–15.

64. Robert H. Wiebe, *The Search for Order, 1877–1920*, 293; Alan Dawley, *Changing the World: American Progressives in War and Revolution*, 285; Cobble, *Other Women's Movement*, 95–96; Dorothy M. Brown, *Setting a Course: American Women in the 1920s*, 85; Katherine Philips Edson, n.d., Box 7, Folder 4, Edson Papers, University of California at Los Angeles, University Research Library, Department of Special Collections; Braitman, "Katherine Phillips Edson," x.

65. Dawley, *Changing the World*, 285; Cobble, *Other Women's Movement*, 95–96.

66. Hundley, "Katherine Phillips Edson," 271, 281–85; Braitman, "Katherine Phillips Edson," x; National Industrial Conference Board, *Wages in the United States, 1914–1930*, 52, 59.

67. This term correctly identifies how female-dominated these largely dead-end jobs became in the twentieth century. However, because the term itself was not

coined until 1977 I have chosen not to use it here (Cobble, *Other Women's Movement*, 231n2).

68. Young, *Pilgrims of Russian-Town*, 252, 27.

69. "Short History of the Japanese YWCA Magnolia Residence," Box 3, Folder 1, Los Angeles Young Women's Christian Association Collection, Urban Archives Center, California State University, Northridge; "Short Historical Sketch of the Los Angeles Y.W.C.A."; "Talkies Strike at Extra's Job," *Los Angeles Times*, February 23, 1930.

70. Perry and Perry, *Los Angeles Labor Movement*, 199; Montgomery, *Fall of the House of Labor*, 332; Fogelson, *Fragmented Metropolis*, 128–29; Gottlieb and Wolt, *Thinking Big*, 156.

Epilogue

1. Edson, n.d., Box 7, Folder 4, Edson Papers, University of California at Los Angeles, University Research Library, Department of Special Collections; Braitman, "Katherine Phillips Edson," x; Fogelson, *Fragmented Metropolis*, 128–29, 131; Fred V. Viehe, "Black Gold Suburbs: The Influence of the Extractive Industry on the Suburbanization of Los Angeles, 1890–1930," 13; J. Laslett and Tyler, *ILGWU in Los Angeles*, 19.

2. "Jobless in City Few," *Los Angeles Times*, September 5, 1930.

3. "Hats of Easter Aid 2,000 Women," *Los Angeles Times*, April 23, 1930; "Rouge for the Unemployed," *Los Angeles Times*, February 28, 1932; "Mission's Shop Provides Jobs," *Los Angeles Times*, July 4, 1932; Alma Whitaker, "Needy Women's Distress Great," *Los Angeles Times*, September 12, 1932.

4. Dawley, *Changing the World*, 285; Cobble, *Other Women's Movement*, 95–96.

5. "Group Merges Aid for Women," *Los Angeles Times*, April 4, 1932; "Unemployed Women Aided," *Los Angeles Times*, January 4, 1935; "S.E.R.A. to Start Works," *Los Angeles Times*, May 3, 1934; "Director of Placements Concentrates on Work Problem of Women Under SERA," *Los Angeles Times*, July 18, 1934; "Women Aid Plan Backed," *Los Angeles Times*, October 15, 1935; "Women's Return to Sewing Project Asked of Hopkins," *Los Angeles Times*, November 12, 1936; "Supervisors Face Sit-Down," *Los Angeles Times*, February 24, 1938; "Sewing Fund Inquiry Asked," *Los Angeles Times*, February 26, 1938; "WPA to Drop Hundreds Today," *Los Angeles Times*, January 5, 1939.

6. Cobble, *Other Women's Movement*, 5, 16; J. Laslett and Tyler, *ILGWU in Los Angeles*, 27.

7. "The Situation in the Waist and Dress Industry in Los Angeles," *Los Angeles Citizen*, August 20, 1920; Castro interview (see introduction, n. 1).

8. J. Laslett and Tyler, *ILGWU in Los Angeles*, 28.

9. Laslett, "Gender, Class, or Ethno-cultural Struggle?" 23–26; Rose Pesotta, *Bread Upon the Waters*, 19–21; Cobble, *Other Women's Movement*, 3.

10. Pesotta, *Bread Upon the Waters*, 19; Gerald Sorin, "Rose Pesotta in the Far West: The Triumphs and Travails of a Jewish Woman Labor Organizer," 137–41;

Castro interview; "End of Strike Today Sought," *Los Angeles Times,* October 31, 1933; J. Laslett, "Gender, Class, or Ethno-cultural Struggle?" 31.

11. "Studios Boast Banner Month," *Los Angeles Times,* October 14, 1933; Jaher, *Urban Establishment,* 669; McWilliams, *Southern California Country,* 348.

12. Sanchez, *Becoming Mexican American,* 143, 197, 201–2.

13. For a discussion of Mexican American women and popular culture, see Vicki Ruiz, *From Out of the Shadows: Mexican Women in Twentieth-Century America,* esp. chap. 3.

14. Bette Yarbrough Cox, *Central Avenue: Its Rise and Fall, 1890–1955,* 23; McWilliams, *Southern California Country,* 325.

15. Takaki, *Strangers From a Different Shore,* 267.

16. Haynes, "Negroes in Domestic Service," 425, 435; Dudden, *Serving Women,* 240; Kessler-Harris, *Out to Work,* 112; Norwood, *Labor's Flaming Youth,* 307–9.

17. Nash, *American West,* 193–95; Cobble, *Other Women's Movement,* 3. On women's work in California during World War II, see, for example, Roger W. Lotchin, *The Bad City in the Good War: San Francisco, Los Angeles, Oakland, and San Diego,* 75, 77, 83.

18. Enstad, *Ladies of Labor,* 13.

SELECTED BIBLIOGRAPHY

―――――――

Manuscript Collections

Braun Research Library, Southwest Museum, Autry National Center, Los Angeles
    Casa de Adobe Collection
California State University, Long Beach
    Virtual Oral/Aural History Archive
Huntington Library, San Marino, California
    Bullocks Department Store Photo Collection
    Clara (Bradley) Burdette Collection
    Friday Morning Club Scrapbooks
    Caroline Maria (Seymour) Severance Collection
Southern California Library for Social Studies Research, Los Angeles
    Charlotta A. Bass Papers
    California Eagle Photograph Collection
    Register of the International Ladies' Garment Workers' Union, Project File, 1914–1993
    Register of the International Typographical Union Records, 1903–1986
Thomas and Dorothy Leavey Center for the Study of Los Angeles, Research Collection, Loyola Marymount University, Los Angeles
    Workman Family Papers
University of California at Los Angeles, University Archives
    Biographical Files
University of California at Los Angeles, University Research Library, Department of Special Collections
    Katherine Phillips Edson Papers
    Frances Noel Papers
University of Southern California, Special Collections Department, Los Angeles
    Coulter Dry Goods Collection
Urban Archives Center, California State University, Northridge
    Los Angeles Young Women's Christian Association Collection

Newspapers and Periodicals

Common Sense
Los Angeles Citizen
Los Angeles Eagle
Los Angeles Examiner
Los Angeles Express
Los Angeles Herald
Los Angeles Record
Los Angeles Times
Los Angeles Tribune
Los Angeles Union Labor News
Sunset

Other Sources

Abbott, Edith. *Women in Industry: A Study in American Economic History.* New York: D. Appelton, 1913.

Abel, Emily K. *Suffering in the Land of Sunshine: A Los Angeles Illness Narrative.* New Brunswick: Rutgers University Press, 2006.

Almaguer, Tomas. *Racial Fault Lines: The Historical Origins of White Supremacy in California.* Berkeley and Los Angeles: University of California Press, 1994.

Alpern, Sara, Joyce Antler, Elisabeth Israels Perry, and Ingred Winther Scobie, eds. *The Challenge of Feminist Biography: Writing the Lives of Modern American Women.* Urbana: University of Illinois Press, 1992.

Anthony, Susan B., and Ida Husted Harper. *History of Woman Suffrage.* Vol. 4, *1883–1900.* 1902. Reprint, New York: Arno and the New York Times, 1969.

Apostol, Jane. "Mary Emily Foy: 'Miss Los Angeles Herself.'" *Southern California Quarterly* 78, no. 2 (1996): 109–37.

———. "They Said It With Flowers: The Los Angeles Flower Festival Society." *Southern California Quarterly* 62 (Spring 1980): 67–78.

———. "Why Women Should Not Have the Vote: Anti-Suffrage Views in the Southland in 1911." *Southern California Quarterly* 70, no. 1 (Spring 1988): 29–41.

Appier, Janis. *The Sexual Politics of Law Enforcement and the LAPD.* Philadelphia: Temple University Press, 1998.

Armitage, Susan. "Women and Men in Western History: A Stereoptical Vision." *Western Historical Quarterly* 16, no. 4 (October 1985).

Baker, Paula. "The Domestication of Politics: Women and American Political Society, 1780–1920." *American Historical Review* 89, no. 3 (June 1984): 620–47.

Banks, Elizabeth. *The Remaking of an American.* Gainesville: University Press of Florida, 2000.

Barrett, James R. "Americanization From the Bottom Up: Immigration and the

Remaking of the Working Class in the United States, 1880–1930." *Journal of American History* 79, no. 3 (December 1992): 996–1020.

Bartlett, Dana W. *The Better City: A Sociological Study of a Modern City.* Los Angeles: Neuner, 1907.

Bass, Charlotta A. *Forty Years: Memoirs From the Pages of a Newspaper.* Los Angeles: by the author, 1960.

Baur, John E. *The Health Seekers of Southern California, 1870–1900.* San Marino, Calif.: Huntington Library, 1959.

Bean, Walton, and James J. Rawls. *California: An Interpretive History.* 5th ed. New York: McGraw-Hill, 1988.

Beasley, Delilah L. *The Negro Trail Blazers of California.* 1919. Reprint, New York: Negro Universities Press, 1969.

Belletti, Valeria. *Adventures of a Hollywood Secretary: Her Private Letters From Inside the Studios of the 1920s.* Edited by Cari Beauchamp. Berkeley and Los Angeles: University of California Press, 2006.

Benson, Susan Porter. *Counter Cultures: Saleswomen, Managers, and Customers in American Department Stores, 1890–1940.* Urbana: University of Illinois Press, 1986.

Berokoff, John K. *Molokans in America.* Los Angeles: privately printed, 1969.

Boris, Eileen. *Home to Work: Motherhood and the Politics of Industrial Homework in the United States.* Cambridge: Cambridge University Press, 1994.

Boris, Eileen, and Angelique Janssens. "Complicating Categories: An Introduction." *International Review of Social History,* supp. 7, *Complicating Categories: Gender, Class, Race, and Ethnicity* 44 (1999): 1–13.

Braitman, Jacqueline R. "A California Stateswoman: The Public Career of Katherine Phillips Edson." *California History* (June 1986): 82–95.

———. "Katherine Phillips Edson: A Progressive-Feminist in California's Era of Reform." Ph.D. diss., University of California at Los Angeles, 1988.

Briegel, Kaye Lynn. "Alianza Hispano-Americana, 1894–1965: A Mexican American Fraternal Insurance Society." Ph.D. diss., University of Southern California, 1974.

Brode, Alverda June. "History of the University Section, Los Angeles." *Annual Publications of the Historical Society of Southern California* 12 (1922): 72–108.

Brook, Harry Ellington. *Los Angeles, California: The City and County.* Los Angeles: Los Angeles Chamber of Commerce, 1909.

Broussard, Albert. *Black San Francisco: The Struggle for Racial Equality in the West, 1900–1954.* Lawrence: University Press of Kansas, 1993.

Brown, Dorothy M. *Setting a Course: American Women in the 1920s.* Boston: Twayne, 1987.

Brown, Martin Louis. "A Historical Economic Analysis of the Wage Structure of the California Fruit and Vegetable Canning Industry." Ph.D. diss., University of California at Berkeley, 1981.

Brumberg, Joan Jacobs, and Nancy Tomes. "Women in the Professions: A Research

Agenda for American Historians." *Reviews in American History* 10, no. 2 (June 1982): 275–96.

"Bullard, Rose Talbott." In *Greater Los Angeles and Southern California: Portraits and Personal Memoranda*, edited by Robert J. Burdette. Los Angeles: Lewis Publishing, 1910.

Bunch, Lonnie G. "A Past Not Necessarily Prologue: The Afro-American in Los Angeles." In *Twentieth-Century Los Angeles: Power, Promotion, and Social Conflict*, edited by Norman M. Klein and Martin J. Schiesl. Claremont, Calif.: Regina, 1990.

Butler, Anne M. *Daughters of Joy, Sisters of Misery: Prostitutes in the American West, 1865–90*. Urbana: University of Illinois Press, 1985.

Byrkit, James W. *Forging the Copper Collar: Arizona's Labor-Management War of 1901–1921*. Tucson: University of Arizona Press, 1982.

Camarillo, Albert. *Chicano in a Changing Society: From Mexican Pueblos to American Barrios in Santa Barbara and Southern California, 1848–1930*. Cambridge: Harvard University Press, 1979.

Castaneda, Antonia I. "The Political Economy of Nineteenth-Century Stereotypes of Californianas." In *Between Borders: Essays on Mexicana/Chicana History*, edited by Adelaida R. Del Castillo, 213–36. Mountain View, Calif.: Floricanto Press, 2005.

Chàvez-García, Miroslava. *Negotiating Conquest: Gender and Power in California, 1770s to 1880s*. Tucson: University of Arizona Press, 2004.

Cheng, Lucie, and Suellen Cheng. "Chinese Women of Los Angles: A Social Historical Survey." In *Linking Our Lives: Chinese American Women of Los Angeles*, 1–25. Los Angeles: Chinese Historical Society of Southern California, 1984.

Christman, Anastasia J. "The Best-Laid Plans: Women's Clubs and City Planning in Los Angeles, 1890–1930." Ph.D. diss., University of California at Los Angeles, 2000.

Clark, Thomas. "Law, Rights, and Local Labor Politics in California, 1901–1911: Reflections on Recent Labor Law Historiography." *Studies in American Political Development* 11, no. 1 (Spring 1997): 325–46.

Clark, Victor S. *Mexican Labor in the United States*. Bureau of Labor Bulletin, no. 78. Washington, D.C.: Department of Commerce and Labor, 1908. Reprinted in *The Mexican American*. New York: Arno Press, 1974. Page references are to the 1974 edition.

Clement, Elizabeth Alice. *Love for Sale: Courting, Treating, and Prostitution in New York City, 1900–1945*. Chapel Hill: University of North Carolina Press, 2006.

Cloud, Roy W. *Education in California: Leaders, Organizations, and Accomplishments of the First Hundred Years*. Stanford: Stanford University Press, 1952.

Cobble, Dorothy Sue. *Dishing It Out: Waitresses and Their Union in the Twentieth Century*. Urbana: University of Illinois Press, 1991.

———. *The Other Women's Movement: Workplace Justice and Social Rights in Modern America*. Princeton: Princeton University Press, 2004.

Cohen, Jeffrey E. *The Politics of Telecommunications Regulation: The States and the Divestiture of AT&T*. New York: M. E. Sharpe, 1992.

Committee on Women in Industry of the Advisory Council of National Defense. Washington, D.C.: Government Printing Office, 1918.

Conk, Margo A. "Accuracy, Efficiency, and Bias: The Interpretation of Women's Work in the U.S. Census of Occupations, 1890–1940." *Historical Methods* 14, no. 2 (Spring 1981): 68.

Cornford, Daniel A. *Workers and Dissent in the Redwood Empire.* Philadelphia: Temple University Press, 1987.

Cott, Nancy F. "What's in a Name? The Limits of 'Social Feminism'; or, Expanding the Vocabulary of Women's History." *Journal of American History* 76, no. 3 (December 1989): 809–29.

Cowan, Geoffrey. *The People vs. Clarence Darrow: The Bribery Trial of America's Greatest Lawyer.* New York: Times Books, 1993.

Cowan, Robert G. *A Backward Glance, 1901–1915.* Los Angeles: Torrez Press, 1969.

Cox, Bette Yarbrough. *Central Avenue: Its Rise and Fall, 1890–1955.* Los Angeles: BEEM Publications, 1996.

Craig, Maxine Leeds. *Ain't I a Beauty Queen: Black Women, Beauty, and the Politics of Race.* New York: Oxford University Press, 2002.

Crockett, Earl C. "The History of California Labor Legislation, 1910–1930." Ph.D. diss., University of California at Berkeley, 1931.

Davis, Allen T. "The Campaign for the Industrial Relations Commission, 1911–1913." *Mid-America: An Historical Review* 45, no. 4 (October 1963): 211–28.

Davis, Clark. *Company Men: White-Collar Life and Corporate Cultures in Los Angeles, 1892–1941.* Baltimore: Johns Hopkins University Press, 2000.

Davis, Elizabeth Lindsay. *Lifting as They Climb.* Washington, D.C.: National Association of Colored Women, 1933.

Dawley, Alan. *Changing the World: American Progressives in War and Revolution.* Princeton: Princeton University Press, 2003.

de Graaf, Lawrence B. "Race, Sex, and Region: Black Women in the American West, 1850–1920." *Pacific Historical Review* 49 (May 1980): 285–313.

de Graaf, Lawrence B., Kevin Mulroy, and Quintard Taylor, eds. *Seeking El Dorado: African Americans in California.* Los Angeles: Autry Museum of Western Heritage, 2001.

Deutsch, Sarah. *No Separate Refuge: Culture, Class, and Gender on an Anglo-Hispanic Frontier, 1880–1940.* New York: Oxford University Press, 1987.

———. *Women and the City: Gender, Space, and Power in Boston, 1870–1940.* New York: Oxford University Press, 2000.

"The Development of the Telephone in Los Angeles." *Pacific Telephone* (January 1913).

Deverell, William. *Whitewashed Adobe: The Rise of Los Angeles and the Remaking of Its Mexican Past.* Berkeley and Los Angeles: University of California Press, 2004.

"Dorsey, Susan Almira Miller." In *Notable American Women, 1607–1950: A Biographical Dictionary,* edited by Edward T. James, 506–8. Cambridge: Harvard University Press, 1971.

Douglas, John Aubrey. *The California Idea and American Higher Education: 1850 to the 1960 Master Plan.* Stanford: Stanford University Press, 2000.

Dublin, Thomas. *Women at Work: The Transformation of Work and Community in Lowell, Massachusetts, 1826–1860.* New York: Columbia University Press, 1979.

Dudden, Faye E. *Serving Women: Household Service in Nineteenth-Century America.* Hanover, N.H.: Wesleyan University Press, 1983.

Dumke, Glenn S. *The Boom of the Eighties in Southern California.* 5th ed. San Marino, Calif.: Henry E. Huntington Library and Art Gallery, 1970.

Edwards, Rebecca. *Angels in the Machinery: Gender in American Party Politics From the Civil War to the Progressive Era.* New York: Oxford University Press, 1997.

Edwards, William A., M.D., and Beatrice Harraden. *Two Health-Seekers in Southern California.* Philadelphia: J. B. Lippincott, 1897.

Engh, Michael E., S.J. "Female, Catholic, and Progressive: The Women of the Brownson Settlement House of Los Angeles, 1901–1920." *Records of the American Catholic Historical Society of Philadelphia* 109, no. 1–2 (1999): 113–26.

———. "Mary Julia Workman, the Catholic Conscience of Los Angeles." *California History* (Spring 1993): 3–19.

Enstad, Nan. *Ladies of Labor, Girls of Adventure: Working Women, Popular Culture, and Labor Politics at the Turn of the Twentieth Century.* New York: Columbia University Press, 1999.

Fields, Barbara J. "Ideology and Race in American History." In *Region, Race, and Reconstruction: Essays in Honor of C. Van Woodward,* ed. J. Morgan Kousser and James McPherson, 143–77. New York: Oxford University Press, 1982.

Flamming, Douglas. *Bound for Freedom: Black Los Angeles in Jim Crow America.* Berkeley and Los Angeles: University of California Press, 2005.

Flanagan, Maureen A. *Seeing With Their Hearts: Chicago Women and the Vision of the Good City, 1871–1933.* Princeton: Princeton University Press, 2002.

Flexner, Eleanor. *Century of Struggle.* Cambridge: Harvard University Press, 1959.

Fogelson, Robert M. *The Fragmented Metropolis: Los Angeles, 1850–1930.* Cambridge: Harvard University Press, 1967.

Francis, E. K. "Variables in the Formation of So-called 'Minority Groups.'" *American Journal of Sociology* 60, no. 1 (July 1954): 6–14.

Frank, Dana. "White Working-Class Women and the Race Question." *International Labor and Working-Class History* no. 54 (Fall 1998): 80–102.

Franks, Kenny A., and Paul F. Lambert. *Early California Oil: A Photographic History, 1865–1940.* College Station: Texas A&M Press, 1985.

Freedman, Estelle. *Maternal Justice: Miriam Van Waters and the Female Reform Tradition.* Chicago: University of Chicago Press, 1996.

———. "Separatism as Strategy: Female Institution Building and American Feminism, 1870–1930." *Feminist Studies* 5, no. 3 (Fall 1979): 512–29.

Friday, Chris. *Organizing Asian American Labor: The Pacific Coast Canned-Salmon Industry, 1870–1942.* Philadelphia: Temple University Press, 1994.

Friedricks, William B. "Capital and Labor in Los Angeles: Henry E. Huntington vs. Organized Labor, 1900–1920." *Pacific Historical Review* 59, no. 3 (August 1990): 375–95.

Gamo, Manuel. *The Life Story of the Mexican Immigrant.* New York: Dover Publications, 1971.

Garcia, Matt. *A World of Its Own: Race, Labor, and Citrus in the Making of Greater Los Angeles, 1900–1970.* Chapel Hill: University of North Carolina Press, 2001.

Gemmill, Paul F. "Equity: The Actor's Trade Union." *Quarterly Journal of Economics* 41, no. 1 (November 1926): 129–45.

Gill, Tiffany Melissa. "'I Had My Own Business . . . So I Didn't Have to Worry': Beauty Salons, Beauty Culturists, and the Politics of African American Female Entrepreneurship." In *Beauty and Business: Commerce, Gender, and Culture in Modern America,* edited by Phillip Scanton, 169–94. New York: Routledge, 2000.

Glenn, Evelyn Nakano. "The Dialectics of Wage Work: Japanese-American Women and Domestic Service, 1905–1940." *Feminist Studies* 6, no. 3 (Fall 1980): 432–71.

Goldin, Claudia. *Understanding the Gender Gap: An Economic History of American Women.* New York: Oxford University Press, 1990.

Gómez-Quiñones, Juan. *Mexican American Labor, 1790–1900.* Albuquerque: University of New Mexico Press, 1994.

Gonzalez, Deena J. *Refusing the Favor: The Spanish-Mexican Women of Santa Fe, 1820–1880.* New York: Oxford University Press, 1999.

———. "The Widowed Women of Santa Fe: Assessments of the Lives of an Unmarried Population, 1850–1880." In *Unequal Sisters: A Multicultural Reader in U.S. Women's History,* edited by Ellen Carol DuBois and Vicki L. Ruiz, 34–50. New York: Routledge, 1990.

Gordon, Linda. "Black and White Visions of Welfare: Women's Welfare Activism, 1890–1945." *Journal of American History* 78, no. 2 (September 1991): 559–90.

Gottlieb, Robert, and Irene Wolt. *Thinking Big: The Story of the "Los Angeles Times," Its Publishers, and Their Influence on Southern California.* New York: G. P. Putnam's Sons, 1977.

Green, Venus. *Race on the Line: Gender, Labor, and Technology in the Bell System, 1880–1980.* Durham: Duke University Press, 2001.

Greenstein, Paul. *Bread and Hyacinths: The Rise and Fall of Utopian Los Angeles.* Los Angeles: California Classic Books, 1992.

Griswold del Castillo, Richard. "La Familia": Chicano Families in the Urban Southwest, 1848 to the Present. Notre Dame: University of Notre Dame Press, 1984.

———. *The Los Angeles Barrio, 1850–1890: A Social History.* Berkeley and Los Angeles: University of California Press, 1979.

Groneman, Carol. "'She Earns as a Child; She Pays as a Man': Women Workers in a Mid-Nineteenth-Century New York City Community." In *Class, Sex, and the Woman Worker,* edited by Milton Cantor and Bruce Laurie, 83–100. Westport, Conn.: Greenwood Press, 1977.

Gullett, Gayle. *Becoming Citizens: The Emergence and Development of the California Women's Movement, 1880–1911.* Urbana: University of Illinois Press, 2000.

———. "Constructing the Woman Citizen and Struggling for the Vote in California, 1896–1911." *Pacific Historical Review* 69, no. 4 (2000): 573–93.

———. "Women Progressives and the Politics of Americanization in California, 1915–1920." *Pacific Historical Review* 64, no. 1 (February 1995): 71–94.

Haarsager, Sandra. *Organized Womanhood: Cultural Politics in the Pacific Northwest, 1840–1920.* Norman: University of Oklahoma Press, 1997.

Haas, Lisbeth. *Conquest and Historical Identities in California, 1769–1936.* Berkeley and Los Angeles: University of California Press, 1995.

Hall, Stuart. "Race, Articulation, and Societies Structured in Dominance." In *Sociological Theories: Race and Colonialism*, 305–45. Poole, England: Sydenhams Printers, 1980.

Hansen, Debra Gold, Karen F. Gracy, and Sheri D. Irvin. "At the Pleasure of the Board: Women Librarians and the Los Angeles Public Library, 1880–1905." *Libraries and Cultures* 34, no. 4 (Fall 1999): 311–46.

Harding, Alfred. *The Revolt of the Actors.* 1929. Reprint, Westport, Conn.: Greenwood Press, 1973.

Harris, Cheryl I. "Whiteness as Property." In *Critical Race Theory: The Key Writings That Formed the Movement,* edited by Kimberlé Crenshaw et al., 276–91. New York: New Press, 1995.

Hawley, A. T. *Condition, Progress, and Advantages of Los Angeles City and County, Southern California.* Los Angeles: Los Angeles Chamber of Commerce, 1876.

Hayden, Dolores. "Biddy Mason's Los Angeles, 1856–1891." *California History* 68, no. 3 (Fall 1989): 86–99.

Hayes, Benjamin. *Pioneer Notes.* Los Angeles: privately printed, 1929.

Haynes, Elizabeth Ross. "Negroes in Domestic Service in the United States: Introduction." *Journal of Negro History* 8, no. 4 (October 1923): 384–442.

Heath, Sarah. "Negotiating White Womanhood: The Cincinnati YWCA and White Wage-Earning Women, 1918–1929." In *Men and Women Adrift: The YMCA and the YWCA in the City,* edited by Nina Mjagkij and Margaret Spratt, 86–109. New York: New York University Press, 1997.

Hembold, Lois Rita, and Ann Schofield. "Women's Labor History, 1790–1945." *Reviews in American History* 17, no. 4 (December 1989): 501–18.

Hernandez, Jose Amaro. *Mutual Aid for Survival: The Case of the Mexican American.* Malabar, Fla.: Robert E. Krieger Publishing, 1983.

Herr, Elizabeth. "Women, Marital Status, and Work Opportunities in 1880 Colorado." *Journal of Economic History* 55, no. 2 (June 1995): 339–66.

Hewitt, Nancy A. *Southern Discomfort: Women's Activism in Tampa, Florida, 1880s–1920s.* Urbana: University of Illinois Press, 2001.

Higginbotham, Evelyn Brooks. "African-American Women's History and the Metalanguage of Race." *Signs: Journal of Women in Culture and Society* 17, no. 21 (Winter 1992): 251–74.

Hill, Joseph A. *Women in Gainful Occupations, 1870–1920: A Study of the Trend of Recent Changes in the Numbers, Occupational Distribution, and Family Relationship of Women Reported in the Census as Following a Gainful Occupation.* Washington, D.C.: Government Printing Office, 1929.

Hirata, Lucie Chen. "Chinese Immigrant Women in Nineteenth-Century California." In *Women of America: A History,* edited by Carol Ruth Berkin and Mary Beth Norton, 223–44. Boston: Houghton Mifflin, 1979.

Holliday, Wendy. "Hollywood's Modern Women: Screenwriting, Work Culture, and Feminism, 1910–1950." Ph.D. diss., New York University, 1995.

Hooks, Janet. *Women's Occupations Through Seven Decades.* Bulletin of the Women's Bureau, no. 218. Washington, D.C.: Government Printing Office, 1947.

Hundley, Norris. "Katherine Phillips Edson and the Fight for California's Minimum Wage Law, 1912–1923," *Pacific Historical Review* 29 (1960): 271–86.

Index to the Laws of California, 1850–1893: Index to Statutes, the State Edition of the Codes, 1872, and Subsequent Amendments, and the Constitution of 1879; Prepared Under the Supervision of A. J. Johnson. San Francisco: Bancroft-Whitney, 1894.

Industrial Welfare Commission of the State of California. *First Biennial Report of the Industrial Welfare Commission of the State of California, 1913–1914.* Sacramento: California State Printing Office, 1915.

———. *Second Biennial Report of the Industrial Welfare Commission of the State of California, 1915–1916.* Sacramento: California State Printing Office, 1916.

———. *Third Biennial Report of the Industrial Welfare Commission of the State of California, 1917–1918.* Sacramento: California State Printing Office, 1919.

Issel, William. "'Citizens Outside the Government': Business and Urban Policy in San Francisco and Los Angeles, 1890–1932." *Pacific Historical Review* 57, no. 2 (May 1988): 117–45.

Jaher, Frederic Cople. *The Urban Establishment: Upper Strata in Boston, New York, Charleston, Chicago, and Los Angeles.* Urbana: University of Illinois Press, 1982.

Jameson, Elizabeth, and Susan Armitage, eds. *Writing the Range: Race, Class, and Cultures in the Women's West.* Norman: University of Oklahoma Press, 1997.

Jenkins, J. Craig. *The Politics of Insurgency: The Farm Worker Movement in the 1960s.* New York: Columbia University Press, 1985.

Jensen, Joan M., and Gloria Ricci Lothrop. *California Women: A History.* San Francisco: Boyd and Fraser Publishing, 1987.

Jensen, Joan M., and Darlis A. Miller. "The Gentle Tamers Revisited." *Pacific Historical Review* 49, no. 2 (May 1980): 173–213.

Johnson, Daniel J. "'No Make-Believe Class Struggle': The Socialist Municipal Campaign in Los Angeles, 1911." *Labor History* 41, no. 1 (2000): 25–45.

Johnson, Susan Lee. "'A Memory Sweet to Soldiers': The Significance of Gender in the

History of the American West." *Western Historical Quarterly* 24, no. 4 (November 1993).

————. *Roaring Camp: The Social World of the California Gold Rush.* New York: W. W. Norton, 2000.

Jones, Adrienne Lash. "Struggle Among Saints: African-American Women and the YWCA, 1870–1920." In *Men and Women Adrift: The YMCA and the YWCA in the City,* edited by Nina Mjagkij and Margaret Spratt, 161–87. New York: New York University Press, 1997.

"Jordon, M. Evangeline." In *Greater Los Angeles and Southern California: Portraits and Personal Memoranda,* edited by Robert J. Burdette, 66. Los Angeles: Lewis Publishing, 1910.

Katz, Sherry Jeanne. "Dual Commitments: Feminism, Socialism, and Women's Political Activism in California, 1890–1920." Ph.D. diss., University of California at Los Angeles, 1991.

————. "Frances Nacke Noel and 'Sister Movements': Socialism, Feminism, and Trade Unionism in Los Angeles, 1909–1916." *California History* 67, no. 3 (September 1988): 180–91.

Katzman, David M. *Seven Days a Week: Women and Domestic Service in Industrializing America.* New York: Oxford University Press, 1978.

Kazin, Michael. *Barons of Labor: The San Francisco Building Trades and Union Power in the Progressive Era.* Urbana: University of Illinois Press, 1987.

————. "The Great Exception Revisited: Organized Labor and Politics in San Francisco and Los Angeles, 1870–1940." *Pacific Historical Review* 55, no. 3 (August 1986): 371–402.

Kelly, Joan. "The Doubled Vision of Feminist Theory." In *Women, History, and Theory.* Chicago: University of Chicago Press, 1984.

"Kenney, Elizabeth L." In *Greater Los Angeles and Southern California: Portraits and Personal Memoranda,* edited by Robert J. Burdette, 247. Los Angeles: Lewis Publishing, 1910.

Kessler-Harris, Alice. "Organizing the Unorganizable: Three Jewish Women and Their Unions." In *Class, Sex, and the Woman Worker,* edited by Milton Cantor and Bruce Laurie, 144–65. Westport, Conn.: Greenwood Press, 1977.

————. *Out to Work: A History of Wage-Earning Women in the United States.* New York: Oxford University Press, 1982.

————. "'Where Are the Organized Women Workers?'" In *A Heritage of Her Own,* edited by Nancy F. Cott and Elizabeth H. Pleck, 367–92. New York: Simon and Schuster, 1979.

Kim, Richard, Kane K. Nakamura, and Gisele Fong, with Ron Cabarloc, Barbara Jung, and Sung Lee. "A Preliminary Investigation: Asian Immigrant Women Garment Workers in Los Angeles." *Amerasia Journal* 18, no. 1 (1992): 69–82.

Kleinberg, Susan J. "Technology and Woman's Work: The Lives of Working-Class Women in Pittsburgh, 1870–1900." *Labor History* 17 (Winter 1976): 58–72.

Knight, Peter. *The Plain People of Boston, 1830–1860: A Study of City Growth*. New York: Oxford University Press, 1971.

Koslow, Jennifer Lisa. "Eden's Underbelly: Female Reformers and Public Health in Los Angeles, 1889–1932." Ph.D. diss., University of California at Los Angeles, 2001.

Kraditor, Aileen. *The Ideas of the Woman Suffrage Movement, 1890–1920*. New York: Columbia University Press, 1965.

Kraft, James P. "The Fall of Job Harriman's Socialist Party: Violence, Gender, and Politics in Los Angeles, 1911." *Southern California Quarterly* 70, no. 1 (Spring 1988): 43–67.

Kramer, William M., and Norton B. Stern. "Birdie Stodel: Los Angeles Patriot." *Western States Jewish History* 20, no. 2 (1998): 109–16.

Kropp, Phoebe S. *California "Vieja": Culture and Memory in a Modern American Place*. Berkeley and Los Angeles: University of California Press, 2006.

Lamar, Howard. "From Bondage to Contract: Ethnic Labor in the American West." In *The Countryside in the Age of Capitalist Transformation: Essays in the Social History of Rural America*, edited by Steven Hahn and Jonathan Prude. Chapel Hill: University of North Carolina Press, 1985.

Larson, T. A. "Women's Role in the American West." *Montana: The Magazine of Western History* 24 (Summer 1974): 2–11.

Laslett, Barbara. "Social Change and the Family: Los Angeles, California, 1850–1870." *American Sociological Review* 42 (April 1977): 268–91.

———. "Women's Work in Late-Nineteenth-Century Los Angeles: Class, Gender, and the Culture of New Womanhood." *Continuity and Change* 5, no. 3 (1990): 417–41.

Laslett, John H. M. "Gender, Class, or Ethno-cultural Struggle? The Problematic Relationship Between Rose Pesotta and the Los Angeles ILGWU." *California History* 71, no. 1 (1993): 20–39.

Laslett, John H. M., and Mary Tyler. *The ILGWU in Los Angeles, 1907–1988*. Inglewood, Calif.: Ten Star Press, 1989.

Laville, Helen. "'If the Time Is Not Ripe, Then You Must Ripen the Time!': The Transformation of the YWCA in the United States From a Segregated Association to an Interracial Organization, 1930–1965." *Women's History Review* 15, no. 3 (2006): 359–83.

Lerner, Gerda. *The Grimké Sisters From South Carolina: Pioneers for Women's Rights and Abolition*. New York: Shocken Books, 1967.

Levine, Louis. *The Women's Garment Workers: A History of the International Ladies' Garment Workers' Union*. New York: B. W. Huebsch, 1924.

Limerick, Patricia Nelson. *The Legacy of Conquest: The Unbroken Past of the American West*. New York: W. W. Norton, 1987.

Locke, Mary Lou. "'Like a Machine or an Animal': Working Women of the Late-Nineteenth-Century Urban Far West, in San Francisco, Portland, and Los Angeles." Ph.D. diss., University of California at San Diego, 1982.

———. "Out of the Shadows and Into the Western Sun: Working Women of the Late-Nineteenth-Century Urban Far West." *Journal of Urban History* 16, no. 2 (February 1990): 175–205.

"Lopez, Maria De G. E." In *Woman's Who's Who of America: A Biographical Dictionary of Contemporary Women of the United States and Canada, 1914–1915.* New York: American Commonwealth, 1914.

Los Angeles, 1900–1961. Los Angeles: History Division of the Los Angeles County Museum, 1962.

Los Angeles Chamber of Commerce. *Facts and Figures Concerning Southern California City and County.* Los Angeles: Los Angeles Chamber of Commerce, 1889.

———. *Research Reveals the Sixty Years of Progress of Los Angeles.* Los Angeles: Los Angeles Chamber of Commerce, 1948.

Los Angeles City Directory, 1901. Los Angeles: Los Angeles Directory, 1901.

Los Angeles City Directory, 1907. Los Angeles: Los Angeles Directory, 1907.

Los Angeles City Directory, 1911. Los Angeles: Los Angeles Directory, 1911.

Los Angeles City Directory, 1913. Los Angeles: Los Angeles Directory, 1913.

Lotchin, Roger W. *The Bad City in the Good War: San Francisco, Los Angeles, Oakland, and San Diego.* Bloomington: Indiana University Press, 2003.

Lothrop, Gloria Ricci. "Westering Women and the Ladies of Los Angeles: Some Similarities and Differences." *South Dakota Review* 19, nos. 1–2 (Spring–Summer 1981): 41–67.

Loughlin, Patricia. "In Search of Capable Allies: Frances Nacke Noel and Women's Labor Activism in Los Angeles." *Southern California Quarterly* 82, no. 1 (Spring 2000): 61–74.

Luckingham, Bradford. "The American Southwest: An Urban View." *Western Historical Quarterly* 15, no. 3 (July 1984).

Malone, Michael P., and Richard Etulain. *The American West: A Twentieth-Century History.* Lincoln: University of Nebraska Press, 1989.

Mason, Karen Oppenheim, and Barbara Laslett. "Women's Work in the American West: Los Angeles, 1880–1890, and Its Contrast With Essex County, Massachusetts, in 1890." Research report, Population Studies Center, University of Minnesota, June 1983.

Mason, Karen Oppenheim, Maxine Weinstein, and Barbara Laslett. "The Decline of Fertility in Los Angeles, California, 1880–1900." *Population Studies* 41, no. 3 (November 1987): 483–99.

McGroarty, John Steven. *California of the South: A History.* Vol. 5, *Biographies.* Chicago: S. J. Clarke, 1935.

McWilliams, Carey. *California, the Great Exception.* New York: Current Books, 1949.

———. *Southern California Country: An Island on the Land.* New York: Duell, Sloan, and Pearce, 1946.

Mead, Rebecca J. "'Let the Women Get Their Wages as Men Do': Trade Union Women and the Legislated Minimum Wage in California." *Pacific Historical Review* 67, no. 3 (August 1998): 317–48.

Meyerowitz, Joanne J. *Women Adrift: Independent Wage Earners in Chicago, 1880–1930.* Chicago: University of Chicago Press, 1988.

Milkman, Ruth. *Gender at Work: The Dynamics of Job Segregation by Sex During World War II.* Urbana: University of Illinois Press, 1987.

———, ed. *Women Work and Protest: A Century of U.S. Women's Labor History.* New York: Routledge and Kegan Paul, 1985.

Mink, Gwendolyn. "The Lady and the Tramp: Gender, Race, and the Origins of the American Welfare State." In *Women, the State, and Welfare,* edited by Linda Gordon, 92–121. Madison: University of Wisconsin Press, 1990.

Modell, John. "Japanese-Americans: Some Costs of Group Achievement." In *Ethnic Conflict in California History,* edited by Charles Wollenberg, 101–20. Los Angeles: Tinnon-Brown, 1978.

Mohl, Raymond A. "Cultural Pluralism in Immigrant Education: The YWCA's International Institutes, 1910–1940." In *Men and Women Adrift: The YMCA and the YWCA in the City,* edited by Nina Mjagkij and Margaret Spratt, 111–37. New York: New York University Press, 1997.

Mohun, Arwen P. *Steam Laundries: Gender, Technology, and Work in the United States and Great Britain, 1880–1940.* Baltimore: Johns Hopkins University Press, 1999.

Molina, Natalia. *Fit to Be Citizens? Public Health and Race in Los Angeles, 1879–1939.* Berkeley and Los Angeles: University of California Press, 2006.

Monroy, Douglas. *Rebirth: Mexican Los Angeles From the Great Migration to the Great Depression.* Berkeley and Los Angeles: University of California Press, 1999.

Montgomery, David. *The Fall of the House of Labor: The Workplace, the State, and American Labor Activism, 1865–1925.* Cambridge: Cambridge University Press, 1987.

Morawska, Ewa. "The Sociology and Historiography of Immigration." In *Immigration Reconsidered: History, Sociology, and Politics,* edited by Virginia Yans-McLaughlen. New York: Oxford University Press, 1990.

Muncy, Robyn. *Creating a Female Dominion in American Reform, 1890–1935.* New York: Oxford University Press, 1991.

Nash, Gerald. *The American West in the Twentieth Century: A Short History of an Urban Oasis.* 2nd ed. Englewood Cliffs, N.J.: Prentice-Hall, 1973.

———. *World War II and the West: Reshaping the Economy.* Lincoln: University of Nebraska Press, 1990.

National Industrial Conference Board. *Wages in the United States, 1914–1930.* New York: National Industrial Conference Board, 1931.

Nelson, Barbara J. "The Origins of the Two-Channel Welfare State: Workmen's Compensation and Mother's Aid." In *Women, the State, and Welfare,* edited by Linda Gordon, 123–51. Madison: University of Wisconsin Press, 1990.

Newmark, Harris. *Sixty Years in Southern California, 1853–1913.* Edited by Maurice H. and Marco R. Newmark. 4th ed. Los Angeles: Zeitlin and Ver Brugge, 1970.

Nicolaides, Becky M. "'Where the Working Man Is Welcomed': Working-Class Suburbs in Los Angeles, 1900–1940." *Pacific Historical Review* 68, no. 4 (November 1999): 517–41.

Nieto-Phillips, John M. *The Language of Blood: The Making of Spanish-American Identity in New Mexico, 1880–1930s.* Albuquerque: University of New Mexico Press, 2004.

Nolan, Jay P., and Gilberto M. Hinojosa, eds. *Mexican Americans and the Catholic Church, 1900–1965.* Notre Dame: University of Notre Dame Press, 1994.

Norwood, Stephen H. *Labor's Flaming Youth: Telephone Operators and Worker Militancy, 1878–1923.* Urbana: University of Illinois Press, 1990.

Odem, Mary E. *Delinquent Daughters: Protecting and Policing Adolescent Female Sexuality in the United States, 1885–1920.* Chapel Hill: University of North Carolina Press, 1995.

Olin, Spencer C., Jr. *California's Prodigal Sons: Hiram Johnson and the Progressives, 1911–1917.* Berkeley and Los Angeles: University of California Press, 1968.

Orozco, Cynthia E. "Beyond Machismo, *la Familia,* and Ladies Auxiliaries: A Historiography of Mexican-Origin Women's Participation in Voluntary Associations and Politics in the United States, 1870–1990." *Perspectives in Mexican American Studies* 5 (1995): 1–34.

Orsi, Richard J. *Sunset Limited: The Southern Pacific Railroad and the Development of the American West, 1850–1930.* Berkeley and Los Angeles: University of California Press, 2005.

Oxnam, G. Bromley. *The Mexican in Los Angeles: Los Angeles City Survey.* Los Angeles: Los Angeles City Survey, 1920.

Page, Margaret Jimenez. "The Adobes of San Gabriel, California." Master's thesis, California State University at Los Angeles, 1976.

Pascoe, Peggy. *Relations of Rescue: The Search for Female Moral Authority in the American West, 1874–1939.* New York: Oxford University Press, 1990.

Peavy, Linda, and Ursula Smith. *Women in Waiting in the Westward Movement.* Norman: University of Oklahoma Press, 1994.

Peiss, Kathy. *Cheap Amusements: Working Women and Leisure in Turn-of-the-Century New York.* Philadelphia: Temple University Press, 1986.

———. *Hope in a Jar: The Making of American Beauty Culture.* New York: Metropolitan Books, 1998.

Perry, Louis B., and Richard S. Perry. *A History of the Los Angeles Labor Movement, 1911–1941.* Berkeley and Los Angeles: University of California Press, 1963.

Pesotta, Rose. *Bread Upon the Waters.* 1944. Reprint, Ithaca: Cornell University Press, 1987.

Pichardo, Nelson A. "The Establishment and Development of Chicano Voluntary Associations in California, 1910–1930." *Aztlan* 19, no. 2 (Fall 1988–1990): 93–155.

Pomeroy, Earl. *The Pacific Slope: A History of California, Oregon, Washington, Idaho, Utah, and Nevada*. New York: Alfred A. Knopf, 1965.

Price, V. Barrett. "The Ultimate Western City." *South Dakota Review* 19, nos. 1–2 (Spring–Summer 1981): 24–29.

Privett, Stephen A., S.J. *The U.S. Catholic Church and Its Hispanic Members: The Pastoral Vision of Archbishop Robert E. Lucey*. San Antonio: Trinity University Press, 1988.

Putnam, John C. *Class and Gender Politics in Progressive-Era Seattle*. Reno: University of Nevada Press, 2008.

Raferty, Judith Rosenberg. *Land of Fair Promise: Politics and Reform in Los Angeles Schools, 1885–1941*. Stanford: Stanford University Press, 1992.

Richter, Amy G. *Home on the Rails: Women, the Railroad, and the Rise of Public Domesticity*. Chapel Hill: University of North Carolina Press, 2005.

Riley, Glenda. *The Female Frontier: A Comparative View of Women on the Prairie and the Plains*. Lawrence: University Press of Kansas, 1988.

Roediger, David R. *The Wages of Whiteness: Race and the Making of the American Working Class*. New York: Verso, 1991.

Rolle, Andrew F. *California, a History*. 3rd ed. Chicago: AHM Publishing, 1978.

Romo, Ricardo. *East Los Angeles: History of a Barrio*. Austin: University of Texas Press, 1983.

Ross, Kristin. *The Emergence of Social Space: Rimbaud and the Paris Commune: Theory and History of Literature*. Vol. 60. Minneapolis: University of Minnesota Press, 1988.

Ross, Sara. "The Americanization of Tsuru Aoki: Orientalism, Melodrama, Star Image, and the New Woman." *Camera Obscura* 20, no. 3 (2005): 129–56.

Ruddy, Ella Giles. *The Mother of Clubs: Caroline M. Seymour Severance*. Los Angeles: Baumgardt, 1906.

Ruiz, Vicki. *Cannery Women, Cannery Lives: Mexican Women, Unionization, and the California Food Processing Industry, 1930–1950*. Albuquerque: University of New Mexico Press, 1987.

———. *From Out of the Shadows: Mexican Women in Twentieth-Century America*. New York: Oxford University Press, 1998.

Ryan, Mary P. *Civic Wars: Democracy and Public Life in the American City During the Nineteenth Century*. Berkeley and Los Angeles: University of California Press, 1997.

Salmon, Lucy M. *Domestic Service*. 2nd ed. New York: Macmillan, 1901.

Sanborn, Kate. *A Truthful Woman in Southern California*. New York: D. Appleton, 1895.

Sanchez, George. *Becoming Mexican American: Ethnicity, Culture, and Identity in Chicano Los Angeles, 1900–1945*. New York: Oxford University Press, 1993.

———. "'Go After the Women': Americanization and the Mexican Immigrant Woman, 1915–1929." In *Unequal Sisters: A Multicultural Reader in U.S. Women's*

History, edited by Ellen Carol DuBois and Vicki L. Ruiz, 250–63. New York: Routledge, 1990.

Sánchez, Rosaura. *Telling Identities: The "Californio Testimonios."* Minneapolis: University of Minnesota Press, 1995.

Saunders, Charles Frances. *Under the Sky in California.* New York: McBride, Nast, 1913.

Schwartz, Stephen. *From West to East: California and the Making of the American Mind.* New York: Free Press, 1998.

Scott, Joan Wallach. "Gender: A Useful Category of Historical Analysis." In *Gender and the Politics of History.* New York: Columbia University Press, 1988.

———. "Women's History." In *Gender and the Politics of History.* New York: Columbia University Press, 1988.

Shaffer, Ralph E. "Radicalism in California, 1869–1929." Ph.D. diss., University of California at Berkeley, 1962.

Shapiro, Herbert. "The McNamara Case: A Window on Class Antagonism in the Progressive Era." *Southern California Quarterly* 70, no. 1 (Spring 1988): 69–95.

Sides, Josh. *L.A. City Limits: African-American Los Angeles From the Great Depression to the Present.* Berkeley and Los Angeles: University of California Press, 2003.

Simpson, Lee. *Selling the City: Gender, Class, and the California Growth Machine, 1880–1940.* Stanford: Stanford University Press, 2004.

Sitton, Tom, and William Deverell, eds. *California Progressivism Revisited.* Berkeley and Los Angeles: University of California Press, 1994.

———. *Metropolis in the Making: Los Angeles in the 1920s.* Berkeley and Los Angeles: University of California Press, 2001.

Slosser, Charles O. "Social Mobility in Nineteenth-Century Los Angeles, 1880–1890." Ph.D. diss., University of California at Los Angeles, 1978.

Smith-Rosenberg, Carroll. "The Female World of Love and Ritual: Relations Between Women in Nineteenth-Century America." *Signs* 1 (1975–1976): 1–29.

Sokoloff, Lillian. *The Russians in Los Angeles.* Studies in Sociology. Los Angeles: Southern California Sociological Society, University of Southern California, 1918.

Sorin, Gerald. "Rose Pesotta in the Far West: The Triumphs and Travails of a Jewish Woman Labor Organizer." *Western States Jewish History* 28, no. 2 (January 1996): 133–43.

Sparks, Edith. *Capital Intentions: Female Proprietors in San Francisco, 1850–1920.* Chapel Hill: University of North Carolina Press, 2006.

Stanley, Norman S. *No Little Plans: The Story of the Los Angeles Chamber of Commerce.* Los Angeles: Los Angeles Chamber of Commerce, 1956.

Stansell, Christine. *City of Women: Sex and Class in New York, 1789–1860.* Urbana: University of Chicago Press, 1982.

Starr, Kevin. *Americans and the California Dream, 1850–1915.* Santa Barbara: P. Smith, 1981.

———. *Inventing the Dream : California Through the Progressive Era.* New York: Oxford Press, 1985.

Stimson, Grace Heilman. *Rise of the Labor Movement in Los Angeles.* Berkeley and Los Angeles: University of California Press, 1955.

The Story of the Bell System. Seattle: Pacific Telephone and Telegraph, 1932.

"Sunset" Magazine: A Century of Western Living, 1898–1998. Stanford: Stanford University Libraries, 1998.

Takaki, Ronald. *Strangers From a Different Shore: A History of Asian Americans.* Boston: Little, Brown, 1989.

Taylor, Paul S. "Mexican Women in Los Angeles Industry in 1928." *Aztlan* 11, no. 1 (Spring 1980): 99–131.

Taylor, Quintard. *In Search of the Racial Frontier: African Americans in the American West, 1528–1990.* New York: W. W. Norton, 1998.

Thernstrom, Stephan. *Poverty and Progress: Social Mobility in a Nineteenth-Century City.* Cambridge: Harvard University Press, 1964.

Tyack, David B. *The One Best System: A History of American Urban Education.* Cambridge: Harvard University Press, 1974.

U.S. Bureau of the Census. "Census of Steam Laundries." In *Manufactures: 1909.* Washington, D.C.: Government Printing Office, 1910.

———. *Thirteenth Census of the United States Taken in the Year 1910.* Vol. 1, *Population.* Washington, D.C.: Government Printing Office, 1910.

———. *Fifteenth Census of the United States.* Vol. 1, *Population.* Washington, D.C.: Government Printing Office, 1931.

U.S. Department of Labor. *The Development of Minimum Wage Laws in the United States, 1912 to 1927.* Bulletin of the Women's Bureau, no. 61. Washington, D.C.: Government Printing Office, 1928.

———. *Fourth Annual Report: Working Women in Large Cities.* Washington, D.C.: Government Printing Office, 1889.

Viehe, Fred V. "Black Gold Suburbs: The Influence of the Extractive Industry on the Suburbanization of Los Angeles, 1890–1930." *Journal of Urban History* 8, no. 1 (November 1981): 3–26.

Wallis, Eileen V. "At Work in the Urban West: Gender, Ethnicity, and Employment in Los Angeles, 1883–1920." Ph.D. diss., University of Utah, 2004.

———. "Mexican-American Women, Clubs, and the 'Spanish' Auxiliary in Southern California, 1880–1930." Paper given at the Pacific Coast Branch American Historical Association annual meeting, Honolulu, July 25, 2007.

Ward, David. *Cities and Immigrants: A Geography of Change in Nineteenth-Century America.* New York: Oxford University Press, 1971.

Weaver, John D. *Los Angeles: The Enormous Village, 1781–1981.* Santa Barbara: Capra Press, 1980.

Weiner, Lynn Y. *From Working Girl to Working Mother: The Female Labor Force in the United States, 1820–1980.* Chapel Hill: University of North Carolina Press, 1985.

Weisenfeld, Judith. *African-American Women and Christian Activism: New York's Black YWCA, 1905–1945.* Cambridge: Harvard University Press, 1998.

Wertheimer, Barbara Mayer. *We Were There: The Story of Working Women in America*. New York: Pantheon Books, 1977.

White, Gerald T. *Formative Years in the Far West: A History of Standard Oil Company of California and Predecessors Through 1919*. New York: Appelton-Century-Crofts, 1962.

White, Richard. *"It's Your Misfortune and None of My Own": A History of the American West*. Norman: University of Oklahoma Press, 1991.

Wiebe, Robert H. *The Search for Order, 1877–1920*. New York: Hill and Wang, 1967.

Wild, Mark. *Street Meeting: Multiethnic Neighborhoods in Early-Twentieth-Century Los Angeles*. Berkeley and Los Angeles: University of California Press, 2005.

Winther, Oscar Osburn. "The Use of Climate as a Means of Promoting Migration to Southern California." *Mississippi Valley Historical Review* 33, no. 3 (December 1946): 411–24.

Woloch, Nancy. *"Muller v. Oregon": A Brief History With Documents*. New York: Bedford Books of St. Martin's Press, 1996.

Wood, Sharon E. *The Freedom of the Streets: Work, Citizenship, and Sexuality in a Gilded Age City*. Chapel Hill: University of North Carolina Press, 2005.

Woods, Robert A., and Albert J. Kennedy, eds. *Handbook of Settlements*. New York: New York Charities Publication Committee, 1911.

Young, Pauline V. *The Pilgrims of Russian-Town*. Chicago: University of Chicago Press, 1932.

———. "The Russian Molokan Community in Los Angeles." *American Journal of Sociology* 35, no. 3 (November 1929): 393–402.

Zimmerman, Tom. "Paradise Promoted: Boosterism and the Los Angeles Chamber of Commerce." *California History* 64, no. 1 (Winter 1985): 22–33.

INDEX